# Checkbook Zionism

# Checkbook Zionism

*Philanthropy and Power in the
Israel-Diaspora Relationship*

ERIC FLEISCH

RUTGERS UNIVERSITY PRESS

NEW BRUNSWICK, CAMDEN, AND NEWARK, NEW JERSEY

LONDON AND OXFORD

Rutgers University Press is a department of Rutgers, The State University of New Jersey, one of the leading public research universities in the nation. By publishing worldwide, it furthers the University's mission of dedication to excellence in teaching, scholarship, research, and clinical care.

Library of Congress Cataloging-in-Publication Data

Names: Fleisch, Eric, 1975– author.

Title: Checkbook Zionism: philanthropy and power in the Israel-Diaspora relationship / Eric Fleisch.

Description: New Brunswick: Rutgers University Press, [2024] | Includes bibliographical references and index.

Identifiers: LCCN 2023018809 | ISBN 9781978819948 (paperback) | ISBN 9781978819955 (hardback) | ISBN 9781978819962 (epub) | ISBN 9781978819986 (pdf)

Subjects: LCSH: Zionism—United States—History. | Jews—United States—Attitudes toward Israel. | Jews—United States—Charities. | Israel and the diaspora. | United States—Ethnic relations.

Classification: LCC DS149.5.U6 F54 2024 | DDC 320.540956940973—dc23/eng/20230427

LC record available at https://lccn.loc.gov/2023018809

A British Cataloging-in-Publication record for this book is available from the British Library.

References to internet websites (URLs) were accurate at the time of writing. Neither the author nor Rutgers University Press is responsible for URLs that may have expired or changed since the manuscript was prepared.

♾ The paper used in this publication meets the requirements of the American National Standard for Information Sciences—Permanence of Paper for Printed Library Materials, ANSI Z39.48–1992.

rutgersuniversitypress.org

*For Oren, Eli, and Emmett who light up my world.*

# Contents

# Abbreviations

| | |
|---|---|
| ABI | American-born Israelis |
| AFNCI | American Friends of New Communities in Israel |
| AFPI | American Fund for Palestine Institutions |
| APN | Americans for Peace Now |
| CCA | Committee for Control and Authorization of Campaigns |
| CJF | Council of Jewish Federations |
| CSO | Civil Society Organization |
| FAZ | Federation of American Zionists |
| FCII | Federated Council of Israel Institutions |
| ICDF | Israel Community Development Fund |
| IEC | Israel Emergency Campaign |
| IEF | Israel Education Fund |
| JDC | Joint Distribution Committee |
| JFNA | Jewish Federations of North America |
| JNF | Jewish National Fund |
| NGO | nongovernmental organization |
| NIF | New Israel Fund |
| OIF | One Israel Fund |
| ONAD | Overseas Needs Assessment and Distribution Committee |
| PEC | Palestine Economic Corporation |
| PEF | Palestine Endowment Fund |
| RHR | Rabbis for Human Rights |

| | |
|---|---|
| RHR-NA | Rabbis for Human Rights-North America |
| SJS | Sheikh Jarrah Solidarity |
| UIA | United Israel Appeal |
| UJA | United Jewish Appeal |
| UJC | United Jewish Communities |
| WZO | World Zionist Organization |
| ZOA | Zionist Organization of America |

# Checkbook Zionism

# Introduction

There is a satirical but telling scene in the classic 1964 Israeli film *Sallah Shabati*. Several *halutzim* are planting trees in an area slated by the Jewish National Fund (JNF) to become a forest. While they are hoeing and digging, a man working for the JNF drives up the dirt path in a car, takes a sign out of the car reading "Simon Birnbaum Forest New York, NY," and hammers it into the ground next to a newly planted tree. Just as he finishes, another car pulls up chauffeuring a wealthy American couple. The Americans, ill dressed for the rugged terrain, get out of the car and awkwardly follow the JNF officer to the tree. The officer says in broken English, "Mrs. and Mr. Birnbaum. *This* is your forest!" The Americans look admiringly at the tree and all of the *halutzim* planting more like it, appear pleased, snap some pictures, and then get back into their car and drive away. No sooner than they are out of sight does the JNF officer take down the sign with the Birnbaums' name on it and hammers in a sign next to the same tree that says "Mrs. Pearl Sonnenschein Forest Detroit." A moment later, the Sonnenscheins also drive up, are also greeted by the JNF officer welcoming them to "their" forest in the same broken English, and are also pleased to be seeing what they are making possible through their generosity.[1]

The scene parodies a peculiar dynamic often at play in relationships between those living in a given "homeland" (be it real or imagined) and their associated diaspora populations. On the surface, the relationship appears to be between well-meaning supporters from afar wanting to aid financially in the development of their homeland and those on the ground in the homeland happy to receive donations. But the subtext of the interaction tells a very different story. Though we do not know how the JNF was going to actually use the funds donated by the Birnbaums and Sonnenscheins, a few points can be inferred: (1) The funds were not going to be used as the donors thought, (2) the donors would almost certainly not be consulted on their actual use, and (3) the recipient JNF officer did not seem to have any problems with deceiving the donors.

What might explain what is really going on here behind the curtain?

One might think that needy recipients—of which Israelis in the 1950s certainly were—principally would appreciate the help (and, secondarily, would hope that the donor would give again in the future). What, then, does it say that the JNF officer does not have any qualms about manipulating the seemingly well-meaning donors? The officer, most likely, would go to such lengths of acting unethically and—maybe even more importantly—possibly jeopardizing the relationships only if he felt very strongly that he did not want the donors to be involved in deciding how the money was actually to be used.

But why might he feel so strongly? Is it that he did not trust donors' ability to accurately evaluate how best to use the money? Perhaps, yes.

But if that were the case, why would the officer not be more forthright and tactfully explain the reason why Israelis believed that they, as the people who lived there, naturally had a clearer understanding of where money was most needed? Genuinely well-meaning donors might actually respond well to such an honest assessment. Maybe it was because the officer's concerns were deeper than just having low confidence in the donors' judgment.

What if his real issue was that he questioned whether the donors' *motives* were truly as "well-meaning" as they appeared? What if, instead of being chiefly driven by an altruistic desire to help, donors wanted the money they contributed to be used for some other purpose that was more in line with their own visions for what Israel's priorities should be—but not necessarily what *Israel* actually needed? In other words, maybe planting new forests fit with the donors' ideas for what the new state most needed, but according to those who lived there it did not.

If this were indeed the case, one could understand why the JNF could want to maintain control over the money badly enough that its officers would be willing to lie to donors.

These issues—of communication and control, divergent agendas and sometime deception—have classically been central features of the American Jewish-Israeli relationship parodied in *Sallah Shabati*, but they apply far beyond this one case to homeland-diaspora relationships all over the world. Often, despite a veneer of partnership and collaboration in relationships between diaspora populations donating money to their homeland and those in the homeland receiving it, these types of dynamics linger right below the surface.

## The Challenges and Opportunities of Diaspora Philanthropy

The nature of philanthropic relationships between homelands and diasporas has become increasingly important in international relations in the emerging twenty-first-century global picture.[2] With human migration at an all-time high,[3] and with communities of migrant expatriates not necessarily rapidly assimilating into the majority cultures where they live,[4] diasporas are springing up and taking root all over the globe.

Over time, it is not uncommon for diasporans to attain greater wealth than those remaining in their homelands and still retain an ongoing desire to "help" those back in the "old country." One of the chief ways many diasporas do so is through philanthropy—mobilizing to bear some of the financial burden of their often less developed homeland.[5]

Depending on the sizes of homeland and diaspora populations and relative economic clout, overseas donation totals can have an outsized proportion of influence on a still-emerging economy. Therefore, whoever gets to decide how to allocate funds coming in from diasporas can hold considerable sway in shaping how a homeland develops—what work should be prioritized, according to which agendas, and so forth.[6] Determining exactly who makes expenditure decisions is of great importance.

States with diasporas usually understand the unique opportunity that can come with having populations living outside of their geographical boundaries who are *specifically dedicated* to supporting their state's betterment. World Bank economist Dilip Ratha argued in 2011 that governments should view their diasporas as "an untapped pool of oil," ripe to be cultivated to aid in their future development.[7] While it is true that ethnically linked diasporas are not the only source of foreign financial assistance available for developing societies, unlike with most other forms of foreign investment/support that are largely initiated for the purpose of bringing the investor/investor country financial and/or strategic benefits, diaspora support for the development of their homeland is thought, at least in part, to be typically motivated by donors holding altruistic concern for and/or identification with the homeland.[8]

On the one hand, most states with significant diaspora populations have recognized this and attempted, on some level, to mobilize diaspora philanthropic support—both for the extra stream of funding itself but also *specifically* for the relatively fewer constraints they expect than are attached to other forms of foreign investment and aid.[9] Scholars have noted the uptick in countries attempting to cultivate diaspora involvement. As Kathleen Newland, Aaron Terrazas, and Roberto Munster explain, "Migrant-sending countries are . . . trying to integrate their native citizens abroad into efforts to promote development at home" because they are "increasingly recognizing the development potential of their diasporas.[10]

But on the other hand, Jennifer Brinkerhoff, perhaps the leading scholar on diaspora philanthropy, offers a more cautious perspective. She argues that there is a broad range of attitudes home countries hold to their diasporas, spanning from actively seeking their involvement to ignoring them and to seeing their activity as inappropriately politically motivated, or worse.[11] Some states worry that their diasporas could use the leverage donated money gives them to push for agendas that may not be in the home country's best interest.

So how true might Brinkerhoff's assessment be? Diasporans donating to their homeland indeed are giving of themselves and mostly claim to be doing so, in part, out of love or patriotism. However, the literature suggests that the stated altruistic intent by diaspora donors may not be quite as good for the homelands as it sounds. For one, diaspora donors are usually motivated, in part, by other, less altruistic motivations as well (e.g., achieving personal gain or status).[12] Matthias Lücke, Omar Mahmoud Toman, and Peuker Christian have termed this phenomenon "impure altruism."[13] But perhaps more importantly, as numerous scholars have argued, even if diaspora populations truly believe they are giving philanthropy with the "best interest" of their homeland in mind, those living in the homeland may have different ideas of what "best interest" means.[14]

One way this sometimes manifests, for example, is when certain groups within a society that do not represent mainstream opinions are able to successfully connect with affluent like-minded supporters abroad to bankroll and empower their more fringe ideas.[15] As Johnson, Johnson, and Kingman explain, when, in such cases, priorities of homelands and diasporas are "not . . . fully congruent . . . , heavy reliance on foreign donations . . . [can] raise issues of legitimacy agenda setting, and public perception."[16] Is it true when empowered, engaged nonnative donors choose to get involved in what might otherwise be regarded as the internal affairs of *another state* that they are in some way undermining that state's sovereignty—especially if they are pushing agendas not necessarily shared by some sufficient part of a state's citizens?

What happens (or should happen) in these cases when the priorities of a homeland and its diaspora donors diverge? Who should determine how donated money to a sovereign country should be spent: The givers from abroad? Those affected by the spending decisions on the ground? The two in concert? And, if so, on what basis should the sides mediate their differences?

On one extreme of the argument is the idea that donors should be understood, more or less, like consumers: they should get to decide how their hard-earned money is spent, as they would with any other purchasing decision. In this formulation, donors choose projects, watch budgets, monitor outcomes, and continually evaluate the merits of their ongoing "investment" in these projects.[17] The opposite extreme holds that only those living in a country should be entitled to make important decisions that impact the future of that country. In this view, the interests of foreign donors are regarded as irrelevant; even more, overseas donors using their philanthropy to push along agendas in a country other than their own is tantamount to inappropriate foreign influence in a sovereign state that should not be tolerated.[18]

These questions have far-reaching effects on both the self-identities of home-land and diaspora communities alike, as well as the relationship between the two. But unfortunately, since research on diaspora philanthropy to date has been sparse—especially regarding issues like power, control, and state sovereignty[19]—there are not yet well-developed theoretical frameworks to draw from in cate-gorizing the contours of philanthropic relations between homelands and diasporas. Those scholars who have broadly surveyed the phenomenon of dias-pora philanthropy recognize that the field is, as Brinkerhoff put it, "in its infancy" or, as Johnson says, is "one of the least understood subfields of philanthropy."[20]

In the absence of a more well-developed literature, therefore, it is helpful to borrow ideas about partnership relationships from the related field of interna-tional development.

Typically, international development relationships are predicated on wealth-ier "developed" states providing funding for projects in poorer "developing" states.[21] Some in the field argue that though the agendas of funding organizations likely differ in key ways from states receiving aid, there are nonetheless myriad potential (and actualized) opportunities for building trust and mutually bene-ficial relationships between the sides.[22]

Other perspectives assert, on the other hand, that the inherent power asym-metries between the two sides make partnership difficult and typically lead to wealthier actors using their financial leverage *specifically* to advance proprietary agendas not necessarily aligned with the best interests of the recipient coun-tries,[23] or even for the express purpose of institutionalizing power discrepan-cies longer term.[24]

Willem Elbers and Lau Schulpen explain that a functioning, mutually ben-eficial partnership would theoretically include features such as "shared goals, bal-ance of power, shared responsibilities, trust, mutual respect and accountability, reflecting the ideal of a mutually dependent relationship based on equality."[25] However, numerous scholars in the field usually see these types of relationships as illusory. Sally Reith, for example, echoing a common perspective in the field, identifies partnership in this context as "something of a Trojan Horse, disguising the reality of the complex relationships in imbalances of power and inequality, often . . . through the control and flow of money."[26] Elbers goes even further, arguing that rather than "partnership," a more appropriate characterization of the relationship between donor populations and recipient societies is "partner-ship paradox," in which monied stakeholders maintain or exacerbate a gap between principles and practices of actual partnership.[27]

This book builds on the ideas and contributes to a new literature within dias-pora studies on what partnership and power sharing look like in philanthropic relationships between homelands and diasporas. Through an analysis of a sin-gle, specific homeland-diaspora relationship, that between American Jews and

Israelis, this book looks at these questions of money, partnership, influence, and control, offering ideas that are applicable to such relationships across the world.

## THE CASE OF AMERICAN JEWS AND ISRAELIS

In a number of ways, the Israel-diaspora relationship is an excellent—and arguably even an ideal—window into how these larger issues play out in philanthropic relationships between homelands and diaspora populations. On the one hand, due to both its historical longevity and the depth of affinity diasporans hold toward the homeland, the Israel-diaspora relationship has been pointed to as perhaps the paradigmatic homeland-diaspora relationship.[28] But on the other, the case of the Israel-diaspora relationship is somewhat unique in the level of maturation it has reached. The relationship is now between a diaspora community among the wealthiest, most established, and most integrated in the world and a modern, developed state—which raises the questions of how a relationship might develop after the inherent dynamics of haves versus have-nots has receded. Finally, with a long modern history of over a hundred years, this relationship offers the opportunity to be scrutinized for how numerous factors (motivations, behavior norms, communication patterns, structural mechanisms, etc.) have developed over time.

### Background

Zionism had originally imagined a Jewish society created exclusively by hardworking, entrepreneurial *halutzim* on the ground in Palestine, but the truth is that Israel was, in large measure, built by diaspora donations. *Halutzim* did the physical construction, but the bill for society building was simply more than the cash-strapped *olim* could foot. Fortunately for Zionist settlers—at least from a pragmatic standpoint—hundreds of thousands or more of diaspora Jews saw the need and were eager to support the unfolding drama of Jewish history from a comfortable distance by financially supporting the building of Zion. Indeed from the beginnings of the Zionist settlement in Palestine in the late nineteenth century through the present, American Jews—the largest and most affluent diaspora community—have donated more than $30 billion to support projects in Israel.[29] Collectively, the funds have had a major impact on nearly every sector of Israeli society throughout the years: from building of infrastructure and absorbing immigrants early on to ongoing economic and civil society development through the present.[30] This has given American Jews the opportunity to leave their fingerprints all over the Israeli state and has raised concerns for Israelis about inappropriate outside influence. This relationship pattern of Jews from abroad funding Israel's development has sometimes been derisively referred to as Checkbook Zionism.

Israelis long had a complicated perspective on the Checkbook Zionism relationship formula. It was true that money was deeply important to the young state,
but the point of Zionism was to be a solution to the problems of diaspora life, not
a movement existing alongside it.[31] The spartan realities of the Zionist settlement
project and the early Israeli state, however, necessitated that the state's leaders
accept and, even more, actively seek out money from American Jews. And so they
put on a good face, kept their often disparaging opinions about diaspora Jews to
themselves,[32] and placated their benefactors enough to keep the funds flowing.[33]
The one red line they maintained was that they would not accept American Jews
having a significant voice in the conversation over how to use the funds. In theory, they would have happily welcomed American Jews as equal participants in
planning Israel's development if the Americans immigrated. But in the opinion
of Israelis, so long as Americans could not be inconvenienced enough to surren-
der the comforts of their lives and truly be Zionists by providing the young state
the manpower it so badly needed, they should be due neither full participation
nor even full respect. To Israelis, the term "Checkbook Zionism" was therefore a
derogatory label they used among themselves as a way to denigrate Americans'
insufficient participation in the "real work" of Zionism.[34]

The mainstream American perspective on the Checkbook Zionism relationship was less complicated. Simply put, American Jews typically saw no shame
in their role. Most believed giving with no intention of immigrating was a perfectly legitimate way of expressing their support, especially when Israel so badly
needed money and they had the means to provide it.[35] They regarded the decision to immigrate to Israel as a personal choice—not an obligation—for Jews.
Most reasoned, furthermore, that it was rather foolish to abandon the comfort
and acceptance they believed they had achieved as American Jews in favor of
picking up and moving to a small, underdeveloped piece of land in the Middle
East—not to mention that it could risk undermining the status they had worked
so hard to achieve as loyal Americans.[36] Therefore, most believed that if they
cared about Israel, it was perfectly legitimate and maybe even better to stay put
and write checks.[37]

———

This book's study of power sharing in the Israeli American Jewish diaspora is
both historical and contemporary. What started as a partnership of necessity
between the doers and the absentee payers—the Zionists and the Checkbook
Zionists—took shape in the first decades of the twentieth century and first began
to seriously falter only in the 1980s. What has risen in its wake has, to date,
received very little attention.

At the core of the inquiry are a number of seemingly technical questions:
What are the priorities of the various players? How do they communicate? Who

sets the narrative? How and why do donors stay engaged? But it also hones in on larger questions surrounding money, control, and sovereignty: Can some kind of equal "partnership" exist in which both Americans and Israelis are adequately competent and deemed so? Should there be partnership? Which agendas are legitimate for diasporas to support and which are not? Does homeland "belong" to only those who live there? Do the sides see merit in the relationship remaining in a similar state to how it has been? If so, what does that mean for how each views both its role and that of its counterpart in the relationship?

### Structure and Methodology

Part I of this book documents and recounts the history of the rise and fall of the Checkbook Zionist relationship—what it was, how it operated, and why it declined. It focuses on two principles at the heart of the relationship: (1) use of collective or "federated" philanthropy as the best way for organizing donors and addressing communal priorities and (2) a built-in deference—an almost automatic trust that American Jewish leaders had in their counterparts in Israel.

Chapter 1 examines these ideas from an institutional perspective. It looks at the vast organizational infrastructure American Jews and Israelis collectively built in the first half of the twentieth century in order to facilitate an efficient and plentiful flow of donations for Israel. It explains the rise of federation as a principle and how it helped transform a haphazard hodgepodge of giving channels into an efficient fundraising machine (headed by the United Jewish Appeal [UJA] in America and the Jewish Agency in Israel) that would be instrumental in building important components of Israeli society and in the process instill ideas of collective action, collective planning, and mandatory personal obligation to give within American Jewry.[38]

Chapter 2 looks at Checkbook Zionism from a cultural perspective, investigating ideas of priorities, collaboration, and trust. It tells the story of two competing philosophies over how the diaspora and Israel should share power in allocating donated funds. The ideas—each championed by a leading voice from the Zionist movement of the day—were premised on differing understandings of the rights of the diaspora to have a say over the use of the money that they contributed. The chapter recounts the process through which the idea pushed by Chaim Weizmann—calling for de facto American Jewish deference to Israeli decision makers—ultimately became the dominant viewpoint. It then details the meticulous process that American and Israeli proponents of Weizmann's ideas undertook to entrench them within the UJA–Jewish Agency system.

Chapter 3 begins at the peak of Checkbook Zionism when federation and deference were celebrated norms underlaying the fundraising enterprise that brought in huge sums annually (the UJA–Jewish Agency structure controlled over 80 percent of American Jewish donations for Israel)[39] and vested decision-making authority in the hands of Israelis, with only rare public criticisms from

Americans.[40] The chapter traces the swift decline of the system explaining how cracks in the relationship increasingly developed from the 1967 War on—and in a pronounced way in the 1980s and early 1990s—with the result being a drop in UJA campaign receipts year after year. Some commentators viewed the decline in giving numbers—despite growing American Jewish affluence—as a sign of diminishing American interest in Israel overall.[41] The chapter argues that a closer look reveals that though the traditional giving numbers were indeed falling, a much larger change was afoot. Americans were not less interested in Israel but rather were simply changing *how* they gave.[42] Rather than giving through the traditional organizational channels, increasing numbers of American Jews were choosing to donate to new organizations that afforded them more opportunity to decide how their funds would be used. Every year, dozens of additional American Jewish organizations collecting money for projects in Israel first appeared on the scene to rival the traditional centralized collection campaigns.[43] The diversity of possible organizations and the opportunities for earmarking donations that they introduced allowed Americans to choose the causes in Israel they wanted to help bankroll much more directly. By 2018, the number of organizations raising funds for projects in Israel had reached nearly a thousand and covered every conceivable charitable stratum—from mainstream causes like hospitals, museums, *yeshivot*, and universities to more boutique causes like guide dogs for the blind, oceanography, orphanages, cystic fibrosis research, missile defense, lacrosse leagues, dentistry, and many others.[44] In an apparent departure from the years of Checkbook Zionism, American Jews were increasingly exercising choice over where to direct their money from the many new giving options.

The second half of the book explores power sharing in the philanthropic relationship in the wake of these major transitions. For as little as the history of philanthropy and power sharing have received adequate scholarly treatment, the years since the 1990s have received even less, likely due to how unwieldy the field became. The fact that as of 2020 there were thousands of distinct philanthropic channels means that old analyses of the philanthropic relationship that were largely based on the single UJA–Jewish Agency channel of philanthropy to Israel could no longer be considered valid. Chapters 4 to 7 sort through the confusion to explore how power is shared in a new and vastly different environment and evaluate the degree to which the characteristics of the Checkbook Zionism of old might still remain.

The task of sorting through the changed philanthropic environment to study power sharing is more than daunting. The two large institutions that classically anchored Checkbook Zionism (the UJA and the Jewish Agency) have receded from importance and been supplanted by hundreds if not thousands of institutional actors. The solution this study used to work around the barrier of the enormity of the field was to identify a number of case studies from the current field of nongovernmental organizations (NGOs) in Israel supported heavily by

American Jews and to analyze power-sharing dynamics between case study organizations and their funders.

In order to best achieve an "apples to apples comparison" in what is a very large field of organizations and donors, it was determined that the sample of selected organizations should ideally all do work on the same general issue; and that issue should be one that (1) draws a broad variety of organizations (in form, ideology, strategies, etc.) and (2) attracts the support of American Jews of all kinds.

The issue identified as best meeting these criteria was the debate over Israel's West Bank settlement project. Numerous Israeli NGOs do work related to the settlement issue, most of which have important philanthropic support from a passionate American donor base. From the large pool of organizations working on settlement, sixteen were selected for in-depth case examination. Collectively the selected organizations represent ideological diversity—eight support the health/expansion of the settlement project in some way, and eight oppose or work to mitigate the effects of the settlements. Some are old. Some are new. Some are big. Some are small. They use a full variety of advocacy techniques, including lobbying, media work, protest, and classic Israeli grassroots activism. All have in common that they seek and rely on support from American Jews for their vitality and, in some cases, their very survival.

For each of the organizations, issues of power sharing were studied closely. Research methods included field observation, document analysis, and over a hundred interviews with NGO leaders, activists, and a subset of their donors. Main research questions included the following: How do NGOs and their donors regard one another? In the opinion of Israelis, does the migration of American donors toward more donor-driven philanthropic vehicles suggest that they want an enhanced role in decision making over use of funds beyond what American Jews had formerly wanted? And, if so, how receptive are the Israelis to this?

Chapters 4 to 7 analyze the nature of their power-sharing dynamics from three different perspectives, with an eye to how much the supposed revolution in the philanthropic relationship is indeed that.

Chapter 4 introduces a number of tools and frames necessary for understanding the contemporary analysis presented in the subsequent chapters, including a primer on new forms of philanthropic organization, relevant American tax law regarding overseas donations, Israeli NGO development, and brief introductions of the sixteen organizations in the sample.

The fact alone that as of 2007 American Jewish donors gave over 93 percent of total contributed funds to Israel through some kind of directed choice—be it giving to the general campaigns of organizations they have handpicked themselves ("new federated" relationships) or to specific projects within them (direct giving)—seems to confirm that Americans are interested in having some degree of say in how their donations are used in Israel.[45] In 2014, more than half of all

American Jewish donations to Israel were through new federated relationships and another 25 to 35 percent were via direct giving relationships.[46] While the degree to which the American principals in the new federated relationships attempt to exercise control over their donations is looked at in chapter 7, it is less clear how much American donors who are engaged in direct giving arrangements view their relationships with the NGOs they support through a frame of influence (e.g., as a struggle for influence, an abdication of influence, etc.). Classically, as sociologist Charles Liebman observed in his groundbreaking work on American Jews and Israel, *Pressure without Sanctions: The Influence of World Jewry on Israeli Policy*, American Jews did *not* view their relationships in this way. They maintained a much more hands-off relationship in how they supported Israel than in anything else they supported because, as Liebman noted, American Jews simply did not "regard Israel as a suitable object of . . . influence."[47] While there have not been any comprehensive follow-ups to Liebman's 1977 work, it remains to be seen how much this attitude has actually changed in the decades since.[48]

The original intent of this book had been to answer this question of how much Americans seek to exercise influence through their giving—as well as other key aspects of power sharing—by equally capturing the experiences and sentiments of all parties to these relationships. However, it became clear early on that there was a major methodological challenge to doing so, as Israeli organizations engaged in direct giving relationships do not publish the identities of their donors and are generally cautious about sharing such information. And though in the process of research each of the NGOs did share some contact information for a small portion of their donors, it was not a large enough data set collectively to be considered representative of the broader donor pool contributing to the organizations in this case study. So the question of how much the typical American Jewish donors giving directly want to use their donations as leverage to shape Israel is not known. Whatever donors' experiences were captured could not be regarded as more than anecdotal.

However, there was a way around this methodological obstacle to still get at some of the most central aspects underlying the contemporary power-sharing relationship. In traditional Checkbook Zionism, Israelis mostly called the shots. Any changes to that relationship, therefore, would necessarily include the Israelis in positions of decision-making authority actively and knowingly—but not necessarily willingly—relinquishing some of their power to donors. In contrast to this study's limited access to donors, it was able to identify and involve nearly all top leaders and fundraisers at each of the sixteen NGOs. Collectively, their experiences and impressions represented a comprehensive data set for this case. By looking at the experience of the Israeli principals at the NGOs, alone, therefore, one can see much about how power relationships may have changed, opinions of American Jews notwithstanding.

It is also important to acknowledge that although the arguments made in this book often speak about American Jews broadly, the community is not, and never was, monolithic. Within the community, there has always been a broad range of observance, affiliation, identity, and feelings about Israel/Zionism. This study's treatment of American Jewish behavior and attitudes mostly focuses on macro observations and, as such, admittedly does not address much of the diversity and nuance that comprise the community.

Chapter 5 examines how willing Israelis are to consider changing the terms of the relationship with American donors. The question of Israeli willingness to even *engage* in a reconceptualization of the relationship, as mentioned, would be a necessary prerequisite to any significant changes actually taking place and is therefore a crucially important component in evaluating the contemporary state of power sharing.

Chapter 6 builds on the conclusions from chapter 5. As it turns out, though there are caveats and conditions under which some Israelis would consider reevaluating power sharing, most Israeli interviewees indicated a strong desire to maintain the classic grip on decision-making power. In light of this, chapter 6 looks at how Israelis have attempted to hold on to their power in direct giving relationships—irrespective of what the Americans in the relationships choosing to give directly may actually want out of the relationships. It additionally assesses the degree to which the Israeli attempts to maintain power appear to be successful.

Chapter 7 looks at what encounters are like in "new federated" relationships—those between Israeli NGOs and American-based 501(c)(3) nonprofit donor organizations that collect money from (and purport to represent) American Jewish donors and allocate to the Israeli NGOs. Unlike the unidentifiable American donors involved in direct giving relationships, those making decisions for the American funding organizations are publicly identifiable and accordingly were recruited to participate in this study. This chapter is thus more able to pinpoint how and when the agendas of Americans and Israelis aligned and how and when they were at cross purposes and, in those instances, how tensions over influence and control were negotiated.

———

The book closes by offering hypotheses that address the trajectory of the power-sharing relationship between American Jewish donors and Israeli activists as we begin the third decade of the twenty-first century. Explored questions include the following: What shape is this one specific relationship taking, and what can that teach more broadly about homeland-diaspora relationships going forward? Are American Jews still inadvertently acting like the Birnbaums and the Sonnenscheins from *Sallah Shabati*? Even though American Jews express increased interest in directing the use of their donations and have far more access to information about Israel, are they still dependent on a version of Israel shown to them by Israeli fundraising professionals? And likewise, are Israelis still operating like the JNF representative in *Sallah Shabati*—putting on a convincing enough show to woo well-meaning but still underinformed donors, and then essentially doing what they wish with the money they collect? The ideas it suggests will shed light on the dynamics of homeland-diaspora philanthropic relationships beyond this single case and indeed will contribute to a greater understanding of the increasingly prevalent and significant global trends around the growth of diasporas.

PART I

# The Rise and Fall of Checkbook Zionism

# CHAPTER 1

# The Mechanics of Checkbook Zionism

Between the turn of the twentieth century and the late 1980s, American Jews cumulatively donated billions of dollars to support the development of the Yishuv/Israel. During this period, the communal leadership on both sides of the ocean collectively created a series of mechanisms, relational patterns, and norms for how best to harness the enormous power of the funds to shape on-the-ground realities in the Yishuv/Israel. This chapter explores the main institutional "planks" they crafted that gave rise to and anchored the Checkbook Zionism relationship for nearly a century: (1) federated giving, (2) an "Israel orientation," (3) a reimagined generosity, and (4) a tightly controlled allocations mechanism. It explores the origins, evolution, and legacies of each of the planks. Through doing so, it both frames the institutional history of Checkbook Zionism and provides important background for understanding the contemporary case study presented in later chapters.

## PLANK 1: THE COLLECTIVE POT—"FEDERATED" GIVING

At the peak of Checkbook Zionism in the 1970s and 1980s, the process of collecting funds from American Jews was orderly and streamlined, bringing in big sums annually and efficiently distributing them to what the community determined to be its top needs and priorities, both domestically and overseas. But, as this section recounts, it was not always this way.

### Chaotic Origins

From the earliest days of Jewish settlement in America, communal life in larger communities typically centered around a single synagogue that provided a variety of religious and social functions. While in the eighteenth and early nineteenth centuries, there were not yet dedicated social service organizations for

Jews outside of this model, Jacob Rader Marcus identifies an ad hoc culture within the communities of "nearly always" providing social services and mutual aid opportunities for their most needy.[1] But as Jonathan Sarna explains, it was not until the mid-1800s and the splintering of the "synagogue-community" model that the Jewish community required the establishment of new types of organizations to meet their various needs.[2] Until the late nineteenth century, these consisted mostly of local, community-based institutions like *chevrot kadisha* (burial societies), fraternal lodges, and mutual aid societies[3]—there was little need for much else.[4] It was not until the last decades of the nineteenth century and the massive influx of Eastern European Jews that American Jewry needed a more complex communal structuring.

Within a generation, the number of Jews in America grew more than tenfold, reaching approximately 3.6 million by 1920.[5] Most came poor and in need of services, including education and social and health support. In response, American Jews established thousands of new organizations to meet the needs of the new immigrants. In New York City alone, for example, as of 1918, 3,637 separate Jewish organizations had been established to meet the community's swelling needs.[6] The establishment of so many organizations in New York and other Jewish communities throughout the country during these years created problems of inefficiency and duplication. Prospective donors looking to support the flow of Jews in need, in the American Jewish tradition, were subject to solicitations by multiple charitable organizations who claimed to serve the same populations. Donors had little way of knowing which organizations were effective and efficient as well as whether they were truly focused on the immigrant community's most pressing needs. With little coordination or planning between them, groups provided redundant services and allocated resources poorly—both of which they could ill afford to do when so many people needed services and the financial resources to support them were so limited.[7]

Against this backdrop, leaders of the American Jewish community convened the first National Conference of Jewish Charities in 1900. At the meeting, leadership argued that in the current state of fast-growing populations of needy immigrants, something needed to be done to better coordinate. As conference president Max Senior put it, "The loose, benevolent, but spasmodic organizations of the past" were simply "not equipped" to deal with the present state of the community.[8] It was in this environment that the idea of federated fundraising for charity organizations gained some initial support as a solution. Community-wide federated fundraising essentially worked like a funnel. It called for the individual Jewish charitable organizations within a given city to suspend their individual fundraising efforts and instead fundraise collectively with other organizations in the community. The idea was that this would maximize the dollars in their collective pot, and the organizations would then together decide

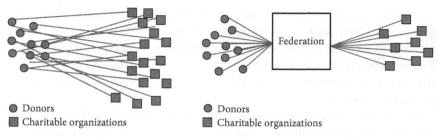

Donors

Charitable organizations

Donors

Charitable organizations

Figure 1.1. The collective pot (federated) model: In the haphazard manner of pre-federated giving in American Jewish communities (left), there were no centralized intermediary bodies to help donors sort through the numerous charities or organizations to efficiently connect with donors. The federated model (right) established a single destination for giving that would identify communal needs and more efficiently distribute resources. In communities that adopted a federated model, the total amount raised increased—in some cases substantially.

how to strategically divide the money among themselves to best meet the needs of the community at large (see figure 1.1).[9]

The Boston and Cincinnati Jewish communities had begun experimenting with this idea a few years earlier, as had a handful of wider nonsectarian communities throughout the United States, to positive effect. But until then it was not a mainstream idea.

In the years following the conference, additional communities initiated federated community-wide fundraising. Generally, they were pleased with the results and confident that they were raising more money than individual constituent organizations could have on their own. Yet, the idea of federated fundraising and allocating only gradually spread.[10] Many Jewish communities were reluctant to move to a federated system, some fearing that a unified campaign would raise less than separate organizational appeals would on their own. By the outbreak of World War I only fourteen other Jewish communities had launched such joint communal appeals.[11]

### Disorganization in Overseas Funding

In the first decades of the twentieth century, fundraising for overseas Jewish causes was even less organized than it was for domestic charities. Though the largely poor American Jewish immigrant community was struggling to work its way up and provide for its own local needs in the late nineteenth and early twentieth centuries, it still found a way to provide some resources to help its even poorer coreligionists abroad. At the root of this was the classic Jewish notion of K'lal Yisrael—that all Jews were responsible for the welfare of Jews everywhere.[12] The chief destinations for overseas giving were to support needy Jews in Europe and, to a lesser extent, in Palestine.

American Jews supported those in Europe primarily through *landsman-schaften*, fraternal lodges established by immigrants principally for social and mutual aid purposes in their new home communities. But as specific lodges were typically composed of members from a specific town or region of origin,[13] hundreds of them also raised money to fund their specific corresponding towns and villages in Europe.[14]

Donations American Jews made to support communities in Palestine during this era fell into two main categories. The first was *halukkah*, the age-old tradition in which diaspora Jews collected charitable funds to support the tiny, impoverished Jewish community living in the Holy Land. The collection and distribution of *halukkah* was not classically known for being an especially orderly process.[15]

The second was support for the welfare and development of the nascent Zionist agricultural settlement communities. The most prominent avenue for this type of giving was the Keren Kayemet L'Yisrael, or Jewish National Fund (JNF). Established in 1901 to be the financial arm of the World Zionist Organization (WZO), the JNF's principal activity was the purchase and rehabilitation of land for the establishment of Zionist settlements in the Yishuv.[16] Fundraising for JNF activities was conducted by a patchwork of independent Zionist organizations located in communities throughout the United States. These organizations were loosely affiliated with the Federation of American Zionists (FAZ), a mostly powerless national American Zionist umbrella. Local Zionist groups determined their own agendas,[17] with many of them focusing more on promoting cultural and educational activities in their communities than on remitting money overseas.[18] The total proceeds raised in the first twenty years of the JNF were very small, even by the standards of the day. Until World War I, American Jews who supported the Zionist pioneering effort donated only about $10,000 to $12,000 total per year (less than $300,000 per year in 2019 terms) (see figure 1.2).[19]

### The Rise of Federation

World War I proved to be a significant turning point in the organization of American Jewish philanthropic efforts. Europe's Jewish communities—often lying right in the middle of battlefields on the eastern war front—faced dire humanitarian needs on a massive scale. American Jews scrambled to become better organized in order to maximize the impact of their donations. By 1915, several smaller Jewish organizations, who had begun raising money for the embattled communities, fused their fundraising operations to create a joint federated body they named the American Jewish Joint Distribution Committee (JDC).[20] Through the JDC, American Jews interested in supporting imperiled Jewish communities in Europe now had a central address that they quickly came to believe they could trust to run well-coordinated fundraising and allocations

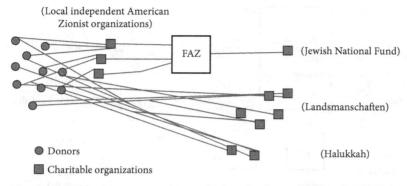

Figure 1.2. Collective overseas giving vehicles—*landsmanschaften, halukkah,*
and local Zionist organizations—reflected that though Jews in America indeed
were interested in supporting needy Jews overseas, systems for doing so were
even more ad hoc than those for domestic giving.

processes, in contradistinction to the piecemeal efforts of *landsmanschaften* and
other small organizations.

The JDC's efforts proved to be successful, raising $63 million between 1914
and 1924—truly astonishing sums well beyond what American Jews had ever
donated (equivalent to $1.15 billion in 2019 terms).[21] In addition, the success
enjoyed by the JDC would forever change American Jewish giving culture, in
both total sums donated and proclivity toward federating their charitable efforts.
Reflecting on the era, in which the broader American nonsectarian community
also had a similar experience with the benefits of federating, Robert Bremner,
preeminent scholar on the history of American philanthropy, noted that the lessons of World War I increasingly taught more and more American communities that federating charities was the ideal model for maximizing receipts and
efficient allocations. Because, as Bremner argued, federating "reduced competition and promoted rational distribution of charitable profits. It expanded the
number of givers [and] increased the amount of money available for social work
(figure 1.3).[22]

Domestically, Jewish federations caught on in community after community
following World War I (just as the counterpart nonsectarian "community chests"
did). Conventional wisdom came to understand that through creating centralized fundraising instruments, charitable giving would flourish—it would be
more efficient and more effective in promoting the most important work and in
drawing in more donors. As Bremner explained, the collective community funding vehicle led American Jews to view giving "less an act of personal charity
than a form of community citizenship, almost as essential as the payment of
taxes."[23] In the next years, this would become even more pronounced within the
Jewish community, with most American Jews contributing something.[24]

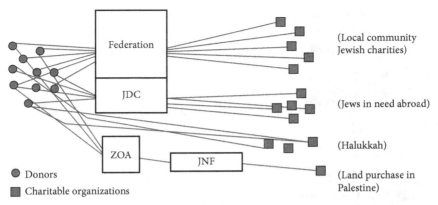

Figure 1.3. The advent of the JDC brought most non-Zionist overseas Jewish philanthropy under a federated umbrella. (By this point, the FAZ had been renamed as the
Zionist Organization of America [ZOA].) Source: Melvin I. Urofsky, *American Zionism
from Herzl to the Holocaust* (Garden City, NY: Anchor Press / Doubleday, 1976), 134.

Indeed, in the years after the war, collective fundraising and allocating were
becoming central parts of the DNA of American Jewish philanthropy. While the
rate at which community-wide federation campaigns blossomed was high all
around, it was even greater in Jewish communities.[25]

## Plank 2: A Shift Toward an "Israel Orientation"

Despite the advances in both organization and proceeds donated to most overseas Jewish communities, the enterprise of giving to Jews in Palestine lagged
behind broader trends. This was not altogether surprising, as the Zionist movement was, at that point, a fringe focus for American Jews. But from the mid-1940s
through the early 1950s, American Zionist leaders would seize upon a feeble and
disorganized system raising scant sums for the Zionist movement and transform
it into an organized fundraising machine that would come to command the
majority of American Jewish communal giving. In less than two decades, the
leaders of the Zionist movement in America, with support from allies in Israel,
would successfully employ an emotionally persuasive campaign that would
change giving mindsets and profoundly tilt allocations patterns toward Israel.[26]
Their efforts would bring in hundreds of millions of additional dollars and forever change giving and allocations outlooks.

### Meager Beginnings for Zionist Fundraising

During World War I, the FAZ—the loosely organized American Zionist
umbrella—tried to emulate the vast success of the JDC by launching its own federated campaign for relief and development in Palestine. Though the sums it

raised marked an improvement over previous efforts——$5.74 million from 1914 to 1921[27]—they were still a fraction of the $63 million raised by the JDC. The Zionist leadership based in the Yishuv launched a handful of other fundraising efforts in America after the war, but they too failed to gain much traction. American Jews contributed only $260,000 to the Keren Hakhana (Preparation Fund) in 1918 and $900,000 to the Keren Geulah (Restoration Fund) in 1919 (approximately $4.1 and $12.2 million in 2019 terms, respectively).[28]

By the mid-1920s, the leadership of the governing body of the worldwide Zionist movement—the WZO—recognized that it had to dramatically revamp its strategies in order to raise from American Jews the capital the Zionist movement needed so badly. In addition to the ever-increasing belief in the wisdom of federating campaigns, the WZO believed that it needed to make supporting Jews in Palestine a greater priority for American Jews. One problem it identified was that it needed to simplify its messaging to American Jews since the actual work of building a Jewish society in Palestine was a much more distant and difficult cause for American Jews to understand than charitable projects going on in their own local Jewish communities. The WZO reasoned that a unified campaign would be more successful than the then existing hodgepodge of Zionist-oriented charities that had, by then, started to fundraise in America.[29] In addition to the JNF, these included campaigns run by a number of Zionist political parties, the Zionist labor union Histadrut, the Yishuv-based medical organization Hadassah, the new Hebrew University in Jerusalem, as well as Keren Hayesod (Foundation Fund), a new fund the WZO had launched in 1921 (to name a subset). In 1925, the WZO spearheaded the federating of these various Zionist campaigns into a new collective umbrella body known as the United Palestine Appeal (UPA). By design, the UPA would collect money on behalf of the various constituent organizations and remit it to the newly founded Jewish Agency, the Yishuv-based governing body (also under the aegis of the WZO) for distribution.

Though the result of the new joint UPA campaign was better, it was still not by nearly as much as Zionist leaders had wished.[30] In the first two years of its existence, the UPA brought in $5.2 million (around $35 to $40 million per year in 2019 terms). The vast majority of American Jewish donations were still going to domestic causes; and even among overseas donations, the JDC's receipts more than doubled those of the UPA (figure 1.4).[31]

### Rivalry for Overseas Allocations Dollars

With the onset of the worldwide economic depression in 1929–1930, things worsened considerably for Zionist fundraising efforts in America. The supply of American Jewish charitable funds for all causes shrank dramatically. This was especially the case for overseas giving, ironically just as the needs of overseas Jewish communities became greater, with the rise of fascism in Europe and escalating tensions in Palestine.[32] In this lean environment, the need for efficiency

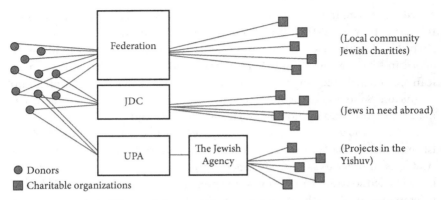

Figure 1.4. The UPA and the streamlining of giving to projects in the Yishuv.

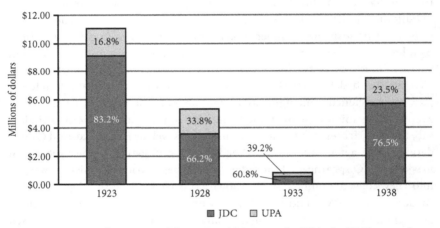

Figure 1.5. Prior to the merger of the JDC and UPA into the UJA, the JDC's annual receipts (shown here in millions of dollars) consistently dwarfed those of the UPA.

in fundraising was greater than ever.[33] In 1930, the Council of Jewish Federations and Welfare Funds—the recently established umbrella body of the domestic American Jewish federation system—intervened, attempting to push the national leadership of the UPA and JDC to form a unified overseas campaign to maximize receipts. It argued a union would yield greater results than the two bodies could achieve on their own.

However, the UPA and JDC opposed merging their campaigns since they had divergent and in some ways contradictory goals. The UPA believed the future of the embattled European Jewish community was in Palestine, while the largely non-Zionist leadership of the JDC wanted to preserve Jewish communities throughout the diaspora. They saw partnership, therefore, as undermining their philosophies and, as a result, likely their overall efficacies (see figure 1.5).

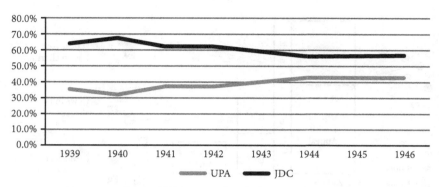

Figure 1.6. Share of UJA proceeds split between UPA and JDC.

But the pressures of the day finally motivated the two organizations to agree to a joint national effort: first, temporarily in 1930 in the so-called Allied Jewish Campaign; and permanently in 1938 after the shock of the Kristallnacht pogrom in Germany made clear to the UPA and JDC just how grave of an imminent crisis world Jewry faced. The two organizations agreed they would no longer allow their differences to stand in the way of maximizing collective campaign revenue, agreeing to a permanent fundraising pact in 1939 known as the United Jewish Appeal (UJA).[34] From then on, the two groups would be committed to a joint campaign, resolving to jockey for maximum allocations for their respective causes under a UJA umbrella, rather than walking away from the partnership. Each year, the JDC and UPA negotiated how they would divide UJA proceeds between themselves based on what they perceived as the most pressing needs of the day.[35] In the first four years of this arrangement from 1938 to 1941, the JDC received 65.4 percent and the UPA 34.6 percent of the roughly $40 million shared between the two organizations (figure 1.6).[36]

In light of the crises facing world Jewry in the early 1940s, the domestic federation system and overseas UJA reached a partnership arrangement. Though they would still remain separate organizations, the UJA and federation system decided to fundraise together and split the pot. Local federations would instruct their donors to make all domestic and overseas donations to them, and they would in turn allocate a certain percentage of the funds they collected to the UJA, which the federation system would now consider its sister organization for overseas projects (figure 1.7).

Within this joint federation/UJA relationship, the domestic-focused federation system still wielded most of the power. It had a much bigger organizational infrastructure and commanded the majority of donor attention. Yet, nevertheless, it agreed in the 1940s to an allocation formula that temporarily would tilt to support overseas needs.[37] It regarded such a split to be appropriate at the time in order to save lives and to a lesser extent attempt to build a soon-to-be Jewish

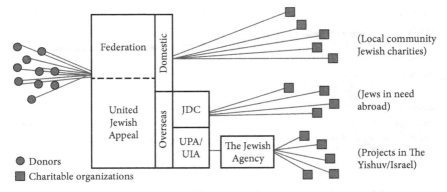

Figure 1.7. With the establishment of the UJA as the sister organization of the federation system, the vast majority of domestic and overseas American Jewish giving was finally under one overarching federated system, nearly fifty years after the federating process began.

state. This was further made possible because American Jewry had by then grown a generation or two from its immigrant status and enjoyed a level of affluence that diminished its need to devote quite as much funding for the American Jewish social infrastructure it was originally created to support.[38]

### An Explosion in Sums Raised

During the 1940s, the amount of money raised from American Jews and allocated to the UPA/UIA's partner organization in Israel, the Jewish Agency, grew by nearly twenty times, from $4.3 million in 1942 to $85 million in 1948 ($65 million and $906 million in 2019 terms, respectively).[39] This was due to dramatic changes both in the portion of the collective fundraising pie growing allotted to the UJA as well as the pie itself growing to a far larger size than previously thought possible.

The enormous growth can be partly explained by the new realities in the Jewish world brought on by the Holocaust and the establishment of the state of Israel (not to mention a rise in American Jewish prosperity). In addition, there was a dramatic shift during these years in how total funds donated by American Jews would be divided up from then on: the Zionist project, which had long been on the fringes of American Jewish communal priorities, was thrust to the center of the American Jewish agenda in the 1940s.[40] New arrangements for sharing allocations between domestic and overseas work and between the UPA and JDC were both drafted in the 1940s at the height of crisis in the Jewish world. They would become the new norm for splitting proceeds long after the height of the crises passed.

For the first several years following its establishment, the UJA had been more focused on supporting and rescuing Jews in Europe than it was on sup-

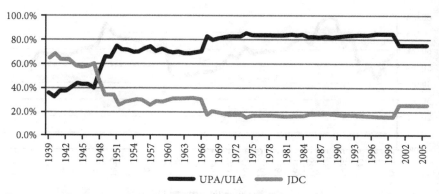

Figure 1.8. The UPA/UIA came to dominate the overall portion of overseas distribution of fundraising over its partner organization, the JDC.

porting Zionist efforts in Palestine. But by 1947, this had changed. As it had become clear the degree to which the Holocaust had decimated European Jewry, the still active battleground for the Jewish future was now in Palestine, with an impending United Nations partition vote and a likely Jewish-Arab war looming. So after years as the junior partner in the UJA, the UPA for the first time in 1948 commanded a majority of UJA's allocations (55.5 percent). By the early 1950s—when the UPA had then, for obvious reasons, changed its name from the United Palestine Appeal to the United Israel Appeal (UIA)—the UIA had cemented its place as the preferred overseas destination of American Jewish philanthropy, even though the immediate crises of 1948 had passed. The UIA would never again be the junior partner to the JDC. From then on, it received roughly 70 to 75 percent of annual UJA allocations to the JDC's 25 to 30 percent (see figure 1.8).[41]

### Changing Focus on Overseas versus Local Needs

While the UPA/UIA and JDC had been busy competing for their share of UJA allocations during the 1940s, the UJA was engaged in a similar hard-fought battle with individual community federations in the 1940s and early 1950s in order to ensure that as high as possible a percentage of the funds they raised would be devoted to overseas causes rather than to local needs. Irving Bernstein recounts the story of UJA leadership traveling across the country during this time, waging a domineering community-by-community campaign to push individual federations to change their allocations culture from mainly domestic-oriented to much more overseas in their focus: "[UJA leaders] forc[ed] their way into resistant communities, tearing up pledge cards they thought were inadequate, locking doors to rooms so that no one could leave. They pounded on tables until they splintered, arguing and fighting to make their fellow Jews realize that the fate of the new Jewish State and the lives of its people were at stake."[42] UJA efforts proved

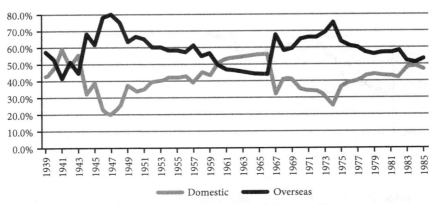

Figure 1.9. Domestic-overseas split in federation allocation.

effective in shifting the mindset of federation leaders—not just for the period of immediate concern but in the years beyond as well. Even during the relatively quiet decade in Israel following the 1948 war, the UJA was able to effectively press its case within the federation orbit for maintaining a greater commitment to overseas needs. Each year from 1949 to 1959, overseas allocations remained the chief beneficiary of the federation system, with the UJA pulling in an annual average of 60 percent of the total federation/UJA budget. Eventually the split tapered down toward even and by the early 1960s again tilted slightly toward domestic giving—but even then, never less than 44 percent.[43] But the 1967 and 1973 wars demonstrably shifted the balance back toward overseas giving. As figure 1.9 indicates, once the advocates for overseas spending were successful in pushing the greater relative importance of their work, there was no looking back. Note, for example, that even a decade after Israel's last war for survival (1973), the money still flowed disproportionately to support overseas causes; the UJA consistently received between 55 and 60 percent of all federation expenditures from 1967 through the late 1980s.[44]

## PLANK 3: A REIMAGINED "GENEROSITY"

Perhaps even more important than the UIA's success in attaining an increased *percentage* of the total federation pie was the work the UJA did to grow the *total size* of the pie itself. Longtime UJA director Henry Montor is often credited with having changed American Jewish fundraising forever. The work he spearheaded grew total amounts American Jews donated annually to new levels that would be sustained for almost half a century thereafter. Noting that American Jews as a whole gave an average of only $39.4 million per year to the combined domestic/overseas federation/UJA campaign between 1941 and 1945, Montor, as Stock put it, recognized a "latent capacity for increased giving" among American

Jews.[45] In response, he introduced a series of revolutionary fundraising practices that would succeed in growing the national federation/UJA campaign to a previously unfathomable size.

Montor realized that a campaign's success was dependent on its wealthiest donors.[46] By his estimate, 20 percent of the donors gave 90 percent of the donations. The best way to increase giving among this population, he reasoned, was to develop ways by which donors would be made publicly accountable for their gifts. One way to do this was to arrange small "parlor meetings" and rig their outcomes in advance. Stock gives an example of how such a meeting was carried out: "A wealthy individual invites a dozen or more of his friends. Two or three among those attending are 'pre-solicited' by a UJA professional and then planted among the rest. After a talk by a prominent Israeli guest, the host throws out his challenge: 'Most of you give $2,000 or $3,000. I would like to see one man get up and give $20,000 this year!' As had been pre-arranged, one man does get up to announce a startling increase over his last gift last year. Others follow suit."[47] In addition, larger meetings were likewise designed to leverage peer pressure into higher giving levels. In such meetings, all attendees had to publicly declare their level of commitment to the common cause. Raphael explains this phenomenon: "Following a brief but inspirational speech by someone with the latest report from Europe or Palestine, the host called each man's name, [announced how much he had given the previous year and then directed] . . . the man to 'stand and publicly pledge' before 'friends and neighbors' [how much he wanted to give]."[48]

This method, known as "card calling," would become standard federation/UJA practice for years to come.[49] By drawing on base human emotions like peer pressure, bravado, and shame,[50] card calling compelled people to make huge increases in their giving. The sum total of these efforts would forever change American Jewish ideas of the appropriate ranges for giving to the communal pot.

In 1946, total federation-UJA campaign receipts soared to $131.7 million, up from $57.3 million in 1945 (which to that point had been an all-time high). In 1947, they jumped to $157.8 million, and in 1948, to $205 million.[51] And in inflation-adjusted terms, receipts continued to grow from there.

As figure 1.10 shows, in inflation-adjusted terms, remissions to the Jewish Agency doubled from the early 1940s (interval 1) to the 1950s / early 1960s (interval 2), and nearly doubled a second time by the mid-1970s through late 1980s (interval 3). After each spike in American Jewish giving to the UJA/UIA following a moment of existential crisis for Israel—such as the wars of 1948, 1967, and 1973—giving levels plateaued. But each time, the plateau resettled at a higher level. It was not until around 1990 that remission totals began a real decline (interval 4) that by the end of the first decade of the twenty-first century were finally again below 1950s levels and again approaching the remission levels of the early 1940s.

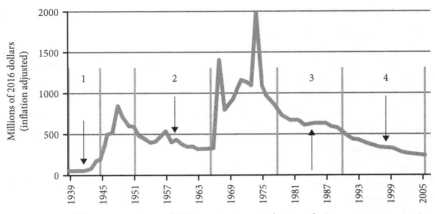

Figure 1.10. Annual UIA remissions to the Jewish Agency.

The point is that even more than the *share* of the pie of American Jewish collective giving that went to Israel, it was the *size* of the pie that made such a difference. American Jews grew in this period in their level of comfort in how much they could/should send to Israel. And for decades, there was no looking back.

### PLANK 4: A TIGHTLY CONTROLLED ALLOCATIONS MECHANISM

Over the decades that American Jews were increasingly giving more to more organized federated bodies and shifting a greater portion of it to support Israel, leadership of the Yishuv / new Jewish state were undertaking a series of steps to ensure that one single body would be the recipient of and allocator for the preponderance of American Jewish funds. Generally speaking, David Ben-Gurion and his allies in the Yishuv/Israel favored the idea of consolidating power in the state and state-aligned bodies at the expense of smaller, independent organizations. So it was unsurprising that they supported having a single centralized body for allocating overseas donations and conducting activities. As believers in the merits of federated collecting and allocating, the leaders of the American system also preferred having a lone allied Israeli partner organization.

### *A Single Israeli Allocations Body*

The 1922 Mandate for Palestine designated the creation of a "Jewish Agency" to administer and oversee the development of the Jewish settlement in Palestine. While the British Mandate administration was officially the legal body in charge, it invited this Jewish Agency (technically a subsidiary body of the WZO) and the associated bodies it funded, Knesset Israel and Va'ad Leumi (National Council), to establish their own structures for self-governance in many areas of Jewish Palestine,[52] including service provision and economic development. Prior to the Mandate period, the range of available social services in the Yishuv had been inadequate to serve even the needs of its small population. But as the Jewish population in the Yishuv surged in the 1920s (more than tripling from 50,000 to 162,000),[53] their shortcomings were magnified. The growing population needed health care, education, transitional absorption services for immigrants, child care, and old age services.[54] While Knesset Israel and Va'ad Leumi provided some services,[55] the Agency would need well more funding than could be raised from the Yishuv's residents alone. The burden of providing adequate social services, therefore, fell predominantly on world Jewry. And while groups such as the JDC and the American Zionist medical organization, Hadassah, did offer important services to Palestine's Jews, the primary provider for the community's needs was the Jewish Agency.[56] The Agency ran or at least funded services ranging from immigrant absorption to settlement construction, education, public health, and social services.[57]

Eventually, the Jewish Agency came to be almost wholly bankrolled by diaspora Jews. In the Agency's 1935 budget, for example, 76 percent of its revenue came from the UPA and its sister fundraising organization in other diaspora communities, Keren Hayesod—with most coming from American Jewry. Of the remaining 24 percent, most came from loans (19 percent), demonstrating further the degree to which the Jewish Agency's only means for income generation for which it would not later be liable were the donations it received from diaspora Jews.[58] Despite some very lean years during the Great Depression, American Jews provided roughly $100 million, or 70 percent of all diaspora philanthropy remitted to the Jewish Agency from the time of its inception in 1920 until statehood was achieved in 1948.[59] It was a natural fit that the WZO-run organization most responsible for Jews in the Yishuv would become the primary destination for the UPA, the WZO-created fundraising body in the diaspora.

From the time of its establishment, a big part of the Jewish Agency's driving ethos was to consolidate nation-building activities under its own aegis. When it did not have the capacity to provide services itself, it would often offer grants to other organizations to do so. For example, the Jewish Agency outsourced many of the social services that it funded in the Yishuv to the network of small organizations run by various political parties in the Yishuv. In fact, of the hundreds of social service organizations operating in the Yishuv in the 1920s and 1930s, most were run by political parties.[60]

In addition to using these party-linked organizations to carry out the services it wanted provided for the Yishuv's residents, the Jewish Agency was interested in compelling the parties that ran them to suspend their independent fundraising campaigns in the diaspora. The Jewish Agency agreed with the UPA's perspective that consolidating American fundraising efforts under a federated UPA campaign would ultimately increase dollars coming from the American Jewish community to the Yishuv as well as vest greater control for the whole allocations process under the two aligned WZO bodies. Therefore, it urged groups to stop fundraising abroad in exchange for receiving automatic funding from the common Jewish Agency pot. Over time, the Jewish Agency would be largely successful in this endeavor due to the close relationships it cultivated with the parties during these years.

## The Jewish Agency after the Establishment of the State

The Jewish Agency's drive toward consolidation continued on into the state era. Israel's first prime minister David Ben-Gurion had served for years as Jewish Agency chairman. While in that post, he had developed a governing philosophy that he would later term *mamlakhtiyut* (translated as "statism"). It called for the centrality of one central governing body in civic life and culture. When Ben-Gurion transitioned from Jewish Agency chair to prime minister, he implemented the *mamlakhtiyut* philosophy in setting up the power structure in the new state. It would have significant impact in determining the role civil society in general, and the Jewish Agency specifically, would play in Israel.

Upon declaring statehood in 1948, the Israeli government immediately assumed the governing and coordinating roles that the Jewish Agency had played during the Yishuv era. It would stand to reason that as the Jewish Agency lost its modus operandi, it would have ceased to exist at that point. But this was not to be the case for one very important reason. The new state faced the dilemma of how it could continue to receive the critical financial support the Jewish Agency had been receiving from diaspora Jews. This was of paramount importance as the state's own financial position was precarious, amid the multiple challenges it faced in security, societal development, and immigrant absorption. However, since by U.S. law contributions to foreign governments are not considered charitable, and are therefore not tax deductible, the only way American Jews could support the new state through tax-deductible donations was if the funds were instead passed along to an NGO.[61] Without tax deductibility, the total amount of money given by Americans would have dropped, and likely considerably.[62] Since the Jewish Agency was considered an NGO by the U.S. Internal Revenue Service, the Israeli government understood that there was value in keeping the Agency intact, so as to ensure that the large sums raised from American Jewry could continue to flow into Israel. However, to continue to qualify as a tax-exempt organization by American law, the Jewish Agency would have to remain a separate entity from the state with a separate portfolio of activities.

The Israeli government, however, had to determine how a well-funded and independent body like the Jewish Agency could operate in an environment in which it sought to consolidate its own authority. So state leadership and the Jewish Agency's new leadership moved quickly to divide up, but still share, responsibilities. While a rivalry would eventually develop between the two bodies, at this stage the government and Jewish Agency, as Stock notes, were not "eager to take on maximum responsibility at the expense of the other. The contrary was the case at the time: each was conscious of the paucity of means at its disposal and hoped the other would carry a larger share of the burden."[63]

Each side knew its role by late 1948, and an agreed-upon division of responsibilities between the two would be officially codified in 1952 (in the World Zionist Organization—Jewish Agency Status Law). The Jewish Agency would continue to be responsible for a number of tasks, but principally the absorption of new immigrants and the development of settlements and agriculture.[64] It was these tasks that the bulk of diaspora philanthropy coming into Israel would support. In addition, while the Yishuv had had a long history of voluntarism, and its residents had founded over four hundred nonprofit organizations to meet their various needs in the past,[65] over time the emergence of a powerful Israeli welfare state bent on *mamlakhtiyut* would crowd out most other actors. In such an environment, there was not much of a place for independent NGOs.

### Alternative Destinations for American Jewish Philanthropy?

While for reasons described the Jewish Agency's role as chief recipient of diaspora donations was consistent with the state's agenda, it is worthwhile to briefly discuss possible alternatives to the Jewish Agency that might have existed. In other words, did American Jewish philanthropic leaders have any other options for who would allocate the money they raised?

The political-party-run service networks that had been so important in the prestate era were no longer potential partners for overseas donors. During the first years of the state, Israel moved to gradually absorb them into its own ever-expanding service infrastructure.[66] The Israeli NGOs that did continue to exist during the early years of the state fell almost entirely into a category that Israeli nonprofit scholar Benjamin Gidron calls IWWSS organizations, or organizations "Integrated Within the Welfare State System." These groups, though technically independent, had an intimate relationship with the state. Most were established specifically to fill roles that the state preferred to outsource and accordingly were heavily if not entirely funded by the state.[67] Technically, the IWWSS organizations could have been alternative Israeli partners for diaspora donors, but neither the Jewish state nor the Jewish Agency nor the UJA saw them as a necessary or helpful alternative. So long as the UJA was pleased with the Jewish Agency as its dispenser of donations—which it would be for years—there was no driving reason to reach out to these other organizations. Furthermore, as groups receiving their financial lifeblood from the Israeli State, IWWSS organizations had no incentive or interest in bucking the system to seek out diaspora donations.

Indeed, beyond these state-linked bodies there was almost no nonprofit sector in Israel during this period. This was not especially surprising. On the one hand, Israeli citizens did not, themselves, have much inclination to establish independent associations and organizations to meet their various needs as they would eventually do decades later. At this time, most Israelis were content enough turning to political parties or the state and its rapidly expanding welfare services to meet their needs.[68] In addition, the Israeli government did not value and even maligned the appearance of independent organizations. In Ben-Gurion's statist outlook, as Hermann noted, voluntary groups were considered "petty, parochial, and counterproductive to the collective national interest."[69]

Indeed, *mamlakhtiyut*, in both concept and practice, propped the Jewish Agency up as the dominant body in collecting and allocating funds contributed by diaspora Jews by keeping the number of potential institutional partners for diaspora philanthropists limited. The result for the philanthropic relationship between American Jews and Israel was that the Jewish Agency was able to maintain a nearly uncontested grip over American Jewish donations for decades. While leadership in the UJA and Jewish Agency did successfully maintain a close relationship, the choice of the Jewish Agency as the destination for UJA allocations was bolstered by the simple fact that there were few or no other viable choices.

Every five years, the UIA—the Israel-focused subsidiary body within the UJA—would renew its agreement with the Jewish Agency, guaranteeing that the latter would be its exclusive recipient of funds in Israel. However, the renewal process from agreement to agreement was essentially pro forma. Between the UJA's dominance in collections and its use of the Jewish Agency as its exclusive grantee organization in Israel, the Jewish Agency held inordinate power in determining how the use of hundreds of millions of dollars provided by American Jews during this era would be used to tackle enormous challenges Israel faced. It was up to the Jewish Agency to determine both the priorities and how best to address them. There was input and collaboration from the Israeli government and to a much lesser extent the American Jewish community. But by and large, it was within the Jewish Agency's directive to make the decisions.

## Conclusion

As this chapter has recounted, the institutional system that would anchor Checkbook Zionism developed over the course of the first half of the twentieth century from meager beginnings into a streamlined philanthropic engine for Israeli development. At its peak in the 1970s and 1980s, American Jews contributed over $300 million to the UJA annually to support Israeli society[70]—or adjusted for inflation in 2019 dollars, it averaged to over $1 billion every year over the twenty-year period. This type of financial muscle enabled the Jewish Agency to conduct a robust portfolio of activities, including agricultural development, refugee settlement, and youth services as well as the construction of schools, urban renewal for depressed neighborhoods, and absorption services for immigrants from the Soviet Union and Ethiopia.

The consolidation and growth of the federation system, the UJA, the UIA, and Jewish Agency discussed in this chapter provided American Jewish leadership—who were predominantly proponents of the Weizmann school of partnership—with the infrastructure they would need to carry out an effective Checkbook Zionist enterprise: a big pool of money, a common funnel to direct it, and an exclusive relationship with a trusted Israeli partner to allocate it. As detailed, over the first decades of the twentieth century, American Jews had gradually been conditioned to donate—and donate generously—to a common pot. With the federation–UJA–UIA–Jewish Agency nexus set as the common pipeline, American Jews knew that a substantial part of the money they donated would be in support of Israel and passed along into the hands of a reliable body in Israel. They knew that body would channel resources to help address Israel's top priorities. The same things they might have read in the newspaper or heard from visiting Israeli speakers about the need for better farming technology or settling immigrants or building schools were the things that their charitable dollars were specifically going to. This all percolated down into the culture. Giving to Israel was a responsibility, and one that many felt honored—not just obliged—to dispense.[71] American Jews knew that by doing their part in the community and writing that check they were playing an important role in the unfolding drama of Jewish history. They may not have been donning the *cova tembels*, or pick axes—or rifles, for that matter—but they proudly understood that they were footing the bill for many of the critical instruments of state building. Precisely *how* they came to understand themselves in their role as Checkbook Zionists is the subject of the next chapter.

# CHAPTER 2

# The Culture of Checkbook Zionism

A central tenet of early Zionist thought was that the diaspora was a phase of Jewish history that needed to come to a close.[1] To many theoreticians, diaspora represented shame and powerlessness. They believed that Zionism should therefore aim to not only create an empowered alternative path to diaspora life but also push for its total conclusion. This concept was known as *shlilat-ha-galut*, or the "negation of exile." It argued that once a Jewish state was established, there would be no place for a permanent diaspora in the future of Jewish civilization. Diaspora communities would immigrate en masse to the new state. Whatever small number of individual Jews choosing to remain in diaspora would eventually vanish at the hands of either persecution or assimilation.[2] And until that point, Jews living in the Jewish state need not pay much attention to the opinions of remaining Jews abroad. If they were going to be shortsighted and ignore the new reality of the Jewish world, then they were forfeiting any meaningful role in it.

However, even before Israel was established in 1948, it had become clear that most of world Jewry was *not* going to immigrate to the new state as Zionism had ideally envisioned, much less endorse the idea of *shlilat-ha-galut*. The new state therefore faced an immediate challenge with diaspora communities—especially in its relationship with the American Jewish community. If the Zionist position said that Jews living outside of Israel should either immigrate or essentially be written off, then what was an Israeli state—the embodiment of Zionism— supposed to say about the continued existence of a much larger, more powerful, and wealthier American Jewish community that was not going to make mass *aliya*? Israeli leadership may have been ideologically opposed to American Jews' choice to remain in diaspora, but it badly needed their financial and political support.

Israelis quickly realized they had to swallow their pride and allow for those Americans who financially supported the Israeli state to be regarded as respected partners—at least ceremonially, if not practically—in the project of building a strong and secure homeland for Jews. But beneath the veneer of the rhetoric, the view of Israelis toward Jews living outside of Israel deviated little from *shlilat ha-galut* mentality—that those who chose to live in diaspora did not deserve equal respect and certainly not an equal voice in shaping the new state's character and policy.[3] In matters of substance, Israelis believed that Jews living outside of Israel—the Checkbook Zionists—should be no more than a junior partner in the Israeli-diaspora relationship.[4] But how would this view sit with diaspora Jews?

American donors who supported the Zionist movement, and eventually the Israeli state, sought to make an important contribution to the effort. A subset of American Jews believed that since their funds would be put to use for the Zionist effort, they should have some input over how they were allocated. But just how much input would be the subject of intense debate throughout the first half of the twentieth century. Were American Jews merely the financiers, or did they deserve an equal role in shaping this most ambitious project for building a more secure future for world Jewry? Would the overseas patrons of Zionism who shouldered so much of the financial burden be willing to play the role of second fiddle? Or, conversely, should American Jews insist on using their finances to leverage power in decision making? And behind it all loomed a corollary question: what degree of American Jewish involvement would Israelis even tolerate in decisions affecting their society?

This chapter explores the origins of Checkbook Zionism from a cultural—rather than an institutional—perspective. It tells the story of dueling philosophies over money, power, and politics in the relationship between American Jewish and Israeli leadership during the twentieth century. It describes the main schools of thought on philanthropic partnership and how their proponents battled in the first half of the century to control the nature and flow of American Jewish philanthropy to the Yishuv and early state. It then details the extensive steps taken by the eventual winning side (led by future Israeli president Chaim Weizmann, future Israeli prime minister David Ben-Gurion, and their American allies) to permanently entrench Checkbook Zionism—and its core philosophy of American deference to Israelis in allocation decision making—as the dominant mode of philanthropic partnership in the second half of the century. It concludes by assessing how well these efforts worked in defining the nature of the American Jewish relationship to Israel for most of the twentieth century.

## THE QUESTION OF OUTSIDE INFLUENCE

The debate over power and influence between givers and spenders did not arise as simply an intellectual exercise. Early Zionist settlers grappled with it directly.

The first Zionist pioneers in the Yishuv had an unpleasant and deeply formative experience that cemented their thoughts on foreign philanthropic involvement. In the late nineteenth century, French Jewish philanthropist Baron Edmond de Rothschild, perhaps the world's wealthiest Jew at the time, became Zionism's most important financial backer. Rothschild, who nearly single-handedly supported the first Zionist colonies in Palestine, felt it his prerogative to dictate how he wanted what he considered *his* money to be spent on the ground in the Yishuv. Rothschild believed that he, rather than those living in the Zionist colonies, knew what was best for them.[5] To ensure things were executed according to his design, Rothschild deployed a team of administrators to Palestine to oversee the work of the colonists. He went so far as to demand that Zionist pioneers take direct orders from his representatives, dangling threats of grave consequences if they failed to do so. He was known to proclaim that, if pushed on the issue, he might withdraw his "protection and abandon them to themselves."[6] Rothschild clearly cared about Zionist settlement, but had he made good on his threats, he could have endangered both the vitality of the project and the well-being of the individual pioneers. Yet he was so adamant that it needed to be done on his terms, that as the financier, he was willing to take that risk.

Rothschild never did abruptly pull his funding; rather, as he was joined by additional donors, he gradually reduced his commitment over time. Still, the experience left a terrible taste in the mouths of the pioneers.

What made this even more difficult for Zionist pioneers in the Yishuv was that they had already been ambivalent about the idea of accepting funding from diaspora Jews long before their relationship with Rothschild. They saw foreign support as too reminiscent of what they regarded as the shameful indigent past of Jews in the Holy Land accepting *halukkah* from concerned, albeit patronizing coreligionists abroad.[7] As Schama put it, for Zionist pioneers "to acknowledge a continued dependence on outside assistance would have been to subvert the effort to recapture personal dignity and self-affirmation" that was so central to the Zionist ethos.[8] The idea of wealthy benefactors from far away involving themselves in decision making about on-the-ground minutiae in Eretz Yisrael was to mainstream Zionist ideology—as it would eventually be to Israeli ideology—not just arrogant and demeaning but more importantly a fundamentally misplaced locus of authority. Zionists believed that they, the motivated workers risking life and limb, were entitled to be the decision makers on anything involving the Zionist project and that diaspora Jewish financiers, who may have spoken of Zionist commitment but were unwilling to make the personal sacrifices of moving to Palestine, simply were not. Still, the Zionist builders in the Yishuv did not have the luxury of repudiating support from abroad. They were in need of funding, so, like it or not, they had to hold their noses and accept it.

### Philanthropic Partnership after Rothschild: Two Schools of Thought

With these conflicting agendas in mind, the World Zionist Organization (WZO), founded in 1897 to be the organizing congress of the Zionist movement, moved to create a new diaspora funding relationship that would avoid the potential ideological and logistical pitfalls that plagued the pioneers in their dealings with Rothschild. In 1901, the WZO rolled out a community-wide fundraising instrument, known as the Jewish National Fund (JNF). Through the JNF, the WZO would urge all Jews worldwide to pitch in to collectively fund the Zionist enterprise.[9] It was initially unclear how the new funding relationship between pioneers and funders of the JNF (and the various other collective funding instruments that would later follow) would mirror or differ from the relationship with Rothschild.

Zionist pioneers were skeptical of diaspora Jewish philanthropists. They abhorred the dependency they believed that diaspora money implied and were loath to replicate that kind of relationship with future donors.[10] But if the Rothschild experience, at one extreme pole of possible arrangements between diaspora philanthropists and those on the ground in the Yishuv/Israel, was beyond the pale of what could be tolerated, what were the terms under which they would feel comfortable? Could they accept surrendering *any* decision making to those living in the diaspora?

On the other side of the ocean, this was a question as well. While few American Jewish donors had interest in dictating their terms to Zionist pioneers to the degree of Rothschild, per se, some felt that as long as they were writing checks, they should be able to have *some* voice in how that money was being used.

In the first decades of the twentieth century, two main schools of thought regarding diaspora donations came to the fore. One argued that Jews living in the Yishuv were the most qualified and, as the people on the ground literally enduring the trials of building a new society, the most entitled to decide how money should be spent.

The other school held that expenditure decisions should be, at least partially, in the hands of those providing the funds. Not only were donors entitled to decide how to spend their own money, it argued, but also, simply handing funds over to one centralized Yishuv-based body to plot out all allocation decisions could easily lead to issues like deception, politicking, and inefficiency that could mitigate the impact of donations.

The most vocal proponents of each of these two perspectives were also arguably the two most influential Zionist figures of the day—Chaim Weizmann, president of the WZO, and Louis Brandeis, a U.S. Supreme Court justice and America's most out-front Zionist leader. The two would differ on a number of practical matters related Zionism,[11] but perhaps none more than the issue of how decisions should be made regarding the use of funds from Zionism's boosters abroad.

### The Brandeis Model for Philanthropic Partnership

In the first decades of the twentieth century, few American Jews supported the Zionist movement. Most who did were devoted adherents to specific strains of Zionist ideology—labor Zionism, cultural Zionism, religious Zionism, and so forth.[12] The small number of non-party-aligned American Zionists that did exist supported the Federation of American Zionists (FAZ), the American affiliate of the WZO. Though the FAZ was primarily interested in American-based programs promoting Zionist culture and education, it also raised some money for work in the Yishuv. For the most part, those American Zionist leaders responsible for allocating collected donations agreed that the nuts-and-bolts decision making for how exactly to craft the new Jewish society in Zion should be determined by those living there and building it—*not* those in the diaspora. And so the FAZ dependably passed on its proceeds to the WZO without demanding a voice in its use.[13]

It was only first in 1914 when Louis Brandeis became president of the FAZ that Zionism began to gain wider support among American Jews. And it was Brandeis's emergence on the scene that would challenge the FAZ's policy of non-interventive allocation to the WZO.

When Brandeis began his tenure as head of the FAZ, he was a devoted supporter of the WZO. He believed the WZO's purpose was to lead the campaign to advocate for the creation of an internationally recognized modern Jewish homeland. Indeed, when Great Britain issued the Balfour Declaration in 1917, calling for the establishment of a Jewish national home in Palestine, Brandeis applauded the work the WZO had done to help make it happen. At that point Brandeis believed that since the WZO's raison d'être had been achieved, there was therefore no longer a reason for it to exist. Yet the leaders of the WZO disagreed. They instead saw their role as evolving into both the leading political body governing the Jewish community in the Yishuv and, through the JNF, as the financial intermediary between overseas donors and projects in the Yishuv.

Brandeis took great exception to this—especially the WZO's intention to control the use of foreign donations. He believed that, in the interest of generating the most funds and using them with the greatest efficiency, businessmen and technicians should be the ones to recommend the most judicious use of the funds, rather than the Zionist politicians and ideologues associated with the WZO. In addition, Brandeis felt that, rather than simply passing their funds along to someone else to make decisions, American Jewish donors, as the benefactors of the Zionist project, should have a say in how the money would be spent. As scholar Ben Halpern explains, Brandeis and his group of supporters believed such giving "provided for more active, closer personal involvement of American Zionist members." Brandeis felt it would be best if American, and indeed all, diaspora Zionists regarded themselves as something like "stockholders of new Palestinian institutions," through which they "could become involved in the work of reconstruction more fully than by simply contributing."[14]

Brandeis envisioned that donors would identify specific destinations for the use of funds and that the recipients in the Yishuv would then need to be accountable for restricting the use of donated funds for these donor-designated purposes and *only* these donor-designated purposes.[15] In this way, American funds would be used to maximum efficiency and also allow for a meaningful and authentic way for Zionists who were not interested in leaving the diaspora to engage in the Zionist project.

### The Weizmann Model for Philanthropic Partnership

The other school of thought, championed by WZO president Chaim Weizmann, argued that all decisions for the state in the making should be handled by those in the Yishuv. Weizmann's philosophy on philanthropic relations was rooted in *shlilat-ha-galut*. While it certainly did not go as far as the original doctrine in terms of explicit disdain for diaspora existence, it was similar in its view of what the diaspora's appropriate voice should be. He argued that those Jews who had already relocated from the diaspora to Zion were holistically devoting their lives to the Zionist project and were more qualified and, even more so, more entitled to call their own shots. As the official on-the-ground Zionist body in the Yishuv, the WZO (or "Jewish Agency," as it was being rebranded) should therefore decide how to allocate money given by Jews to support the upbuilding of Jewish communities in the Yishuv. Prior to Brandeis, Weizmann had appreciated that Zionist funding bodies throughout the diaspora world mostly comported with his perspective and allowed those in the WZO to make expenditure decisions.

### The Battle over American Jewish Giving Culture: Round 1

In 1920, Brandeis embarked on a campaign to codify his personal philosophy as the official policy of the FAZ, or as it was being renamed, the Zionist Organization of America (ZOA). Until then, the FAZ/ZOA had been an affiliate of the WZO, subject to its direction. Brandeis wanted to break the ZOA out from under WZO yoke and make it an independent American-run body that distributed the money as it saw fit. Brandeis's pitch found a sympathetic audience with leading American Zionists. At the ZOA executive committee meeting in November 1920, a majority of the group's leadership voted in support of Brandeis's restructuring plan. The decision stood to be officially ratified as new ZOA policy at the organization's general meeting the following June.

Weizmann viewed these developments with great alarm. He believed that with this change, the ZOA may be on the verge of working, as Halpern put it, "solely on their own projects without reference to the policy or authority of the

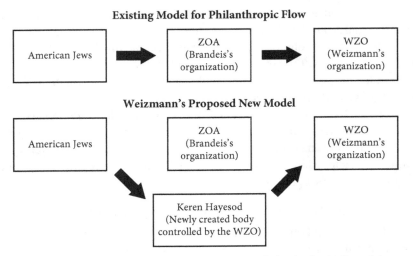

Figure 2.1. The new model proposed by Weizmann helped sidestep Brandeis and the ZOA.

WZO."[16] He knew he had to take action quickly or risk the WZO losing control over its American funding, a crucial part of its operational lifeblood. Weizmann reasoned that his best bet would be to leverage his own fame and prominence to appeal directly to American Jews. So in April 1921 Weizmann came to the United States to personally stop Brandeis's campaign to gain control over the use of American Zionist funding. Rather than going to the ZOA and risking Brandeis's interference, he encouraged American Jews to directly support the WZO through a new fund he had launched called Keren Hayesod (Foundation Fund). If American Jews gave to his new fund instead of the ZOA, Weizmann reasoned that he could cut both Brandeis's organization and what he considered Brandeis's very dangerous ideas on allocations and decision making out of the equation (figure 2.1).

It is not entirely clear which perspective was more of the natural inclination of American Zionists at the time. More likely, as the less ideologically driven wing of world Zionism, American Zionists stood to be swayed by whichever argument was presented in a more convincing manner. Brandeis and Weizmann each appeared to feel that way, as they fought to win over the American Jewish community to their perspectives. Halpern recounts that, to do so, representatives from the two sides "descended on the clubs and affiliates of the ZOA with speakers and rival publications" in what he called "open warfare" from late 1920 to spring 1921.[17] ZOA leadership recognized it needed to ameliorate rising tensions between the two camps and their opposing views, and so put resolution of this issue at the top of its agenda for its general organizational meeting in June 1921.

At the meeting, the two sides emphatically made their cases for how American Jewish donations should be used in the Yishuv. To Weizmann's great relief, he was able to convince enough of the ZOA's delegates of his perspective. And by a vote of 173–71, the ZOA opted to overrule the recommendation of its own executive committee and remain a loyal branch of the WZO. Whether this reflected a sympathetic endorsement of the Weizmann model over the Brandeis model or whether Weizmann just made a more convincing case, the end result was the same. The ZOA would continue to defer decision making over the use of donations to those in the Yishuv.[18]

Unwilling to endorse Weizmann's divergent vision for controlling allocations, Brandeis and thirty-four other delegates resigned their posts with the ZOA.[19] On the one hand, they accepted their defeat. They believed it would be detrimental to the overall Zionist project to wage an ongoing public war for the hearts and minds of the wider American Jewish community. Yet, on the other hand, they wanted to offer donors opportunities for supporting work in the Yishuv in a way more in line with their own philosophy. So they formed their own alternative organizations to facilitate direct philanthropy as well as investment to the Yishuv. The organizations, the Palestine Endowment Fund (PEF) and the Palestine Economic Corporation (PEC), would vest decision-making prerogatives in the hands of the donors. Brandeis saw to it that PEF and PEC conducted their work in a relatively quiet and noncompetitive fashion. Though not an insignificant enterprise, PEF would essentially be a scarcely known alternative mode for philanthropic engagement with the Yishuv/Israel for the next decades.[20]

From the perspective of the Weizmann camp, it appeared that crisis had been averted. Weizmann's victory at the ZOA in 1921 ensured that his perspective on use of funds would remain as ZOA policy going forward. Indeed, over the ensuing two decades, funds raised by Weizmann's organization Keren Hayesod and its successor umbrella bodies, the United Palestine Appeal (UPA) and the United Jewish Appeal (UJA), were forwarded along (via the ZOA) to the WZO/Jewish Agency in the Yishuv to be used at its discretion with minimal incident. But to the dismay of Weizmann's camp, a second battle for control over American Jewish funds would eventually ensue in 1948.

## The Battle over American Jewish Giving Culture: Round 2

Cleveland rabbi Abba Hillel Silver had been one of the junior members of the Brandeis group who had left the ZOA after the defeat in 1921. Unlike most in the group, however, Silver had quietly returned to the ZOA in the late 1920s. Over the next decade and a half, Silver, a charismatic advocate for the creation of a Jewish state, had climbed the ranks of the American Zionist movement. By the 1940s, he had become arguably its most influential figure.[21] However, as heir to the Brandeis school of philanthropic power sharing, Silver took issue with some of the ZOA's positions. He did not view the American Zionist movement exclusively as a tool to help advocate for and fundraise on behalf of Zionists in the Yishuv/Israel forever. He believed instead that once a Jewish state was established, the ZOA should become an independent body, promoting its own agendas and allowing American supporters of the Jewish state to voice their own opinions regardless of whether they necessarily comported with those of the future state's leadership. Silver and his allies, as Raphael recounts, were "concerned that the ZOA not be perceived as merely an arm of a foreign power. . . . He wanted to make certain that the Israeli leaders did not control the diaspora Zionist bodies as they struggled with the challenges of incipient nationhood."[22] This idea had not been at the forefront of Silver's public messaging during his rise to prominence, but once his chief goal of advocating for the creation of a Jewish state finally appeared imminent, the tone of his message shifted.

Legally, the ZOA still maintained discretion over the use of all Yishuv-bound funds raised by the UJA and UPA. Until that point, the ZOA, as a subsidiary of the WZO, had allowed for mostly unfettered flow of these dollars to the WZO–Jewish Agency in Israel. But the ZOA technically had the power to turn off the faucet and redirect the expenditure of UJA funds in any way it wanted. The heirs to the Weizmann school, including soon-to-be Israeli prime minister David Ben-Gurion and much of the other political leadership of the Yishuv as well as their like-minded American allies (notably UJA director Henry Montor and UJA campaign chair and former U.S. treasury secretary Henry Morgenthau), therefore viewed Silver's plans for a restructured relationship with grave concern. They staunchly believed that control over the use of philanthropic funds needed to remain with those on the ground in the soon-to-be state of Israel. They could not accept the kind of American agency in decision making that Silver intimated should become ZOA policy after the state's establishment. To their mind, even after the establishment of Israel, the American fundraising machine should serve principally to get American Jewish donations into the hands of decision makers in Israel and not be a foreign voice trying "to influence the social and political constellation in Israel,"[23] as Montor had accused Silver and his allies of intending. Morgenthau echoed this concern in a 1948 letter he wrote to Jewish Agency and eventual Israeli finance minister Eliezer Kaplan: "What we fear is that certain Jews in the U.S. will dictate to you what you should do with their money," adding, "I have confidence in the Jews of Israel, I have no confidence in the Jews of the U.S. who have control over their money."[24] This stinging indictment of American Jewry by one of the leading figures in the American Jewish community illustrated just how crucial those in the Weizmann camp believed it was to keep American-raised funds under the control of Israelis.

For this reason, Montor, Morgenthau, and their allies in the Yishuv viewed Silver's ambition and stature within the American Jewish community as dangerous. Yet it was clear in the lead-up to 1948 that it was not yet the time to wage a bruising public fight against such a powerful ally in the statehood cause as Sil-

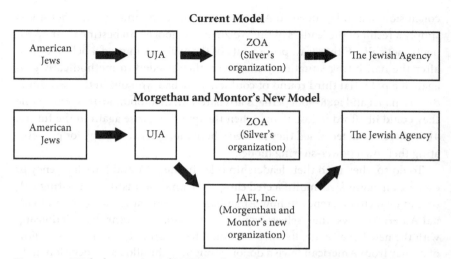

Figure 2.2. With the creation of JAFI, Inc. by Morgenthau and Montor, the Weizmann model once again prevailed over the Brandeis model championed by Silver and his allies.

ver, so they chose to temporarily withhold their criticisms. However, once Israel declared its statehood in May 1948, the Morgenthau-Montor camp went after Silver over the issue.

Still, they feared that if they entered a direct confrontation with Silver, as Weizmann had done with Brandeis in 1920–1921, they could very likely lose to the immensely popular American Zionist leader and individual American Jews could begin calling for a say in the use of their charitable funds in Israel. They calculated that the flamboyant Silver would not be quite as quiescent as Brandeis had been. So, rather than publicly appealing to American Jews, they pulled a procedural stunt to effectively hijack the flow of money. In 1949, Morgenthau and Montor announced a plan to establish a new, independent nonprofit organization— named JAFI, Inc.—that would replace the ZOA as the legal owner of the funds the UJA raised for projects in Israel.[25] They reasoned that, from the perspective of donors, things would look indistinguishable. Donors would still give to the recognizable UJA brand, regardless of whether the organization maintaining discretion over allocation of UJA funds was called the ZOA or JAFI, Inc. (figure 2.2).

With the creation of JAFI, Inc., Silver and his allies in the ZOA well understood what was happening. The ZOA was being legally stripped of its control over UJA funds. Recognizing they had no recourse to prevent it short of publicly declaring a civil war within the American Jewish organizational apparatus, Silver and his allies resigned from their posts in the ZOA.[26]

For the second time, the Weizmann model had prevailed over the Brandeis model. Here again, it was not clear whether this outcome would have been the conclusion of a fully informed American Jewish community or whether it was simply a result of the leaders of the Weizmann school again besting their opponents tactically. Either way, proponents of the Weizmann model believed that, after the nail-biting situation with Silver, they needed to methodically gird against a potential third round of conflict. They had won out in the two showdowns in 1921 and 1948—but perhaps just barely. In their opinion, this was a game they could ill afford to lose if and when the question arose again in the future. They therefore determined they needed a better long-term strategy for perpetuating their own power-sharing model.

To do so, they used their leadership roles in the UJA and Jewish Agency to execute an aggressive, multifaceted campaign aimed at instilling a lasting culture of de facto deference in how American Jewish organizations and individual American Jews, themselves, would regard their philanthropic relationship with the new Israeli state. Its purpose would be to facilitate an unimpeded flow of money from American Jewish donors straight to the allocation decision makers at Jewish Agency and prevent future advocates for Brandeis's model of power sharing from threatening their hold on the system. The leaders at the UJA and Jewish Agency envisioned several ways that their efforts could be undermined. But if they could groom rank-and-file American Jews to believe that the UJA was the only legitimate destination for Israel-oriented giving and if all intermediaries involved in the process of passing money along to the Jewish Agency refrained from injecting differing opinions on allocations along the way, American money could continue to flow smoothly to Israeli decision makers.

### Instilling a Lasting Culture of American Jewish Deference

In reviewing the sum of the UJA and Jewish Agency activities over the ensuing years, one can discern a strategy made up of four distinct components they used to instill an ongoing prevalent attitude among American Jewish leaders as well as rank-and-file donors of deference to Israelis in decision making over use of funds that was so central to Checkbook Zionism: (1) gutting the ranks of the UJA to put their own like-minded allies in place; (2) squelching alternative voices who might be advocating for different philanthropic partnership arrangements; (3) steering potentially independent-minded donors into the UJA fold; (4) controlling the narrative about Israel by appealing directly to donors and pushing their own chosen mythology about what Israel was and what it needed.

#### Gutting the Ranks

As chapter 1 outlined, until the 1940s most American Jews donating to Jewish causes overseas focused on supporting the preservation of Jewish communities in Europe and elsewhere via the Joint Distribution Committee (JDC), rather than supporting Zionist activities in Palestine.[27] But when the Holocaust decimated

European communities and Zionism moved from aspirational vision to action plan for supporting a likely soon-to-be state for Jews, the non-Zionists, as they had been called, suddenly had interest in supporting Zionist efforts in Palestine. For the most part, this was born not out of a newfound belief in classic Zionist ideologies but rather out of a general concern for the welfare of their embattled fellow Jews abroad—many of whom now lived in the Yishuv/Israel. American Jewish communal leader Max Fisher would eventually term this group the "New Zionists."[28]

Notably, these New Zionists included many of America's wealthiest Jews. Montor and Morgenthau wanted to recruit New Zionists to become active participants in the UJA fundraising enterprise for two reasons: so the UJA could gain access to their large and previously untapped financial resources, of course, but also *precisely* because most in this group were not driven by a specific kind of Zionist ideology. Montor and Morgenthau generally regarded ideologically driven Zionists as problematic for their goals. Since ideological Zionists likely had specific visions or even agendas for how they wanted Israeli society to develop—not unlike Abba Hillel Silver had—Montor and Morgenthau feared this group might seek a more active voice in shaping Israel's development, rather than mostly passively bankrolling it. In contrast, the outlook of New Zionists was something like a nonideological philo-Israelism. They were essentially quiescent financial boosters and were mostly fine allowing the Jewish Agency to set the agenda. According to the Weizmann school, this was the ideal paradigm for how diaspora donors should act.

In the next few years, Montor was successful in courting some of the wealthiest and most prominent New Zionists to be national UJA campaign chairs—or the out-front spokespeople for the UJA's fundraising efforts. These included first Morgenthau himself and later also figures such as William Rosenwald, heir to the Sears Roebuck empire, and Edward M. M. Warburg, of the Warburg banking family. If the elite of wealthy and formerly non-Zionist American Jews like Morgenthau, Rosenwald, and Warburg vocally endorsed the Zionist cause, Montor predicted that legions of other wealthy former non-Zionists would follow.[29] And his plan proved correct.[30]

In addition to placing New Zionists as leaders at the top of the UJA, Montor and Morgenthau methodically pushed to remove ideological Zionists from even the lower level fundraising posts they had held for the UJA in communities throughout the country. This was no small act—for decades, these local activists had been the biggest and most tireless American supporters of creating a Jewish state.[31] They were now unceremoniously replaced by New Zionists who had not supported the state building enterprise during its many lean years. But with a crop of New Zionist fundraisers, many of whom came from the leadership ranks of their local communities' federations, the UJA had enlisted as its pitchmen often the most well-connected local leaders. The organization for the first time could now make in-roads all over the country into the formerly non-Zionist elite—often the wealthiest and most generous donors.[32] In addition, these moves helped give rise to a multitude of small- and medium-sized New Zionist donors as well. These donors, though typically not supporters of any specific ideological Zionist party, philosophy, or political program, were nonetheless being swayed by the new local UJA campaign chairmen into a deep commitment to supporting a strong and flourishing Israel.

In all, by replacing those who might espouse their own particularistic agendas for how to shape the character of the new state mainly with figures willing to acknowledge that Israelis probably knew what was best for themselves, Montor and Morgenthau were ensuring a UJA that, for the foreseeable future, would continue to defer expenditure decisions to Israelis.[33]

### Squelching Alternative Voices

By 1948, though the UJA was overwhelmingly the main American Jewish organization raising money to support Israel, dozens of smaller independent fundraising appeals had begun to appear on the American Jewish landscape. Some supported specific causes like education or social welfare. Some were tied to specific Israeli institutions, like universities. And others fashioned themselves as alternatives to the UJA's catch-all umbrella approach of supporting a broad range of causes in Israel.

The UJA and Jewish Agency viewed these alternate appeals as threats to cementing themselves as the dominant fundraising pipeline for American Jews wanting to support Israel. They also believed that in such a critical time, it was vital for Israel's survival that as much money as possible be sent to Israel and that these funds be spent on the young state's most pressing needs. In their eyes, the Jewish Agency was best equipped to define what those needs were. For example, Israel Goldstein of the Jewish Agency expressed this sentiment in a meeting with American Jewish leaders in 1949. "[Independent campaigns] have no right to come to America to confuse the giving public or divert from the basic institutions with which we are concerned," because "they duplicate existing activities [or] . . . they do not represent the legitimate needs [of Israel]."[34]

To address these issues, the UJA and Jewish Agency jointly formed a body in 1949 called the Committee on Control and Authorization of Campaigns (CCA). Its purpose would be to squelch any current and potential future alternate organizations that might appeal directly to donors and/or advocate for different fundraising arrangements than those put forth by the UJA and Jewish Agency. The story of the CCA is a dramatic and, until now, mostly untold story that illustrates the extent to which the UJA and Jewish Agency went to root out competition and maintain their perch atop the American Jewish philanthropic machine.

*Creation of the CCA.* In July 1949, the UJA and Jewish Agency jointly convened a conference in Tel Aviv called the Conference on Multiple Campaigns. Their chief collective agenda at the conference was to advocate for the merits of having the UJA be *the single* federated fundraising body for Israel operating in the United States. In attendance were the top figures in the UJA and Jewish Agency, as well as the Israeli government and other leading American Jewish fundraising organizations—Council of Jewish Federations (CJF), Joint Distribution Committee (JDC), Jewish National Fund (JNF), Hadassah (the Women's Zionist organization), and Labor Zionism's Gewerkschaft campaign.

Henry Montor presented the UJA/Jewish Agency case, noting the increasingly populated and complicated field of new Israel-oriented fundraising appeals in the United States. He argued, "There cannot be on the American scene some sixty organizations from Israel . . . appealing to the American Jewish community without having the basic causes." He continued, "The fact that each agency which comes to America says, and . . . I am not being facetious—each is responsible for the upkeep of the army, the establishment of the State, for immigration, every worthy institution in the land, [as if] there is no difference between the United Jewish Appeal and any other appeal in America."[35] Montor advocated that the assembled group needed to develop a "rigid unbending attitude," in order to ensure that the American fundraising effort for Israel not be diluted by the activity of the new, independent fundraising campaigns.[36]

A few of the smaller players in attendance, such as Hadassah and Gewerkschaft, resisted the severity of Montor's assessment. However, most agreed with Montor's general point and supported the idea of propping up the UJA to be a solitary campaign, for the purpose of maximizing and best utilizing American Jewish donations.

The conference concluded with the establishment of the CCA to oversee the field of organizations fundraising for Israel. Officially operating under the aegis of the Jewish Agency—but in reality closely coordinated by the Agency and the UJA together—the CCA would be responsible for deciding the legitimacy of campaigns. It would "license" a limited number to remain independent, so long as they coordinated their fundraising activities with the UJA. This often meant deferring their own activities to the UJA's fundraising timetable, campaign strategies, and intended donor solicitation lists. As for campaigns that did not receive licenses, the CCA would undertake an unapologetic campaign to eradicate their presence from the American fundraising scene. The CCA operated with a self-understood legitimacy to both speak with an authoritative voice on what was in the best interest of Israel and impose judgments on that basis.

When it chose to eliminate alternate campaigns acting outside of its purview, the CCA made heavy use of collective Jewish communal pressure to enforce its decisions. It drew on the collective organizational backing it received from the most reputable bodies in the community (including the UJA, CJF, JDC, and Jewish Agency) as well as the endorsement it received from the government of Israel.

Upon its establishment, the CCA notified all current and would-be charitable solicitors that its mandate would be to "scrutinize all proposed campaigns in [sic] behalf of Israel with a view to establishing the validity of their claims and their general usefulness."[37] The CCA presented itself as a voluntary instrument acting in everyone's best interest, noting in its own information bulletins that "the Committee is armed not with police power in a free society, but only the power of persuasion based on the prestige of its member organizations [UJA, CJF, JDC, Jewish Agency, etc.]."[38] Its success would therefore depend on organizations operating under the Jewish communal virtue of self-discipline in the interest of the broader Jewish community.

In contrast to the CCA's public statements, however, what transpired was not always a collaborative system of communal self-regulation. CCA activities, at times, entailed heavy-handed policing in cases in which an organization continued to operate in America despite CCA "recommendations."

When the CCA became aware of unlicensed campaigns, or what it referred to as "wildcat campaigns," its first response was to cordially request the operation to cease its fundraising activities. In one case, for example, CCA officials confronted the ultra-Orthodox body Agudat Israel regarding a subsidiary social welfare organization it had established: "Mr. Hamlin has called my attention to . . . your organization 'Homes for Children in Israel.' We appreciate your concern and sincerity for the problem of the housing of religious children in Israel. . . . [But] in order to avoid any difficulties . . . we would urge you to inform us immediately that all of your fundraising activities have been cancelled."[39]

While such "requests" worked in some cases, they did not always. If they did not produce the desired result, the CCA would invoke whatever means of policing power it could conceive of. In numerous cases, the CCA called on Israeli authorities to deny issuing passports to emissaries from small charities set to travel to the United States to fundraise. In some instances, the CCA would request that the Israeli government formally recall its citizens who were allegedly acting in violation of CCA decisions.[40]

To smaller operations not beholden to official Israeli bodies, the CCA responded just as strongly. For example, when a small organization called Achdut Israel was soliciting funds in June 1949 in support of health services for wounded veterans from Israel's War of Independence, the CCA issued a shaming letter to the organization accusing that it "cheapened the name of Israel" by resorting to what it regarded as the deplorable fundraising tactics like engaging in street collections.[41] When Achdut Israel did not back down from its activities, the CCA contacted the Brooklyn Jewish community council, asking it to crack down on Achdut Israel, claiming that its work was "undignified" and resulted in "none of the monies so collected . . . arriv[ing] in Israel."[42]

The CCA did not stop at using in-house methods for policing alternative fundraising for Israel. It believed the work it was doing was important enough to justify airing the community's "dirty laundry" in a broader non-Jewish society. On numerous occasions, when "unauthorized" fundraising bodies did not follow CCA notifications to cease and desist from their activities, the CCA reached outside of the Jewish community, notifying local police departments and welfare agencies of any legal infractions the small organizations may have committed. In one example, the CCA notified the New York City police department that the sound truck solicitations of some organizations may have been violating local sound ordinances and urged the police to shut the groups down.[43] Another example concerned individual *yeshivot* raising money in New York City. A confidential CCA memo referred to "several of the offices of . . . [*yeshivot* having been] closed by the actions of the Committee in conjunction with the Welfare Department of the City of New York."[44]

In this manner, the CCA pushed for exclusive control over American Jewish fundraising for Israel well into the 1980s. It continued to make use of its self-appointed platform to be *the* arbiter of what was worthwhile to support in Israel. And the results of its rather ruthless campaign were, as we shall see, impressive.

### Shepherding Independent-Minded Donors

The third component of the UJA–Jewish Agency plan was to identify what was then a small subset of entrepreneurially oriented American Jewish donors and shepherd as many of them as possible into what the organizations deemed as "acceptable" giving activities—various UJA-controlled or UJA-aligned ventures. These donors had either particular interests that they wanted to support in Israel or, in the case of some larger donors, a desire to work outside of the collective framework in order to make a more personal mark and legacy.

Two groups the UJA and Jewish Agency attempted to co-opt were American supporters of *yeshivot* and arts and cultural organizations in Israel (which were not necessarily supporters of the UJA's general campaign). To do this, they endorsed the continued existence of two small already-existing federated-like campaigns: the Federated Council of Israel Institutions (FCII), which allocated funds to independent *yeshivot*, and the American Fund for Palestine Institutions (AFPI), also known as the Norman Fund, which distributed donations to various small cultural institutions in Israel. The FCII and AFPI were exactly the kinds of organizations that the CCA usually tried to eliminate. But, in these particular cases, UJA and Jewish Agency leadership recognized these two organizations as the best channels for coordinating, collecting, and allocating funds by donors interested in supporting traditional Jewish learning and cultural projects.

The UJA and Jewish Agency leaders strongly preferred this arrangement over alternative solutions. For one, they reasoned that they could not simply eliminate *yeshivot* and cultural institutions in Israel as giving options because that would alienate subsets of American Jews who may have been interested in supporting *only* these types of institutions, but no other work in Israel. Second, leadership believed it was not feasible to integrate individual beneficiary *yeshivot* and cultural groups directly into the Jewish Agency grantee structure, as the Jewish Agency had neither the ability nor the desire to bring dozens or perhaps hundreds of tiny religious and cultural programs under its umbrella. So they decided to allow the FCII and AFPI a limited degree of autonomy in interacting with their American donors and their grantees in Israel, under the condition that the UJA would limit the scope and size of their fundraising activities.[45]

Another group the UJA and Jewish Agency targeted was the more purely ideological Zionist donors. Even though the UJA had recently forced Zionist leaders from its fundraising ranks, it still sought an avenue to keep this rather small but intensely devoted base in the fold. Many of these donors were affiliated with organizations linked to specific political parties in Israel. Until that point, most major Israeli political parties had each maintained their own funding instruments outside of the Jewish Agency that they would use to raise diaspora donations for their own party-run social service networks on the ground in Israel.

But by 1950, the CCA identified these Zionist parties' fundraising campaigns as a potentially harmful competitive challenge to the UJA.[46] UJA and Jewish Agency leaders feared that the passion Zionist leaders had for their own particularistic philosophies and values could prove enticing and therefore potentially disruptive, drawing some rank-and-file nonideological American Jewish donors away from the UJA and toward competing Zionist fundraising efforts. However, any attempts by the CCA to shut those groups down, as they had done with so many other organizations, certainly would have alienated die-hard supporters, among whom numbered some of the most enthusiastic and vocal American Jewish supporters of Israel. The Jewish Agency's solution was therefore to negotiate a series of agreements with the Zionist fundraising organizations that were akin to buyout arrangements. The UJA would provide a small but predictable line-item allocation to each of the various Zionist party-run service networks that would be known as Constructive Enterprise Funds. In return, the parties agreed to abstain from independent fundraising. By the early 1950s, these "buyout agreements" were established with six Israeli political parties (Mizrahi, HaPoel HaMizrahi, Herut, the General Zionists, Agudat Yisrael, and Poalei Agudat Yisrael).

From the perspective of the various recipient groups, giving up fundraising efforts and instead receiving guaranteed funding allocations for their activities in Israel was a worthwhile compromise. And from the UJA's perspective, the agreements eliminated what could have been formidable competition for its efforts. The various motives for such arrangements were well illustrated, for example, in a meeting between the UJA and Agudat Israel in 1949. Rabbi Goldstein, leader of Agudath Israel, argued that such an agreement would be mutually beneficial: "The forces of Agudath Israel, properly harnessed, could do much for the United Jewish Appeal and perhaps bring to UJA more funds than Agudath Israel received."[47] The UJA concurred that it "had been [otherwise] concerned about the failure of the United Jewish Appeal to find a way to obtain the full cooperation of the orthodox groups and that . . . [it] would welcome the help offered by Rabbi Goldstein."[48] With party leaders now instructing their membership to directly support the UJA, previous ideological outliers were brought into the broad UJA tent.

One can only speculate on the long-term impact Constructive Enterprise Funds had in killing the UJA's potential competition, but, at the very least, the creation of these agreements dampened the potential of some advocates who otherwise would have more vocally pushed for alternatives to the UJA.

Finally, there was the issue of how to deal with independent-minded high-dollar donors who wanted to make a greater and more specific impact than just giving to the general campaign. At the time, the UJA did not allow earmarking or donor-directed giving (as it later would), and yet these donors wanted a more specific way to designate their contributions. The UJA largely attempted to confront the challenge by driving donors into one of the CCA-licensed campaigns that supported Israeli universities—funds for the Weizmann Institute of Science, Technion, and Hebrew University. The university campaigns alone could provide opportunities for big givers who wanted to dedicate large capital projects in their names. In fact, university funds focused their American fundraising work exclusively on securing these larger gifts.[49]

In later years, the UJA would institute so-called second line campaigns, which were essentially new ways to generate increased revenue by big, independent-minded donors as well as to excite the donor base with new opportunities for making an impact in Israel.[50] The first second line was launched in 1956 as a one-time effort to help aid the large influx of Jewish immigrants to Israel from North Africa that year.[51] It was so successful in generating additional revenue beyond the annual campaign that the UJA decided to make use of second line campaigns regularly in the years after. In 1964, it launched its first major non-crisis-driven second-line campaign, the Israel Education Fund (IEF). The IEF's purpose was to raise money for the construction of high school buildings and kindergartens in Israel. Over a twenty-year period starting in 1965, the IEF collected funds to build more than five hundred school buildings in Israel, many of which bore the names of the diaspora donors who supported them, such as its first schools, the Rodman school in Kiryat Yam, built with funds donated by

Gertrude and Morris Rodman of Washington, D.C., and the Racoosin Comprehensive High School in Ramleh, supported by Theodore R. Racoosin of New
York.[52]

All told, the phenomenon of the independent-minded donor was still a relatively small part of the American-Israeli philanthropic scene in the first few
decades of the state. At the time, giving norms still valued federation as both a
virtuous and a strategically wise structure for maximizing giving. Tendencies
toward entrepreneurial, nonfederated giving that would eventually come to be
widespread were still limited.

### Controlling the Narrative about Israel

The final piece of the UJA and Jewish Agency's strategy to maintain control over
American Jewish giving culture was to shape the narrative for how American
Jews understood the realities of Israel. Without the bevvy of information sources
that would eventually be available by the 1990s and beyond, the UJA and its allied
bodies were able to largely control the messaging of how Israel was portrayed to
American Jews. Clearly, this long predated social media, blogs, and alternative
news sources about Israel. But this was also before the growth of the vibrant
independent civil society in Israel that would arise in the 1970s and 1980s,[53] so
there was not the proliferation of Israeli NGOs producing glossy publications
and dispensing speakers into the United States as would become the case in the
twenty-first century. Any other potentially competitive voices to the UJA with
information about Israel were to various degrees in league with the UJA. The
big organizations that existed outside of the UJA that circulated speakers in the
United States—such as Hadassah, the Technion, or the JNF—were, in their
capacities as CCA licensees, all at least practically committed to the UJA's self-
designated role as primary purveyor of information about Israel. This was true
even for those licensed organizations not necessarily ideologically aligned with
the UJA's portrayal and priorities. In addition, the UJA cultivated relationships
with synagogues,[54] and by the 1950s it reached what would be a long-standing
détente with the Israel bonds organization.[55]

The methods for American donors to learn about Israel at the local commu-
nity level were therefore mainly through Jewish newspapers and federation- or
UJA-sponsored speaker tours. The local Jewish press, it should be noted, was
often owned or run by the federations, who directly partnered with the UJA.
Regarding speakers, those who wanted to hear about what was happening in
Israel during the 1980s and before would therefore flock to hear whatever speakers federations brought in. Stanley Stone, executive vice president of the Jewish
Federation of Central New Jersey and longtime federation veteran, described the
phenomenon at the time: "We would do a program on Israel. I don't care if we
did it with a lot of time or no time, we were the place to get the information. It
would be subscribed to. Packed. You could bring in a speaker. You could do the

most creative thing. Done. It could be a yutz. But if it said 'coming from Israel' or 'an expert on Israel,' people were dying for that. They wanted it. We were the only place to get it."[56]

As the often exclusive source of information, the UJA could shape the narrative about what was going on in Israel and specifically what causes most needed the support of American Jews. Its leaders could frame the Israeli reality to donors as they saw best. In the 1960s, the UJA pushed the idea that Israel needed high schools built.[57] In the 1980s, it was urban renewal.[58] Whether these were really the most pressing needs at the time was not really something the average American Jewish donor had much ability to validate. By the Jewish Agency setting the agenda for how to allocate diaspora contributions and the UJA-federation agreeing to be its mouthpiece (and the loudest voices available aligned with the chosen messaging), a certain picture of Israel's realities and priorities was projected to American Jews, and most American Jews neither had the wherewithal nor reasons they eventually would have to question the information they were being fed.

## CONCLUSION: A CULTURE OF DEFERENCE ACHIEVED?

Chaim Weizmann and his ideological descendants worked over decades to instill a giving culture of Checkbook Zionism in which American Jews would give money to support Israel and mostly allow Israelis the latitude to spend it as they saw fit. Their multipronged strategy for institutionalizing American Jewish philanthropic deference to their Israeli partners (of clearing the field of alternative advocates, organizations, and messaging) proved to be effective. This becomes clear by looking at two metrics. First, as numbers demonstrate, the UJA and Jewish Agency (as the torchbearers for the Weizmann school) were effective at limiting actual alternate Israel-oriented giving from American Jews. Second, the federation–UJA–Jewish Agency system effectively clamped down on would-be internal critics that could have advocated instead for greater American Jewish input over expenditure decisions, as Louis Brandeis had wanted.

The clearest signs of success of the federation–UJA–Jewish Agency pipeline are the bottom line figures. In these crucial years for the Jewish state, Israel's government tasked the Jewish Agency with several indispensable activities to ensure a secure and thriving Jewish state, such as funding immigrant absorption and agricultural development.[59] From the time that the UJA and Jewish Agency partnered in 1948 to institute a system fostering an airtight financial flow until the system started showing cracks in the 1980s, American Jews put more than $6 billion into the hands of the Jewish Agency.[60] That figure put in 2019 inflation-adjusted terms is more than $30 billion.[61] Each year, funds from the UJA accounted for a substantial portion of the Jewish Agency's budget. Indeed, the overall impact of UJA funds on Israel was undeniable.

The work of the CCA and the Constructive Enterprise Funds proved effective in making the federation-UJA system the principal recipient of American Jewish philanthropy for Israel. One by one, the CCA managed to pick off potential rivals for forty years. The archives abound with numerous examples beyond the ones relayed in this chapter of the CCA effectively shutting down rival campaigns. In total, according to one scholarly estimate made at the peak of UJA dominance, the percentage of total American Jewish philanthropic dollars brought in by non-UJA groups was only around 21 percent.[62] It should be noted that this figure, while low to begin with, also includes all CCA-licensed campaigns, including big-ticket campaigns like development campaigns for Israeli universities. In reality, the total dollars given outside of the UJA and CCA-licensed organizations to the "wildcat campaigns" were insignificant. This is illustrated, for example, by the case of PEF, the most successful of the wildcat campaign. Over the years, PEF, the instrument Brandeis created when he broke with Weizmann and the ZOA in 1921, helped American Jews support hundreds of small, independent projects and organizations in Israel outside of the Jewish Agency orbit. While PEF was a dependable resource for interested donors, the scale of its giving compared to the UJA's was tiny. As a point of comparison, in the twenty years from 1968 to 1987, arguably the heyday of Checkbook Zionism, PEF allocated a little more than $4 million per year in Israel. For comparison, over the same period, the UJA remitted over $200 million per year, roughly fifty times more than PEF.[63] So while some money did go outside of the UJA and its allied CCA-licensed organizations, it was a small fraction of the total pie.

The UJA and Jewish Agency—buttressed by support from the Israeli government—were able to effectively push the importance of supporting Israel to the center of the American Jewish philanthropic agenda.[64] While it is true that Israel had legitimate needs and was in worse financial shape than the American Jewish community, the American Jewish federation system, which coordinated all collective Jewish funding on a local community level, gave a consistently high portion of its campaign receipts to the UJA. Even in the leanest years of federation fundraising campaigns—and at a time when American Jews were simultaneously preoccupied with all kinds of expensive local community needs,[65] including funding their new suburban communal infrastructures (synagogues, Jewish community centers, and day schools)—annual allocations to the UJA never dropped below 44 percent of the federation system's budget in any year until the 1990. And over Israel's first forty years, allocations to the UJA averaged 58 percent of the annual federation campaigns.[66] It is clear that American Jews believed in the importance of funding Israel, and most believed it should be through the federation–UJA–Jewish Agency system.

Beyond the numbers, it is important to examine the extent to which alternative voices in the organized Jewish community may have tried to exert independent influence over the use of funds raised from American Jews. The

Council of Jewish Federations (CJF), the umbrella body of federations, certainly had the leverage to demand a greater say in the use of funds in Israel if it wished. Were it not satisfied, the CJF could have withheld funds, diverted them to domestic causes, or found an alternative partner on the ground in Israel. This all begs the question of how much the federation system may have added its voice to the conversation.

Yet all indications are that it did not put up resistance to Jewish Agency decision making in any significant way. For the most part, if the UJA trusted the Jewish Agency, that was good enough for the CJF. Gottlieb Hammer, executive director of the Jewish Agency's office in New York, the Jewish Agency–American Section, recounted an instance in the mid-1950s that shows how normative it was in American Jewish organizational culture for the federation system to stay at arm's length from the overseas decision making of the UJA (and its constituent body, the JDC). According to Hammer, the Jewish Agency–American Section agreed to a request from the CJF to review the Jewish Agency's budget: "[The JDC chair] was aghast when he heard I had agreed to discuss the Jewish Agency's budget with the CJF committee. I must emphasize the word 'discuss' because our agreement was to give information, not to seek approval or accept disapproval; the representatives of the federation were to be there, not express opinions."[67] Implicit in Hammer's recollection is how the CJF was regarded as little more than a rubber stamp for the Jewish Agency. Considering that the CJF technically held the purse strings, this is an astonishing illustration of just how much latitude the CJF allowed the UJA and Jewish Agency in the use of funds.

There is little evidence that the federation system challenged the UJA and Jewish Agency very much at all. The rare cases that exist usually centered on the federation requesting greater transparency and accountability from the Jewish Agency; and typically, in the end, the UJA was able to convince skeptics that the Jewish Agency should continue to be trusted to create its budget and carry out its work exactly as it saw fit. In one such case, Jewish Agency leadership arranged to personally take the main critics from the CJF on a three-week trip to Israel in 1951 to tour Jewish Agency field operations and discuss Jewish Agency priorities.[68] As Gottlieb Hammer recounted, the trip fully assuaged the concerns of the Jewish Agency's biggest critics: "The reaction . . . was highly favorable. . . . [Howard Glasser, the consultant to CJF who was most concerned about the Jewish Agency] conceded bluntly that we had licked him on the issues he had raised. As far as the CJF was concerned, [worries over the Jewish Agency's efficacy and trustworthiness] would never have to be brought up again."[69] This anecdote speaks to the high level of ingrained deference at the time. Among the organized American Jewish communal leadership, through one short trip alone, the UJA and Jewish Agency were able to quiet the Agency's leading American critics, who not only conceded to maintain the status quo in power relations but also went nearly so far as to apologize that they had even questioned the Jewish Agency in the first place.

Though there is evidence that by the mid-1960s some diaspora donors began murmuring for some role in the governance of the Jewish Agency, as the next chapter will explain, these yearnings did not lead to diaspora Jews pushing the Jewish Agency on the matter in any meaningful ways until at least the 1980s.

In the intervening decades, while the full body of opinions held by leading CJF employees and American Jewish donors was not documented and therefore cannot fully be known, it is reasonable to assume that there were some individual attitudinal deviations along the way. Yet the facts that there was never large-scale conflict between the federation system and the UJA/Jewish Agency and that CJF allocations to the UJA remained consistently high year after year suggest that for decades the most important leadership in the federation system either endorsed or at least tacitly supported deferring allocation decision making to Israelis.

The other place in the pipeline in which different ideas of philanthropic power sharing could have surfaced was the United Israel Appeal (UIA). For reasons related to American tax law, all UJA funds bound for the Jewish Agency had to first pass through the UIA, a small conduit organization. The UIA's legal purpose was to be the final check that the American Jewish tax-exempt donations it received from the UJA were remitted to what U.S. tax law would regard as a legitimate overseas partner organization.[70] It was in the UIA's purview, therefore, to assess that the Jewish Agency used American Jewish funds responsibly. Had the board of the UIA not supported the Weizmann model, it could have easily directed the Jewish Agency to allow for additional American input in allocation decision making or found a different partner organization in Israel that would have. The U.S. Internal Revenue Service not only permitted but would have applauded this exercise of oversight. Yet the UIA never did such things. In fact, although the UIA's organizational bylaws included a provision that its relationship with the Jewish Agency was subject to review and reauthorization every five years, there is no evidence that the UIA viewed its relationship with the Jewish Agency as subject to any serious review. The UIA did not make its passage of funding contingent on any conditions of power sharing. As far as the UIA was concerned, the Jewish Agency was its partner and could spend the money it received as it saw fit.[71]

In this manner, the Checkbook Zionism system hummed along. Billions of dollars flowed overseas into the hands of the Jewish Agency for decades, with no more than minimal discontent. As the next chapter recounts, things began to change in the 1970s and 1980s as more and increasingly louder voices would question and eventually push back against the automatic deference of American organizations to Israelis.

# CHAPTER 3

# The Decline of Checkbook Zionism

In the wee hours of June 5, 1967, Israel launched a surprise attack on three of its bordering countries—Egypt, Syria, and Jordan. Over the previous weeks, the three had taken a series of aggressive steps against Israel. Israel believed it was facing an imminent attack and a potentially existential calamity unless it acted first. The strike proved to be successful, catching its neighbors off guard and, to the surprise of the world, securing a dramatic military victory for Israel. When the dust settled, it had become apparent that in just six days the young state had gone from staring down its possible demise to scoring a resounding victory—more than doubling the amount of territory it controlled and opening up a new chapter of national pride and self-confidence for Israelis. Israel could now truly declare to its longtime hostile neighbors, in no uncertain terms, that it was there to stay.

These events had a major impact on Jews outside of Israel as well. Diaspora Jews from around the world who had previously been only mildly engaged in the affairs of Israel suddenly found themselves passionate supporters of the Jewish state, both in terms of their identities as Jews and in a variety of tangible ways as well—including increased frequency of travel to Israel, growing affinity toward Israeli culture, and even an uptick in immigration.[1] But there is perhaps no better reflection of the increased interest diaspora Jews had in Israel after the Six-Day War than the massive surge that was seen in diaspora philanthropy to Israel. In the days following the outbreak of the war, philanthropic support for Israel flooded in from every stratum of the American Jewish community.[2] As Kaufman recounts, there were "thousands of stories of how Jews who had contributed to the UJA in the past now . . . gave sums ten times or more than their regular contributions, while others who had never donated a penny in the past . . . [now] sent checks and pledged enormous amounts." To illustrate the level of passion expressed by donors at the time, he cited the example of Dallas Jew Jake

Feldman, who "gave $250,000, saying: 'If that isn't enough, you guys tell me what I ought to do, because you guys can have everything I own, for if anything happened to Israel what I had left would be meaningless.'"[3]

These examples epitomized the rise in American Jewish interest in Israel after the war. Describing the almost religious experience American Jews seemed to be undergoing in their love for and desire to be connected to Israel, sociologist Daniel Elazar coined the term "Israelolatry."[4] Whether the Israelolatry felt by American Jews was out of pride in Israel's achievements, fear for its vulnerability, greater awareness of its needs in general, or some combination, the result was unmistakable. An energized American Jewish donor base was engaging with Israel far more than ever before, including sending unprecedented sums to support the state.

Indeed, even after the immediacy of the war died down, the surge in popular Jewish support for Israel did not. For the next several years, giving numbers remained more than triple what they had been before the war. And when Egypt and Syria launched a surprise attack against Israel in 1973, American Jews shattered the philanthropy records they had set six years earlier. Overall, both the sums raised and the proportion of the total federation pie allocated to the UJA/ UIA to support Israel in this era ballooned from what they had been before 1967. From 1967 to 1973, American Jews, incredibly, put a total of $1.2 billion in 1972 inflation-adjusted terms (or almost $7.3 billion in 2019 terms) into the hands of the Jewish Agency. This sum was more than the inflation-adjusted combined total of funds remitted in the *entire forty-six-year period* from the establishment of Keren Hayesod in 1920 through 1966.[5] It is staggering to observe just how much the acute moments of crisis in 1967 and 1973 triggered a new reality in how funds would be given in noncrisis moments going forward as well. In fact, the growth in numbers after the wars did not return to their prewar levels for over thirty years.[6]

Checkbook Zionism appeared on the surface to have reached a golden age. Yet, below the surface, a dramatically different story was unfolding: In this moment of greatest seeming strength, unprecedented attitudinal and behavior changes to the foundations of the system were underway. Indeed, as it would turn out, the increased engagement of American Jews brought on by this moment would prove to be a double-edged sword for the ongoing health of Checkbook Zionism.

The nature of power sharing between American Jews and Israelis had been largely one-sided for Israel's first decades, as the last chapter recounted: an effectively quiescent American Jewish community allowed the Jewish Agency mostly unfettered use of the hundreds of millions of dollars it donated annually. But while the drama of the 1967 and 1973 wars may have motivated more American Jews into giving and giving more, it would become clear that many of the newly energized donors would not be satisfied with the traditionally limited place assigned to diaspora Jews as hands-off, deferential Checkbook Zionists. Increasing numbers of American Jews expressed a desire to play a more impactful role in helping Israel beyond simply writing checks; many sought to have some say in the process of determining the use of their donated funds.

Over the ensuing years, as knee-jerk Checkbook Zionism was called into increasing question, cracks began developing in every section of the funding pipeline. The nearly airtight system of passing funds from American donors to the Jewish Agency, detailed in the past two chapters, began to split apart as American Jews looked for something beyond Checkbook Zionism. Changes were emerging at every level simultaneously. Individual donors began connecting with new partner organizations in Israel on their own. Local federations, rather than giving exclusively through the national federation system, sniffed around for non–Jewish Agency backed projects in Israel that they could support. Even the devoted organizational partner to the Jewish Agency, the federation system/ UJA/UIA, pushed for reform in the Agency's power sharing structure and eventually, after years of frustration, sought alternative partnership opportunities outside of the Agency.

By the 1990s and 2000s, the seeds of increased engagement of American Jewish philanthropists that had originally sprung from the 1967 to 1973 era were coming to fruition. The classic ideals of federation and deference to Israel had drastically weakened, and the Jewish Agency's dominant role in allocating American Jewish donations in Israel had collapsed—as it received less than 10 percent of all American Jewish donations to Israel by 2007.[7]

Yet while American Jews had indeed grown tired of the old relationship form, they had not grown tired of the relationship itself. In fact, looking at total dollars given by American Jews through both old and new giving channels, as of 2016 the philanthropic relationship between American Jews and Israelis was as healthy as ever.[8]

This chapter explores the transformation away from Checkbook Zionism from three levels: the transnational level, the local/national level, and the individual level. The story of how and why the Checkbook Zionism framework collapsed completes the narrative arc introduced in chapters 1 and 2 and serves as important context for the rest of the book's study of the new arrangements in power sharing that have come in the wake of the old system's demise.

## CHANGES AT THE TRANSNATIONAL LEVEL: THE DECLINE OF THE JEWISH AGENCY AS AN ATTRACTIVE PARTNER FOR AMERICAN JEWS

While the windfall of American Jewish support following the 1967 War brought record-breaking charitable receipts to the Jewish Agency, it also created a challenge: How could the Jewish Agency and its American allies in the federation/ UJA system provide a compelling enough vision of diaspora involvement in

Israel to maintain this new surge in interest and engagement by American Jews? To their credit, the Agency and its American allies correctly predicted that the energized donor class would not be fully satisfied with the old relationship patterns of Checkbook Zionism. They reasoned that if the Agency wanted to keep hold of its perch as the dominant voice in deciding how to spend money from American Jews, they would have to address the changing expressed needs of the American donors. But their assessment of exactly *how* to effectively do this was not quite as prophetic.

### Reformulating Checkbook Zionism in a Changing Era

In 1968, the Jewish Agency invited Jews from around the world to Jerusalem for a meeting it called the Conference on Human Needs. Acknowledging in their opening statement that "the Jews of the world are seeking a more personal involvement in what goes on in Israel,"[9] the conference's leadership declared as their purpose to discuss how the Israel-diaspora partnership could be enhanced in the wake of Israel's dramatic battlefield victory a year earlier. They indicated that there had been a maturation in diaspora Jewry's knowledge, interest, and understanding of Israel and, in enthused language, spoke of the new possibilities for "partnership." They proclaimed, "The present relationship of world Jewry and Israel goes beyond the mainly emotional character of earlier years. We are today witnessing growing interest in mutual practical involvement, increasing eagerness for action based on information and understanding."[10] On the surface, it seemed a major change in the relationship was afoot.

With this call for a reexamination of the relationship as a backdrop, Israeli and American participants concluded at the conference that it was time that the Jewish Agency—the classic conduit for getting American Jewish funds into the hands of Israelis—be reimagined to include a greater role for diaspora Jews in formulating strategy and making allocation decisions. Together, they initiated a formal joint process to reform the governance structure of the Agency. Their stated purpose was, as chairman of the Jewish Agency Executive Louis Pincus put it, to "give world Jewry, which raises the funds for Israel, a direct say in the way the funds are spent."[11]

It took three years of planning and negotiations following the conference, but, in 1971, Israeli and diaspora leaders agreed on a formal reconstitution of the governance structure of the Jewish Agency that would purportedly divide decision-making responsibilities equally between Israelis and diaspora Jews.[12] There would be a General Assembly, composed of hundreds of delegates from around the world, that would meet once annually to plan policy. But the nerve center of the reformed Agency would comprise two bodies—the Board of Governors and the Executive. The decision-making power was supposed to lie with the Board of Governors, a body composed of equal numbers of diaspora and Israeli delegates that would be charged with setting Agency agendas and policy.

The Executive, on the other hand, would be more of an administrative and implementation body tasked with running the Agency's day-to-day affairs. For practical purposes, the Executive would be composed mainly of Israelis, as those living in Israel were best equipped to manage regular on-the-ground functions of the organization.

On paper, the change appeared to put the decision-making power of diaspora donors on par with Israelis—a truly revolutionary departure from the Weizmannian philosophy of power sharing.

The reality, however, would prove to be much different. Despite its design as a forum for joint Israeli-diaspora decision making, the Board of Governors effectively remained under Israeli control. When important matters arose, the 50-percent Israeli delegation on the Board would often decide to vote as a bloc, ostensibly to keep diaspora members from having too much of a say. While the designers of the reconstituted Agency structure did not anticipate that Board votes would fall down national lines necessarily, that is how things often unfolded. In such cases, diaspora delegates proved neither organized enough nor sufficiently knowledgeable on specific issues to put together a unified bloc to check their Israeli counterparts when their interests diverged. Raymond Epstein, an American member of the Board of Governors and a former president of American federation system's umbrella body, the Council of Jewish Federations (CJF), observed this dynamic over time. Since meetings were held in Israel, he explained, "Israeli members [of the Board of Governors] attend[ed] meetings far more frequently than diaspora members," and therefore "diaspora Board members were "not equally involved in decision-making."[13]

In addition, the Israeli-controlled Executive proved to not be the purely task-focused administrative body it was designed as; rather, through its control of budgets and appointments, it became the de facto leader in designing much of the Agency's policy. Epstein noted how the Executive effectively usurped much of the Board's power. Not only was "the Board not making the important decisions," he explained, "it . . . [was] not even being kept fully aware of the decisions made by the Executive."[14] *Jerusalem Post* journalist Charles Hoffman, a frequent reporter on Agency affairs, offered a similar assessment, characterizing diaspora Board members as "insiders without inside information."[15]

Despite the promises of a sea change that newly delineated roles would bring, not much changed practically when it came to decision making at the Jewish Agency. In many ways, the reconstitution was no more than a clever repackaging of old relationship dynamics, with Israelis controlling allocations of diaspora funds—a traditional Checkbook Zionist relationship dressed up in a cloak of "equal partnership." Yet, realities aside, it is also important to understand how diaspora Jews—and American Jews specifically—*perceived* their role in power sharing within the new Agency structure in order to fully understand how relationship dynamics evolved.

### American Attitudes toward the Reconstituted Jewish Agency

American Jews involved in Agency governance had a mixed experience in the first years following the reconstitution. On one side of the spectrum was a small but vocal group that had been hoping for real structural changes to power relationships, favoring more of a Brandeisian view of sharing power. But while this group attempted a more active role in the revamped governance structure, it experienced frustrations early on with the lack of transparency and partnership offered by its Israeli counterparts. As Elazar and Dortort explain, the group encountered "budgets that were not budgets, [and] meetings that had no operative dimension but [consisted of] merely being lectured at by Israelis."[16] To this group's dismay, the lack of forum for real communication and collaboration indicated that promises of changes to the power-sharing relationship were not materializing.[17]

On the other hand, many of the American Board members, as well as the vast majority of the Agency's Assembly, though eager to be more involved, had less of an agenda for what that should look like exactly. For this group, the fanfare of the "new partnership" that came with the reconstitution introduced enough new honorific—but essentially superficial—features, so as to amply placate whatever enhanced interest in involvement they had had post-1967. Elazar and Dortort described how in the first decade following the reconstitution, most American participants mainly seemed flattered that they were invited into conversations but did not want any real responsibilities. Diaspora delegates, they explained, were mostly "pleased at the respect and deference with which they are treated by Israeli leaders [but] . . . the last thing they want is more responsibility which would necessitate greater demands on their time."[18] Hoffman concurred, recounting reflections of a longtime observer of the Agency during these years: "Getting them interested in really learning about Agency business was a hopeless task." Instead, he explained, "all they wanted to do was to hear talks by the Defense Minister or other dignitaries."[19]

The net effect was that the majority of diaspora Jews involved in Jewish Agency governance, even though not necessarily as philosophically committed to exclusive Israeli control over use of funds as the UJA had long been, in a de facto sense still acted mostly deferentially to their Israeli counterparts over issues of substance.

### The First Major Challenge to Deference

In 1981, Jewish Agency leadership convened a meeting in Caesarea, Israel, to review the first decade of the reconstitution of the Agency. It was there that the more restive segment of diaspora leadership began to more actively demand real shared governance. The group insisted that a review process be launched in order to "institute reforms or clarifications with regard to the Jewish Agency's goals and objectives."[20] The Agency's Israeli leaders faced at that moment what could have been a major turning point in the development of the Israel-diaspora philanthropic relationship: either they could attempt to accommodate the concerns of the diaspora Board members and yield to some kind of genuine reform in power sharing or they could continue to conduct business as usual, claiming "partnership" but continuing to hold the power in meaningful decision making. To their long-term detriment, as it would eventually turn out, the Israeli leaders mainly opted for the latter. Aside from plenty of rhetoric trumpeting partnership and greater diaspora involvement, they offered restless diaspora members of the Board of Governors a single concession—what was known as the "advise and consent" powers—that they expected would be no more than a token gesture. Originally included as a provision of the 1971 Jewish Agency reconstitution agreement, "advise and consent" powers gave non-Israeli members of the Agency's Board of Governors the power to approve the Israeli leadership's nominations for Jewish Agency department heads. Until 1977, diaspora Jews had refrained from using the powers at all,[21] and until the Caesarea conference, not in any significant way. But this was about to change.[22]

While serving their first decade on the Board, diaspora members had learned that the real power for shaping Agency policy lay with its department chairs. But in the aftermath of their frustrating experience at Caesarea, they came to realize that if they wanted to have a true substantive role in Agency governance, they could make active use of their "advise and consent" role to appoint Agency department chairs and keep watch on how they used their departmental budgets.

When the influential position of Agency treasurer opened up two years later, diaspora delegates were ready to act. The Agency Executive announced its nomination of Rafael Kotlowitz, a close political ally of Israeli prime minister Menachem Begin, as treasurer. As per usual, the Board of Governors was invited by the Executive to evaluate the nomination. But to the surprise of Israelis in the Agency and their close allies in the Israeli government, diaspora Jews, for the first time, vetoed a major nomination. They explained that they regarded Kotlowitz as unqualified for the post and that he received the nomination only as a beneficiary of Israeli political party cronyism.[23] Irritated by the surprise move, the Executive was forced to pull back its nomination. It then advanced the candidacy of Eli Tavin, another ally of Begin's. But again the diaspora contingent on the Board of Governors called the nominee unqualified and vetoed the nomination. Israeli leadership did not take kindly to what it regarded as inappropriate diaspora interference in its own affairs. Begin let his dissatisfaction with diaspora leaders be known by skipping the annual prime ministerial ritual of meeting with the Agency's eight-hundred-plus General Assembly delegates at their annual meeting. The *Jewish Telegraphic Agency* reported that "the unofficial word was that Begin deliberately stayed away because he was angered that the overseas Jewish fundraisers had rejected [the Executive's nominees]."[24]

This new diaspora show of power would not be limited to the cases of Kot-lowitz and Tavin alone. Over the next years, an increasingly emboldened con-tingent within the Board of Governors, who identified themselves as "the committee of 12," blocked several key nominations, including Akiva Lewinsky as Jewish Agency chairman in 1987,[25] three successive nominees to Agency treasurer in 1988,[26] and Yehiel Leket as Agency chairman in 1996.[27] It appeared that the use of "advise and consent" powers was giving diaspora Jews on the Board of Governors legitimate authority at last.

Drama and theatrics aside, however, "advise and consent" would prove to be a relatively toothless power in the end—perhaps more a thorn in the side of Israe-lis at the Agency than anything else. Israeli leadership in the Agency—which was often intimately tied to the leadership in the Israeli government—discovered after several diaspora vetoes that when it *really* wanted to neuter the Board's use of this power, it could. For one, diaspora leaders understood that they eventu-ally had to accept *someone* to fill vacancies at the Agency's top posts. And while they had veto power over specific nominations, they had no voice in the nomi-nation process itself other than to say "no." Israelis, alone, still set the menu of potential candidates. If it so chose, the Israeli Executive could respond to dias-pora vetoes, therefore, by continuing to put forth candidates of a similar ilk until diaspora Jews eventually relented and accepted one of the nominees. Diaspora Jews soon came to understand that they could not win a protracted war of attri-tion over nominations. The best they could do was delay the inevitable.

In addition, Israeli government leadership eventually learned that in certain instances, if it got directly involved—more so than Begin had—it could push the decision making of the Board of Governors to its liking, as the following anec-dote illustrates. Former executive vice chairman of the UIA, Rabbi Daniel Allen, recounted an experience he had while at the Board's "advise and consent" committee's interviews for the new treasurer of the Jewish Agency in the late 1990s. Allen explained that the committee was conducting interviews in Detroit. Diaspora members of the Board of Governors came

> from around the world . . . to interview five Israelis who wanted to be treasurer of the Jewish Agency . . . and in the middle of that meeting . . . the phone rang and it was the Prime Minister. . . . The chairman of the committee said, "may I put it on speaker phone?" And he said, "No." They had the conversation. Put down the phone. The chairman of the committee, [the meeting's host], and I, as the senior staff person, went in another room, had a meeting for 30 nano-seconds and came back and announced the person who would be the treasurer of the Jewish Agency. The Prime Minister called and said "this is my person. Thank you very much for having your committee meeting."

In this case, the diaspora leadership of the Board of Governors, some of the most highly esteemed diaspora Jews, traveled from around the world to exercise what

THE DECLINE OF CHECKBOOK ZIONISM

was supposed to be their most important responsibility in their supposedly "equal" role in power sharing within the Jewish Agency—the main transnational body for Israeli-diaspora partnership. Yet in a moment their power was over-ruled by a word from the Israeli prime minister. Diaspora delegates did not have sufficient will to stand up to the prime minister and push the issue. As Allen explained, "No one was going to argue with the Prime Minister."[28] Diaspora Jew-ish members of the Board of Governors, whether they liked it or not, were com-ing to recognize over time that there was little or no room for them in the Jewish Agency power structure to be more than cheerleaders or, at best, sometime semi-appreciated advisors.

The limited efficacy of real diaspora power notwithstanding, the periodic struggle over nominations and vetoes, alone, nonetheless irked Israeli leadership and laid bare how hollow the rhetoric of "partnership" was and brought to light how little appetite Israelis had for genuine power sharing within the Jewish Agency. After American Jews blocked a candidate in 1988, for example, the chair of the Labor Party—one of Israel's main political parties—complained that Board members from the diaspora should not be allowed to "dictate the elec-tion of candidates." He, instead, longingly recalled the first several years after diaspora Jews were granted "advise and consent" powers in 1971 that basically consisted of the Israeli prime minister sitting down with the American chair of the Board of Governors deciding on candidates "together" in private[29]—which was likely much less of a decision than a one-sided dictation. Attitudes like this were not limited to this one case. In other expressions of discontent, Israeli offi-cials characterized diaspora exercise of agreed upon "advise and consent" pow-ers, for example, as "acting improperly," "subverting democratic principles," and "overstep[ping] their bounds."[30] Most Israelis in leadership positions showed little interest in granting diaspora Jews consequential seats at the decision-making table.

### Lack of Reform and the Decline of the Jewish Agency Grip

Every three years, the UIA and Jewish Agency renewed their "exclusivity agree-ment," guaranteeing that aside from a nominal amount granted to the JDC, the Jewish Agency would be the sole Israeli recipient of UJA-raised funds.[31] The UIA's decision to renew the agreement each time it came up was, as discussed in the last chapter, supposed to be based on its evaluation of the Agency's performance. But time and again, "evaluation" proved to be little more than a formality before the agreement was again automatically renewed. Israeli scholar of phi-lanthropy Eliezer Jaffe, who had long proposed that diaspora Jews become more aware of the breadth of possible uses for their philanthropic dollars in Israel, lamented that in his opinion, diaspora Jews simply considered the Jewish Agency as an institution beyond reproach. Despite knowing the Agency's flaws, he wrote, diaspora Jews maintained a "stubborn insistence . . . to cling to the Agency as 'the principal link between Israel and the Diaspora communities'" that was *not* to their benefit.[32] One major giver to the UJA (quoted by Hoffman) gave voice to a similar viewpoint: "The Jewish Agency is as corrupt and inefficient as anything I've seen," he explained. "But I don't want to stop giving, so I look the other way." Noting that his sentiment was widely shared among major UJA contributors, he continued, "I'd disband the Agency if I could, but I won't say that I'll stop giving until they change things over there."[33] In viewing the disconnect between an unresponsive and arguably poorly run Agency and an unwaveringly loyal American donor base, Jaffe noted that "modern principles of philanthropy, welfare planning, and even elementary business management would never permit the present situation to continue." He added, "Everyone involved knows these facts, yet no one is willing to rock the boat, especially in America."[34] Imperfect as it was, the Jewish Agency remained for years impervious to real evaluation and perpetually endorsed as the body to exclusively allocate UJA-raised funds.

Yet by the late 1980s, 1990s, and early 2000s, this long history of unabated loyalty finally began to give way. More American Jews came to believe that the Israeli conception of partnership at the Jewish Agency was not developing the way many wanted—neither in actuality nor in intent—and an ever-more vocal leadership in the federation/UJA/UIA system began to hold the Jewish Agency to account for what it increasingly criticized as inefficient, wasteful, and overly politicized operating practices.[35] They pushed for changes to the Agency, calling for greater transparency in budgets and expenditures and fewer political appointments to top posts. But their quest for reform was met with a lot of the same response as their predecessor's earlier push for control had been—flattering language and hollow promises.[36] David Polish, former president of the Central Conference of American Rabbis, recounted his organization's experience dealing with an unresponsive Jewish Agency during these years. Recognizing a number of "issues troubling many American Jews," Polish advocated for an expanded dialogue between American Jews and leadership at the Jewish Agency (and Israeli government). However, he lamented, "the sessions were so structured that they were monologues [by Israeli participants], not dialogues. . . . The results were negligible."[37] Polish was not alone.

Gradually, as the Agency's behavior became more apparent and calls for reform went unheeded, automatic diaspora loyalty to the Jewish Agency began to dissipate. Overseas Jewish communities grew less willing to automatically send their funds to such a flawed body, which, as one account characterized, was likely to often "funnel contributions into [its] innumerable bureaucratic pigeonholes."[38] While the Agency took note of the growing chorus of discontent, its responsiveness to diaspora concerns proved true to brand: too little and too late—proclamations without real reforms, as well as a handful of attempts to restructure the giver-recipient relationship in a way that was theoretically designed to allow diaspora Jews a greater role. The most prominent of these restructuring plans, known as Project Renewal, matched specific diaspora communities with "twinned" cities and towns in Israel for the purpose of refurbishing some of the most impoverished neighborhoods in Israel. While Project Renewal did reimagine new ways of involving diaspora Jews in local-based projects and opened up new lines of dialogue, neither it nor its successor project, known as Partnership 2000, meaningfully altered the balance in Israel-diaspora power sharing.[39]

Observing the slow and incomplete manner in which the Jewish Agency was responding to concerned diaspora Jews, Jaffe prophetically proclaimed that such "ad hoc repairs and superficial housecleaning at the Agency will not be enough. . . . [Short of] serious conceptual rethinking of its future role . . . [and] radical restructuring," he argued, "the donors/fundraisers must sooner or later unilaterally and calmly divest themselves of . . . the Agency and take control over policy, spending, and organization."[40]

Polish, likewise, predicted that due to the poor state of communication and responsiveness, the decline of diaspora deference was inevitable: "We cannot indefinitely hold the support of a tranquilized American Jewry that receives simplistic information and is conditioned to believe that it discharges its responsibility to Israel primarily through financial generosity. The children of such a generation will grow up neither tranquil nor generous."[41]

Indeed, in the 1990s and 2000s, more American Jews grew more disenchanted with the process of automatically sending all UJA-raised money to the Jewish Agency to be used at its discretion. As will be laid out, American Jews gradually migrated toward more of a Brandeisian form of giving that increasingly sidestepped the Agency. Through myriad local community and individual efforts to find new Israeli philanthropic partners, allocations to the Agency shrunk. As indicated earlier, by the early 2010s the Agency's role would recede from its long-held mantle of undisputed principal recipient of American Jewish philanthropy into a much smaller piece of the story, controlling less than 10 percent of all American Jewish philanthropy to Israel by the mid-2000s.[42]

Finally by 2011, the pretense of maintaining the Jewish Agency as the unrivaled arbiter of transnational power sharing suffered a fatal blow. Facing considerable upward pressure from its constituents, the CJF/UJA/UIA's eventual successor organization, the Jewish Federations of North America (JFNA), decided for the first time to *not* renew the exclusivity relationship with the Jewish Agency,[43] instead opening the door to hundreds of other organizations to compete for allocation dollars from the centralized American Jewish fundraising system. The remaining sections of this chapter explore how declines in American Jewish deference and commitment to the ideas of federated action to the Jewish Agency at local, national, and individual levels would collectively lead to the collapse of Checkbook Zionism as the dominant mode of Israeli-diaspora philanthropic power sharing.

CHANGES AT THE LOCAL AND NATIONAL LEVELS: INDIVIDUAL FEDERATIONS
BREAK WITH THE UJA AND OTHER NATIONALLY FEDERATED BODIES
*The Slow Revolt at the Margins*

By the mid-1980s, the leadership at the San Francisco federation had become increasingly frustrated with their Israel giving. Unlike with their domestic giving activities, they could track neither how the charitable dollars their community handed to the UJA to be sent off to the Jewish Agency were being spent, nor what their gifts helped achieve. The federation decided to take two steps in response, both of which were at the time unprecedented. First, in 1985, it diverted $100,000 from its automatic annual allocation to the UJA to instead support other NGOs in Israel not affiliated with the Jewish Agency.[44] Although the $100,000 represented only a small portion of the San Francisco federation's total giving to the UJA, it was still a controversial move to break with the protocol of full and automatic allocation of federation-raised funds for Israel to the Jewish Agency.[45]

The other major step the San Francisco federation took was to open its own office in Jerusalem for the purpose of directly observing how the Jewish Agency allocated the funds received from San Francisco (via the UJA/UIA).[46] The presence of an office would enable the federation to gather its own information without a Jewish Agency filter as well as to scout out and suggest new initiatives and programs that the federation might want to support in Israel in addition to the Jewish Agency. These developments signaled that a new moment in the relationship had arrived. For the first time, an important institution in the federation universe—albeit a relatively small piece of the overall pie—began modeling its practices to be more in line with Brandeis's view of power sharing. The San Francisco federation was expressing that it was actively skeptical of handing over its community's money to the Jewish Agency without adding a voice in how it was to be used.

Over the next several years, other federations followed San Francisco's lead, opening Israel offices as well. As one midwestern federation's Israel office director put it, her community was no longer satisfied with a "spray and pray" mentality in having the UJA forward all of their Israel giving to the Jewish Agency with no say and limited accountability.[47] In federation parlance, the national system's unrestricted giving to the Jewish Agency (and a small portfolio of JDC activity in Israel) known as "core" giving, has come to be disparagingly referred to by some federation insiders as "core *shachor*"—an English/Hebrew hybrid term meaning "black hole." The implication was that giving to the Jewish Agency—which was alternately being criticized as a bloated bureaucracy, an inefficient organization, or simply as not always the best NGO provider for services—was tantamount in some ways to throwing money away.

By 2010, twenty additional federations had followed San Francisco's lead and opened their own offices in Israel.[48] Over time, most offices grew to take on increased roles, with functions ranging from observatory to identifying new projects for their individual federation to fund to fully handle their federation's Israel allocations process.

The Israel office of the Metrowest New Jersey Federation is a good example of what a typical federation Israel office had become by the 2010s. According to its representative in Israel, Amir Shacham, Metrowest opened its office in 1998 to better "develop their Israel and overseas agenda," which, as he explained, involved better "identifying needs" in Israel and "building better relationships" with beneficiary communities and organizations.[49] Over time, the office identified specific projects in Israel that it believed better fit the Metrowest community's priorities than general Jewish Agency activity alone. Ultimately, the office helped to facilitate the funding of over a hundred non–Jewish Agency projects in Israel with the Metrowest community's funds. Metrowest leaders indicated in interviews that they believed their experience with so many new hands-on projects and partnerships with Israelis undoubtedly contributed to their own enhanced ability to offer bold, informed perspectives on a variety of Israel-related issues, rather than simply waiting for the centralized federation/UJA system to hand down information and policies.

### Persistent Loyalty to "Core"

As much as there was increased evidence over time of individual federations' discontent with the exclusive relationship with the Jewish Agency as their main funding recipient and source of information, the national federation/UJA/UIA system's loyalty to the Jewish Agency ran deeply. From its perspective, the Jewish Agency had a storied history of meeting Israelis' most pressing needs in times of crisis—be it war, mass immigration, or anything else. So, irrespective of how legitimate critiques of the "old system" of centralized collection and distribution by the Jewish Agency might have been or what positive results federations were experiencing with their non–Jewish Agency giving activity, the central federation umbrella body, the CJF, and its overseas counterpart the UJA were going to stick by their partner. A number of supporters of perpetuating exclusive allocations to the Jewish Agency decried independent activity by federations. In response to the San Francisco federation's Israel work outside of Jewish Agency channels, the Zionist Organization of America, for example, passed a resolution in 1987 stating that it "deplores any action by which public campaign funds of the community are disbursed outside the normal United Jewish Appeal-Federation allocations process." The chairman of the World Zionist Organization urged San Francisco to "abolish" its giving policies, calling its behavior "a breach in the unity of the [community]."[50]

## *Revolt Against Automatic Allocations Intensifies*

Nevertheless, the opinion regarding core allocations as "core *shachor*" grew within the federation world over the decades following San Francisco's first move away from traditional federation behavior. More and more federations experimented over time with the same thing: shifting a portion of their overseas budgets away from core allocations and opting instead to directly fund Israeli NGOs. For the first several years, federations did so with relatively small portions of their budget, but starting in 1997, Cleveland, as Mark Rosen explains, was "the first federation to really break rank in any significant way." Rather than remitting its typical $10 to $11 million to the UJA, the Cleveland federation decided that from then on it would withhold $3 million of its annual UJA contribution—allocating it instead to organizations of its choosing.[51]

This trend had evolved by the end of the 2000s to the point that a handful of larger federations no longer gave *any* automatic grants to the Jewish Agency, instead inviting it to apply for grants from their overseas budget, just as any other Israeli NGO seeking funding would have to do. The most extreme example of this trend was the Philadelphia federation, which, by 2010, began to make its entire overseas budget available to whoever presented the most compelling proposal. As their leaders explained, they identified their communities' priorities and would fund only projects that aligned with them. They would then closely evaluate and measure performance outcomes, with poor performers not getting their grants renewed. A high-ranking executive in the Philadelphia federation explained that with the spike in the number of Israeli NGOs that had taken place since the 1990s her federation determined that "if we want the best provider for a certain project, it's not always going to be [the Jewish Agency]." She added, "It's not that we're not funding core [anymore] . . . we're just not going to fund core because it's core."[52]

However, a more typical example of federation behavior by the early 2010s was the San Francisco federation. Though by 2010 it supported approximately thirty-five other grantees annually to the tune of $2.5 million, in most cases it still chose the Jewish Agency's projects as the best recipients for most of its budget.[53] At the other end of the spectrum, some federations resisted the move toward independent Israel allocations. Federations like Chicago and Baltimore insisted that they believed in the sanctity of core giving and maintained generally disparaging attitudes toward those departing from core. As Linda Epstein, associate vice president of the Jewish United Fund / Jewish Federation of Metropolitan Chicago, explained, in terms of federation giving "Chicago is a community" in which donors have bought into collective action, rather than individual initiative, as the best course for supporting Israel. She added, "You will almost never hear the phrase [from our donors]: 'see what *I* did.'"[54]

Despite voices like these, the trend away from core allocations continued to grow larger within the wider federation system. Increasingly, the growth of Israeli NGOs provided federations even greater opportunity to identify work in Israel that they wanted to support. The more the genie came out of the bottle, the less it seemed that most wanted to put it back in.

## The Revolt Trickles Upward

Eventually, the United Jewish Communities (UJC; established in 1999 as a merger of the CJF, UJA, and UIA) came to realize that it had to accommodate a growing desire from local community federations to find new opportunities for philanthropic partnership outside of the classic Jewish Agency paradigm.[55] Yet it recognized that the shift to federations conducting their own Israel giving outside of the Jewish Agency was an increasingly unwieldy and potentially dangerous trend. In response, in late 1999 it issued a new system-wide protocol for overseas giving, known as ONAD (the Overseas Needs Assessment and Distribution Committee). Under ONAD, federations would be instructed to continue to automatically give 90 percent of their overseas budget to the core but could designate the remaining 10 percent—the so-called elective money—more according to their own specifically determined priorities.[56] The idea was that by doing so the system would, as Rebecca Caspi, senior vice president for Israel and Overseas for JFNA, explained, "*kasher* a process that had been splintering and happening anyway, which was the direct federation-to-program relationships."[57]

Although intended to effectively co-opt the trend of federations making their own choices for their Israel giving, the creation of ONAD's officially endorsed core/elective divide instead exacerbated the splintering process. A problem with ONAD's setup was that elective funding had to still go to the Jewish Agency, the JDC, or one of two other UJC-determined projects.[58] It was, therefore, not surprising that criticisms began to roll in that the elective options were too narrow and did not really give federations the flexibility and control they desired.[59] Federations that did not want to adhere to the limiting ONAD stipulations simply did not. There was nothing to prevent them from going their own way. Participation in the UJC/CJF/UJA's centralized efforts had always been a voluntary decision for local federations, but the traditional culture in most cases since the creation of a centralized system in the first decades of the twentieth century had been for local federations to willingly and consistently submit to the national organization's protocols. Besides this, other federations that had previously never made their own overseas giving choices got a taste under ONAD of the appeal of earmarking funds to projects of their choosing. The result was that, within a short time, more federations began to allocate more of their overseas dollars outside of the system, and the ONAD framework collapsed.[60]

## The Formal Break

The trends of dissatisfaction with the Jewish Agency in satisfying the Israel giving needs of the American Jewish federation movement culminated in the official 2011 decision by the JFNA (which the UJC had been renamed), discussed earlier in the chapter, that formally ended the exclusivity agreement between the JFNA and Jewish Agency.[61] The fact that it did so without adding a new partner organization in its place speaks to just how much the idea of automatic deference had collapsed. In other words, this represented a rejection not only of the Agency but also of a permanent Israeli principal in the relationship at all. American actors would be the ones to identify whom they wanted to work with in Israel. All decisions on the use of funds raised by the JFNA would be by the JFNA, itself, and not Israelis.

This is not to say that this represented the death of institutional deference overall. Each individual federation engaging individual Israeli NGOs as partners has had to negotiate its own relationships. As later chapters will demonstrate, for many donors, whether by choice or habit, some degree of deference has remained as an important aspect of the relationship. In addition, despite the changing relationship between federations and core overseas allocations to the Jewish Agency, there is still a prevailing sense among many in the federation world that the core, while in many ways problematic, remains extremely important. That is why federations that are active with elective work still by and large support a core Jewish Agency budget; for example, between 45 and 65 percent of total UJC funds passed along to the Jewish Agency in 2007 were unrestricted, meaning they were up to the Jewish Agency's own allocations discretion.[62]

The Metrowest New Jersey Federation's director of Israel Operations Amir Shacham explained this phenomenon—why a federation like his, which itself maintains direct partnerships with six different communities in Israel, funding approximately a hundred programs, is still so loyal to supporting the core: "With Metrowest . . . everyone understands that the electives and the partnerships and the building bridges are the bones and heart of what we do and are the best tools to connect us. And on the other hand, everybody understands that we can't really abandon the national system. We are always good soldiers. We will never leave the system or make Shabbat to ourselves and we try to support the core as much as we can."[63]

There is still some trust remaining that, in times of crisis, the Jewish Agency might be the best way to adequately serve Jewish needs, as it has traditionally been.[64] Caspi explained: "If you defund JAFI [the Jewish Agency] . . . to a degree that their ability to continue having certain core competencies or to continue to do . . . certain kinds of activities that in a moment of need could be easily expanded, then you risk going back to a time that hasn't existed for more than half a century where that capacity no longer exists in the Jewish world."[65]

The example of the 2006 Israel Emergency Campaign (IEC) seems to illustrate the state of the drift from commitment to core within the federation system. Launched at the start of the 2006 Lebanon War between Israel and Hezbollah, the IEC demonstrated how the national system can still pull together to raise a lot of money ($350 million) quickly in times of emergency.[66]

However, compared to how smoothly allocations were executed in previous emergency campaigns (e.g., the 1973 emergency campaign in the wake of the October 1973 Yom Kippur War),[67] the allocations process surrounding the 2006 IEC had its problems. One federation employee involved in the IEC who asked to remain nameless relayed a sentiment shared by a number of interviewees:

> We said: "Look, we are giving I don't know how many millions, but we want half a million to go to Sderot, because all the money's going to the North and we are very South-oriented." Now that's a small example, but each federation did that. "We want this and we want that." "Why did Nahariya not get this and that?" "Who told you they didn't get it?" OK. The mayor called the executive of the federation because he knows him and said, "you are giving money and we didn't get it." [It was] a big, big *balagan*. On the one hand, it's good, because it emphasizes the need of transparency and we all want to know that each city got its [part]. On the other hand, the needs were not equal and you need to trust your headquarters and your people to map the needs . . . so there was a lot of money, it was a great success on the one hand. On the other hand . . . it's impossible to work like that.

The Jewish Agency's director of the Division of Priority Regions Offer Isseroff, a critic of the newly fragmented nature of federations' Israel giving, echoed this sentiment: "The whole process took much more time that it should have taken. The various interests within the system stopped a lot of money. Decision making was very slow. Money often came in 3–6 months after it should have."[68] In his opinion, there were too many cooks in the kitchen—too many voices representing too many constituencies who all wanted to have their say for the kind of efficient and effective allocation of resources they believed necessary at the time.

These examples speak to a changing power-sharing environment differing from the classic Checkbook Zionism relationship. While American Jewish deference to Israelis still exists to some degree as a prominent feature in many federations' relationships with Israeli NGOs in the second and third decades of the twenty-first century, it is no longer the blanket phenomenon it long was across American communities; nor is it the universal commitment to federating as the ideal mode of organized giving and allocating.

This has opened the door to new kinds of as yet undefined power-sharing relationships on the communal level.

CHANGES AT THE INDIVIDUAL DONOR LEVEL: DONOR-DIRECTED
GIVING AND NEW OPTIONS FOR PARTNERSHIP

At the root of the changes to local federations' ideas on Israel allocations has been
something of a revolution in giving philosophy and behavior at the individual
level that has developed over time. Depending on one's perspective, an increasingly vocal and independent pool of potential donors has pushed to either com-
plicate or to democratize the process of American Jewish allocations to Israeli
causes.

At the core of changes at the transnational and national levels discussed so
far in this chapter, a major shift was underway during these years in the tectonic
plates of *general* American philanthropy (including Jewish philanthropy, specifically). Federated philanthropic giving, which, as discussed, had been the
dominant mode of American giving in the first portion of the twentieth
century—was being replaced more and more by something broadly called "direct
giving." Direct giving is a manner of philanthropy that vests more control over
the destination of donations into the hands of the donors (at least theoretically).
Direct giving can come in a number of forms. It might be as simple as donors
picking small, more specifically focused organizations of their choosing, rather
than giving to an umbrella fund like a federation. In other cases, direct giving
might entail donors to a specific organization selecting the destination of their
dollars from a menu of projects within the organizations' portfolio of activities.
At its greatest extreme, donors giving directly might set up special "donor-
advised" funds linked to federations or create their own personal or family
foundations, over which they control all allocation decisions.[69]

One of the basic building block of classic Checkbook Zionism for years had
been the trust average American Jewish donors had in the umbrella bodies collecting and distributing their money in Israel. Reflecting on this dynamic, Jaffe
noted that for average individual donors to the federation/UJA it was "extremely
doubtful whether . . . [they had] the slightest understanding of the political
nature of . . . the Jewish Agency." The result, he continued, was that "most donors
[did not] really care, and they settle[d] for sloppy, wasteful philanthropy with
only the crudest kind of 'representation' . . . [which] no one care[d] to stop."[70] But,
over time, just as American Jews involved in the Jewish Agency's Board of Governors and leadership of renegade federations, discussed earlier in this chapter,
began to distrust that old patterns of automatic giving to centralized institutions
still remained as the ideal practice, individual donors underwent a similar
process.

In the 1980s and 1990s, increasing numbers of American Jewish donors began
to see direct giving as a more appealing option than federated giving. The ideal
of supporting the collective, which had been the core tenet at the center of the
American Jewish philanthropic machine for nearly a century, began to recede

in comparative importance to donors.[71] It was being replaced by a new ideal for donors—a variation of Brandeis's vision in which they went their own way in order to maximize impact and not leave allocation decisions in the hands of others.

This trend at the individual level was largely what pushed both local Jewish federations and the national federation/UJA/UIA system to make the changes away from classic patterns of automatic institutional deference discussed earlier in this chapter. Federations were realizing that between the decline in the ideal of federated giving and the explosion in the number of alternative giving options that was simultaneously taking place it would be much harder to retain their donors unless they made adjustments that spoke to the changing desires of their giving bases.[72] As multiple interviewees for this study explained, organizations reasoned, therefore, that by breaking from traditional patterns of deference to larger institutions, wresting some control over allocations, and opening their own activities to some degree of direct giving, they could hopefully keep as many of their donors as possible committed to the federation and away from the newer giving options that allowed them even more freedom and control.

———

To adequately understand the background for how acceleration of direct giving in the decades since the 1980s has reshaped the contours of American Jewish giving to Israel, there are two main questions to explore: Why have donors been drawn to direct giving? And what have the effects of direct giving been on the shifts in attitude and behavior at every cog of the American Jewish philanthropic relationship with Israel?

## The Appeal of Direct Giving

The literature on changing giving patterns among Americans suggests that the main reason that donors have gravitated toward donor-directed giving options over the past generation is that they want some control over how their donations are used.[73] Much of the literature on this issue links donors' desire for control to a corollary desire to have more information on the organizations they are supporting in order to help them make their giving choices and maximize impact.

One formulation has labeled this contemporary giving culture as the era of "new scientific philanthropy." It is characterized by a commonly held assumption among donors, big and small, that charities/NGOs would work much better if they were run more like businesses. By this thinking, all donors—no matter how small—become shareholders of sorts, demanding accountability on the destination and eventual impact of their charitable dollars.[74]

Likewise, some scholars have noted the rise of "venture philanthropy," a type of giving in which a new breed of involved donors supports NGOs that *specifically* focus on doing innovative work.[75] Felicia Herman, a scholar and Jewish foundation professional, describes how, in this model, donors place a high premium on attaining good information to help them make their giving choices, including upfront research on potential grantees and ongoing evaluations on the progress of their work. Peter Frumkin, a scholar of social policy and practice, explains how venture philanthropy views previous modes of giving as not adequately concrete and specific and therefore too often wasteful. He argues that a more "sophisticated" breed of philanthropists today now choose this type of donor-targeted giving because they believe it will "maximize the public benefits of their giving."[76] While venture philanthropy was originally piloted by larger giving organizations, such as corporations and foundations, its appeal of targeted, information-based giving trickled down over time to individual donors as well. Scholar and veteran fundraiser Dvora Blum describes a giving philosophy she terms "strategic philanthropy." In it, donors heavily target their giving in a certain, very specific area and then closely monitor the results of their gifts.[77] Similarly, economist Brian Duncan characterizes the tendency as "impact philanthropy," in which donors want to see the direct impact of their gift rather than support the broader charitable portfolio of an umbrella giving body.[78]

Name and subtle differences of these various categorizations aside, all echo some common characteristics. First, they describe a growing American donor interest in making a greater impact through giving directly to specific causes, organizations, or projects rather than to an intermediary organization.[79] In addition, they suggest that the practices described having initially been carried out by foundations or corporations but that increasingly influence the attitudes and interests of smaller, individual donors.[80]

The various types of direct giving arrangements that donors pursue appear, on the surface, to give them such control. Most donors choosing to give directly likely *believe* that doing so gives them a greater measure of control and choice. But whether they actually have greater control or just the illusion of greater control varies by case.

Before moving on, it is worth briefly noting that in addition to the abovementioned motivations for direct giving that highlight the thought processes of individual donors, there was also a broader political/economic shift underway in the United States (as well as Great Britain, Israel, and other Western states) during these same years that may also help explain the shift to direct giving. During the Reagan-Thatcher deregulatory era of the early 1980s, as the predominant policy perspective moved to a belief that big government programs were not the ideal solution for solving certain social ills, as they had long been heralded to be, perhaps a corollary attitude percolated downward into the minds of individual donors as well, that the big federated charity model of the past half century might need similar reevaluation/retooling as the welfare state.[81] While this idea is somewhat beyond the scope of this study, it would be an interesting idea to explore further. And it will be briefly touched upon in the next chapter as well, regarding the proliferation of third-sector organizations in Israel during the same years.

## The Effects of Direct Giving

Evidence for how the migration from federated giving to direct giving has changed the nature of overall American giving to Israel can be seen through a variety of metrics.

On a micro level, for years federations reported declines in their number of donors,[82] yet, all the while, total giving to Israel was steady or on the rise.[83] One can infer that the simultaneous dip in federation performance and increase in independent funding campaigns by Israeli NGOs reflects some degree of donor disenchantment with the old way of collective giving to the same centralized institutions. Donors still cared about supporting Israel, but apparently wanted new ways to do it. An anecdote relayed by an Israeli fundraiser interviewed for this study relays a type of dissatisfaction American Jews were experiencing when giving blindly to umbrella bodies. He witnessed the experiences his donors had wanting to understand how their community's donations were being used by the Jewish Agency. "[Our American donors] just kept calling the people in the Jewish Agency. And they [Jewish Agency representatives] are just telling them [the donors]: 'Everything's amazing. Everything's amazing. Everything's amazing.' Showing the exact same bomb shelter that they built to 20 different groups [from different communities] and telling everybody this is your money that built this bomb shelter. [Our donors would] hear from people that were here in Israel: 'We're waiting for a bomb shelter to be fixed in our neighborhood.'"[84] Interviews with numerous veteran fundraising professionals echoed the idea that many American Jewish donors like the ones referenced in this case came to believe that the work of the Agency and its centralized funding partners—and perhaps even the overall picture of Israel they were being sold—was in many ways not reality.

Scholar of American Jewish philanthropy Gary Tobin predicted in the early 1990s that, unless properly addressed, this growing feeling at the donor grassroots might upend the traditional system of American Jewish giving to Israel. He told the *Jewish Telegraphic Agency* that increasingly "donors are rethinking previously automatic contributions to 'umbrella agencies,'" considering "the UJA-Federation system as only 'one of many choices.'" He warned that reform to the system to accommodate donor concerns was "urgent" and that, without it, a fundamental realignment of American Jewish giving to Israel loomed.[85] His warning proved to be prophetic.

While it is hard to point to each giving choice by each donor to give in any other way than a federation's general campaign as definitive evidence that that donor necessarily favors direct giving, from a macro perspective it is clear that the center of gravity has shifted since the 1980s and increasingly more so in the first decades of the twenty-first century. As indicated, though total American Jewish giving to Israel has increased, federation giving has significantly declined.[86] As of 2014, the overwhelming proportion of giving to Israel was through Israeli NGOs outside of the Jewish Agency orbit.[87] In addition, as explained earlier, federations have increasingly shifted their portfolios away from the Jewish Agency and offered donors opportunities to designate their choices. This is to say nothing of the rise of individual and family foundations that has taken place during these years that have put big donors directly in contact with Israeli organizations.[88]

Overall, this rise of direct giving has contributed substantially to changing the complexion of how American Jews give to Israel. For one, the number of American Jews actually making spending decisions has vastly increased from the days when it was only leaders of local federations handing funds to their national body and leaders at the UIA automatically passing it to the Jewish Agency. In addition, an important new wrinkle to the dynamics is that those on the Israeli side representing the NGOs or projects seeking American funds now have to negotiate relationships with their individual donors who may, but may not, hold the deferential attitudes of old.

## CONCLUSION

The faith American Jews had in the federation/UJA and the federation/UJA had in the Jewish Agency grounded Israel-diaspora philanthropic relationship for decades. Israelis at the Jewish Agency were able to present Israel as they wanted, and American donors trusted their Israeli "partners" in the field to report on needs, use of funds, and impact—relying on their assessments with minimal pushback. Indeed, there was enormous power for the Jewish Agency in being able to set a narrative that American donors believed. But, as has been discussed throughout this chapter, in the half century since the 1967 War, much of the trust and deference that supported the giving-allocating pipeline has collapsed at every level—the transnational, the national, and the individual. As the Jewish Agency lost the ability to play the role of trusted dispenser of information and American Jewish donors started working with a glut of new Israeli organizations, the days of the starry-eyed American donors began to come to an end. Americans had grown weary of their old roles. They now had access to all kinds of information on Israel, including from increased travel, online sources, and new contacts at Israeli NGOs. The realities of Israel were simply more plain for them to see.

These changes notwithstanding, several questions emerge in evaluating the contemporary state of power sharing between Israeli activists and their American supporters. First, is the old relationship paradigm quite as dead as it may appear on the surface? Have a triumphant age of empowered American Jews and a genuine transnational partnership that would have made Brandeis proud ensued? Or do the same old relationship dynamics of Checkbook Zionism still exist, just with new trimmings? Finally, what is the position of Israelis in this new endeavor? Are they hoping to keep American Jews within the classic Checkbook Zionism frame they supported or allowing for more equal partnership with their now more engaged diaspora allies? The final four chapters of this book represent the first attempt to answer these questions and define the dynamics of the field in the twenty-first century.

# PART II

# Power Sharing in the Contemporary Era

# CHAPTER 4

# An Introduction to the Study of Contemporary Relationship Dynamics

As of 2020, American Jewish giving to Israeli organizations was arguably as healthy as ever. American Jews gave over $2.4 billion/year to Israeli organizations[1]—more than they *ever* gave through the UJA/Jewish Agency pipeline in inflation-adjusted terms (see figure 1.10). The relationship involved hundreds of American Jewish organizations, thousands of Israeli NGOs, and untold hundreds of thousands—perhaps into the millions—of donors. The remaining chapters of this book investigate the new relational patterns that have emerged in a new post–Checkbook Zionism environment. This chapter introduces a number of important frames and concepts necessary for interpreting the case study ahead.

First, it discusses the development of Israel's NGO sector and how it came to supplant the Jewish Agency as the prime destination for American Jewish donations. Next, it examines important aspects of the changed structural landscape of American Jewish philanthropy, including giving culture and relevant tax law—and offers a typology for understanding the plethora of American Jewish giving vehicles established to facilitate donations to Israel over recent decades. It then introduces the specific sixteen Israeli NGOs that compose this study's sample—explaining how they were selected as well as their histories, missions, activities, and perceptions of impact. It closes by discussing the central role American Jewish funding plays in supporting the organizations in this study.

## The Rise of Israeli NGOs as Rivals to the Jewish Agency

For decades, the Jewish Agency maintained its place as the mostly unrivaled dispenser of American Jewish donations in Israel. As discussed in chapter 3, the UIA had few choices for destinations for its annual remissions other than to the

Jewish Agency (whether it would have even wanted alternatives is another question). U.S. tax law dictated that in order for donors to the UJA/UIA to receive tax deductions, their contributions needed to be remitted to an NGO—not a foreign government and not individuals. So it was little more than a formality when the UIA "reevaluated" whether to renew its agreement with the Jewish Agency every five years, guaranteeing that the latter would be its exclusive recipient of funds in Israel. With so few Israeli NGOs operating outside of the Jewish Agency umbrella, the Jewish Agency was really the only choice.

The Israeli government supported the idea that the Jewish Agency—a unitary body with close government ties—was responsible for centrally collecting, planning, and dispensing the foreign donations that were so fundamental to the state's development, especially in the early years. In part, this had to do with the organizational philosophy that Israel's first prime minister, David Ben-Gurion, had set out for the new state. As discussed in chapter 1, Ben-Gurion's *mamlakhtiyut* (translated as "statism") promoted the centrality of the state in Israel's civic life and culture. Moreover, the Jewish Agency's primacy in managing diaspora contributions was consistent with Israeli political culture of the era more broadly. Most Israeli citizens shared the outlook during these years that the state apparatus should play a central role in Israeli society and that there was, therefore, little room for other civil society organizations not tied to government (or, to a smaller degree, political parties).[2]

The effect of this all was that the number of potential institutional partners for diaspora philanthropists was limited to the Jewish Agency and a tiny number of other organizations—most of which were either very small and/or aligned with the Jewish Agency's activity and agenda.

This situation remained static for decades. But starting in the 1970s, changes in both Israeli government philosophy and citizen-initiated activity began to alter the complexion of the Israeli nonprofit sector and eventually open competition to the Jewish Agency for attracting foreign donations.

Following the Likud party's surprise victory in the 1977 Israeli election, Israeli civil society began a dramatic transformation. Unlike the Labor Party, which had run the Yishuv/Israel uninterrupted since the 1930s, Likud pursued an economic policy of privatization. In the name of smaller government and promotion of free enterprise, the Likud government initiated a process to dismantle Israel's then sprawling state-controlled welfare system. Breaking with the idea of *mamlakhtiyut*, it rolled back centralized state programs and looked to outsource many of Israel's education, health care, and social service programs to privately run NGOs. Israel suddenly found itself in need of organizations to fill the service provision and community building roles the state was relinquishing, and, as a result, over the next years Israeli citizens established hundreds of new independent NGOs.[3]

Simultaneously, the Israeli populace was undergoing a mostly unrelated process in its changing attitudes toward government. Over Israel's first several decades, largely due to the paternalistic effects of *mamlakhtiyut*, citizens often acquiesced to societal and political realities in Israel—even some distasteful ones. If they were to express discontent, most Israelis believed that it should be at the ballot box rather than through other forms of protest or advocacy.[4] Yet in the wake of the 1967 and 1973 Wars, a new culture of popular grassroots protest emerged in Israel as a means for expressing disenchantment and advocating for societal changes.[5] In his impressive study on the emergence of protest in Israel, Sam Lehman-Wilzig demonstrates just how much Israeli citizens began turning to extra-parliamentary protest activities in the 1970s and 1980s. Compared to the previous period that he calls the age of "extra-parliamentary quiescence" (1955–1970), from 1971 to 1978 the average annual number of "protest events" in Israel grew by 213 percent (from 38.8 to 121.5). And from 1979 to 1986 it grew another 60 percent to an average of 202 protest events/year.[6]

Starting in the 1980s and 1990s, a portion of Israelis wanting to voice protest recognized they could have greater impact if they incorporated their movements as NGOs, rather than the mass protest movements they had previously been organizing.[7] In addition to voicing discontent, groups incorporating protest movements into NGOs could now raise money—often from overseas supporters— that they could then strategically leverage to influence Israeli policy and society. Though by the end of the 1990s, this category of advocacy NGOs—sometimes referred to civil society organizations (CSOs)—was only a small portion of the overall Israeli NGO sector, it was emerging as the fastest growing category of NGOs in Israel, growing from only 3 percent of all new organizations established at the beginning of the decade to 9 percent by the end.[8]

The result that these two trends—changing government philosophy and changing citizen attitudes—collectively had on the Israeli nonprofit sector was significant. From the beginning of the 1980s to the beginning of the 1990s, the number of NGOs in Israel soared: from 3,000 to 16,000 and by 2005 to 41,000.[9] The sector's importance in Israel's economy grew substantially as well. In the years between 1955 and 1975, the Israeli nonprofit sector composed an annual average of only 6 percent of Israel's GDP. But from 1975 to 1984, the figure rose to 8 percent. By 1991, it reached 11.6 percent.[10]

Indeed, by the end of the 1990s, a robust NGO sector in Israel—including thousands of CSOs—had blossomed just as a maturing American Jewish community, fatigued with the Jewish Agency and classic Checkbook Zionism patterns, was ready to find new partners abroad (as explained in chapter 3). Both CSOs and the more nonpoliticized educational and welfare NGOs would become significant factors in the constellation of diasporic philanthropic relationships from that point forward.

## NGOs as Rival Options for Overseas Donations

As they came of age, many Israeli NGOs encountered problems securing enough of the funding they needed from within Israel alone. Though, as of the 1990s, a fair-sized portion of non-CSO NGOs received state support (41 percent), most did not (59 percent); and an even higher percentage of the CSOs (74 percent) did not.[11] Additionally, Israeli NGOs were often not able to get sufficient charitable contributions from Israelis. Unlike in many other industrialized countries with comparable economies, Israel did not yet have a well-developed culture of philanthropy—due largely to its legacy of looking to government to provide all services and frowning upon independent initiatives. To illustrate just how poor individual Israelis' rate of philanthropic giving was at the time that its CSO sector was beginning to flourish, one can look at Israeli citizens' giving patterns relative to those of Americans at the time. In 1997, for example, Israelis donated the paltry sum of $23.19 in charity annually per capita.[12] This compared to $408.02 given by Americans per capita.[13] To better compare apples to apples, these figures can be looked at relative to median income levels among Americans ($30,282)[14] and Israelis ($18,450) in 1997.[15] By this metric, Americans at the time gave approximately 1.3 percent of their earnings to charity, eleven times as much as Israelis, who gave less than 0.012 percent of the money they earned to charity.

Fortunately for many of these cash-strapped Israeli NGOs in the 1990s and beyond, a variety of foreign contributors had an interest in supporting causes or organizations in Israel. These included various American Christian movements, European state-linked foundations, and diaspora Jewish communities from all around the world. Yet the biggest group of interested foreign donors were American Jews, who, as explained in chapter 3, were at the same time looking for ways to connect philanthropically with Israel outside of the federation/UJA/Jewish Agency pipeline. As a result, thousands of Israeli NGOs began to put themselves onto the international market for philanthropy.

To American Jewish donors, it soon became clear that NGOs held a number of significant advantages over the Jewish Agency. First, these hundreds of newly established Israeli NGOs collectively worked on a much broader range of issues and causes in Israel than the Agency ever did. Potential individual American Jewish donors now had options to specifically support whichever issues they cared most about in Israel (including social justice work, medical research, sports leagues, theater groups, Jewish education, business development associations, and many more). Second, as independent actors free from the influence of the state or Jewish Agency, individual Israeli NGOs did not have to comport with Checkbook Zionism's classic power-sharing model. They could forge whatever kinds of power-sharing arrangements with their benefactors that they pleased.

In addition, to facilitate the flow of overseas donations, in the 1990s and first decades of the twenty-first century, American activists and donors established hundreds of new organizations specifically designed to support charitable work in Israel. By 2010, over 750 such organizations were active each year in raising money from American Jews to support work in Israel.[16] Increasingly more Jews in the United States choosing to contribute to Israeli causes did so by way of these organizations.

These developments would create unprecedented challenges for the Jewish Agency in competing for the large, albeit not unlimited, pot of overseas funds.

## AMERICAN CHARITABLE GIVING CULTURE AND TAX LAW

As indicated earlier, as of 2016, Israeli NGOs outside of the Jewish Agency orbit brought in over $2 billion, representing over 90 percent of all American Jewish donations to Israel.[17] The success Israeli NGOs have had in drawing so many American Jewish donors away from the UJA and Jewish Agency can be explained mostly by the already discussed trends of discontent with the Jewish Agency and appreciation of the variety of causes supported by NGOs. But it also needs to be understood in the context of aspects of American giving culture and U.S. tax law.

### Importance of Tax Deductions

Legally, Americans are allowed to donate their money to any organization they wish, so long as it does not support terrorism.[18] Yet, aside from contributing to political campaigns, most Americans will typically give to a cause in significant quantities only if they can receive a tax deduction for doing so. Scholars of philanthropy agree that if a charity cannot offer donors a tax deduction for their charitable gifts, American donors are likely to give either far less money or maybe even none at all.[19]

There is no evidence to suggest American Jewish donors are any different from the broader American Jewish population in this regard. On the contrary, there are numerous examples that illustrate how American Jews act just like other donors in this regard. One telling case of this took place during the Israeli War of Independence.

As of early 1948, American Jews had been dramatically increasing their financial support to the prestate Yishuv. American Jewish concern for the vitality of the Zionist project and the Jews of Palestine was at an all-time high as startling images like the massacre of the Hadassah medical convoy in Jerusalem in April 1948 filled the Jewish press. Yet in that same month, the UJA experienced a scare when the IRS briefly stripped its tax-exempt status due to an accusation that UJA money was being used to buy arms for the Haganah (the precursor to the Israel Defense Forces).

Leaders within the American Jewish community recognized the intense gravity of the situation. The usually cool-headed, pragmatic UJA chair Henry Montor, for example, sent a panicked cable to Jewish Agency finance minister Eliezer

Kaplan regarding the indispensability of UJA tax exemption. "If the tax ruling stands," Montor explained, "it will mean the collapse of the UJA and perhaps a new kind of campaign without tax exemptions. That will be a terrible kind of campaign to conduct. The proceeds would be minimal . . . I don't know how we could operate under those circumstances and convince people to give any kind of substantial sums."[20]

Staring down what they anticipated would be a dire situation, American Jewish leadership aggressively lobbied to have the decision reversed. Their efforts were successful, and within weeks the IRS reinstituted the UJA's exempt status.

As this example shows, even at a moment in which the future of an Israeli state hung in the balance, American Jewish leaders believed that donors would still be heavily influenced by the issue of tax deductibility.

Interviewees in this study revealed that this feeling is still alive and well. Representatives of fifteen of the sixteen Israeli NGOs in this study's sample indicated they believed their organization would likely not be able to survive if they were not able to facilitate tax deductions for contributions from their overseas donors.

In short, Israeli organizations believe that if they are going to be able to secure ample funding from American Jews, they need to be able to offer their donors tax deductions for their giving.

### Background and Criteria of American Tax Deductions
### for Overseas Giving

The U.S. government began offering American taxpayers deductions for domestic charitable giving in 1917. Over the next decades, it would refine the criteria organizations would need to meet in order for its donors to be eligible for deductions.[21] Eventually, it would stipulate that three requirements be met.[22] First, the organization needed to be nonprofit—in other words, neither board members nor employees could derive financial profit from the group's work.[23] Second, it could not be what is considered "overtly political," which is defined only as groups engaging in excessive lobbying or support of political candidates.[24] Finally, it needed to be dedicated to what the IRS calls either "religious, literary, scientific, educational, recreational, or charitable purposes."[25]

Some have argued that an additional stipulation be added: that an organization supporting work that runs contrary to U.S. policy not be tax-exempt.[26] This perspective stems from the argument that the government is effectively using its tax policy as a way to encourage certain kinds of private charitable giving. By allowing individuals to send what have been termed "otherwise taxable dollars" to private charities rather than paid in taxes, the argument goes, the government is therefore in a de facto way endorsing individuals' support of these organizations. It has been argued that since this is almost tantamount to the U.S. government itself supporting those organizations,[27] organizations be allowed to receive the exemption only so long as they are in line generally with U.S. policy. Nevertheless, to date this has become neither a majority opinion nor a requirement for tax exemption.[28]

In 1938, Congress passed a new revenue act to clarify and refine a number of provisions of federal income tax policy (just as it had more than a dozen times since the federal government had gained the power to levy income tax in 1913).[29] While the rather routine update had focused on a number of only tangentially related provisions, it had the unintended side consequence of introducing language that would call into question the eligibility of certain charitable donations intended for overseas use.[30] To clarify the confusion that would ensue over the next years, the treasury department eventually articulated its position in a 1963 revenue ruling, explaining that the tax deduction benefits it offered for charitable giving extended to *all* charitable giving, regardless of whether the ultimate destination of the donation was a domestic American charity or an overseas charity.[31] With this ruling, it became clear that supporting an orphanage in Cambodia, for example, was, in the eyes of the Treasury department, equally worthy of a U.S. tax deduction as supporting an orphanage in Cleveland. Indeed, nothing was written in the tax code to preference domestic charitable giving over eligible overseas charitable giving, so long as the donation to a foreign NGO met three additional requirements that still stand as of the writing of this book.

First, the donation needed to formally be given directly to an "American" organization—one that is registered in the United States and whose board of directors is 50 percent or more composed of American citizens.[32] The rationale is that, in such an organization, expenditure decisions are theoretically made and monitored by Americans, who, by virtue of being Americans, retain some kind of operative "American interest" (whatever that might mean) in their decision making. Yet, as far as the IRS is concerned, that organization needs neither a domestic agenda nor domestic activities. In fact, if it chooses, the group can remit 100 percent of the donations it receives to foreign NGOs doing work abroad.

The second requirement is that any foreign charitable organization that would be the eventual recipient of American tax-exempt dollars would be able to pass what is known as the "foreign equivalency test," if it were called upon to do so. This means that the American organization must determine whether the foreign NGO it supports falls within the same criteria for tax-exempt organizations that the IRS uses to evaluate American NGOs. Foreign equivalency can be achieved by getting a "determination letter" from the IRS in which the IRS itself investigates the specific foreign NGO and attests to its eligibility. But as this is a complicated and costly process to initiate, the IRS allows American organizations to make their own "equivalency determination" of foreign NGOs.[33] However, it warns American organizations to treat this privilege very seriously, for if it was ever revealed that the foreign NGOs they supported were *not* compliant with the rules governing American nonprofits, the American organization supporting the foreign NGO could itself be stripped of its tax-exempt status and face significant tax and legal penalties.[34]

Last, American organizations granting money to foreign NGOs have to exercise "expenditure responsibility," meaning that they must ensure that granted money is spent exactly as the grantee organization claims it will be spent; and, just as with domestic giving, it can be used only for activities that the IRS considers charitable (religious, literary, scientific, educational, recreational, etc.).[35] This theoretically ensures that tax-deductible U.S. contributions are used only for purposes the IRS believes are legitimately charitable.

While collectively this system is supposed to ensure that all tax-deductible dollars remain under the stewardship of American citizens, who are legally accountable for upholding the letter, if not the spirit, of IRS regulations,[36] it is not difficult for legitimate charitable overseas organizations to meet these three requirements. As a result, untold thousands of overseas NGOs qualify for and receive tax-deductible donations from Americans every year. In the case of American Jewish donation to Israel, as of 2016 more than eight hundred distinct American Jewish organizations existed mostly or entirely for the purpose of collecting funds from American Jews to distribute to Israeli NGOs. Collectively, they supported over two thousand NGOs in Israel.[37]

The emergence of so many new American-based organizations raising money for charitable causes in Israel contributed to—or at least coincided with—the decline of American Jewish support for the UJA/UIA/federation system, which was discussed in chapter 3. To illustrate just how far these organizations had fallen from their long dominant perch, one study argued that as of 2007 the JFNA (the organization formed in 1999 by the merger of the UJA, UIA, and CJF) was bringing in less than 10 percent of all Jewish giving to Israel in a typical year.[38] In the years after, the trend continued to grow.

## TYPES OF AMERICAN JEWISH FUNDING ORGANIZATIONS

In this changing post-JFNA era, the eight-hundred-plus American Jewish organizations raising funds for Israel each fall into one of four organizational types: (1) "friends of" organizations, (2) pass-through organizations, (3) ideological umbrella organizations, and (4) foundations. To understand the intricacies of how the transnational donor-recipient relationships in this new environment resemble or differ from classic patterns of Checkbook Zionism, it is therefore necessary to examine these four organizational forms—how they function and, more importantly, what power-sharing relationships have come to look like between them and the Israeli NGOs they support.

### Organization Type 1: "Friends of" Organizations

The fastest growing sector of American Jewish giving to Israel since the 1980s has been "friends of" organizations.[39] As of 2016, there were over 700 such organizations supporting causes in Israel, a whopping 75 percent increase over the number existing only fifteen years earlier (397 friends of existed by the end of 2000) and more than three times as many as there were twenty-five years prior (209 such organizations existed by the end of 1990).[40] Generally speaking, "friends of" organizations are established to support one specific organization abroad. Though some of these organizations conduct additional domestic activity or have domestic agendas, most do nothing else besides fundraise in the United States and pass the money they raise to their partner Israeli organization. Some have paid professionals and very active boards that take a hands-on role in overseeing the use of funds in Israel. Others, however, are little more than "paper organizations," with just a post office box as the organization's American "headquarters" and a titular, but essentially powerless, board of directors that meets infrequently, if at all, leaving decision making over use of funds to its affiliated Israeli NGO. For this reason, "friends of" organizations have been criticized as mere legal conduits established to funnel tax-exempt money to overseas NGOs.[41] However, as long as everyone involved in the exchange understands that the American board technically retains full legal rights to, at any point, allocate the donations it receives to any charitable cause it wishes without recourse, the IRS does not get involved.[42]

For example, if the board of the American Friends of Hebrew University—an organization established in 1925 for the express purpose of raising money from Americans to support the Hebrew University in Jerusalem[43]—decided that instead of passing the money it raised to Hebrew University it instead wanted to give it to an environmental organization in Zimbabwe, it would be within its legal right to do so. Neither Hebrew University nor the American donors who intended their gifts to go to the university would have any legal recourse to prevent it. Although this option always remains a legal possibility, "friends of" organizations do not typically make drastically different allocation decisions than their donors expect them to. Naturally, that would almost certainly lead to donors discontinuing their support for that organization. But it is worthwhile to note that it is nevertheless technically in the legal jurisdiction of a "friends of" organization to do so.

### Organization Type 2: Pass-Through Organizations

The second organization type is the pass-through. While most of the eight-hundred-plus American organizations that grant money to Israeli organizations are directly linked to a single specific NGO, educational facility, or social service organization in Israel, pass-through organizations enable donors to support Israeli institutions, regardless of whether those organizations have their own affiliated "friends of" organization. For the most part, pass-through organizations do not outwardly espouse any ideology or agenda, nor do they weigh in on allocation decisions. So while they are still required to fulfill IRS requirements for making equivalency determinations of their overseas grantees and maintaining responsibility over allocations, their purpose is to provide an easy way to pass tax-exempt donations from American donors to Israeli NGOs.

The oldest and most well-known pass-through organization is PEF–Israel Endowment Funds. Established by Louis Brandeis and his allies in 1923 for the purpose of offering American Jews opportunities for greater control over their giving,[44] PEF operated as the lone significant pass-through organization for decades. In the era of UJA primacy, it was very small in scope. For example, PEF's total giving to Israel in 1984 was $8 million, compared to $243 million given by the UJA.[45] But from 1990 onward, coinciding with the decline of UJA dominance, PEF grew dramatically, cementing itself as the largest in what has become a burgeoning subsector of pass-through organizations. In 2017, for example, PEF facilitated a total of $104 million to over twelve hundred Israeli NGOs.[46]

Another of the older pass-through organizations, Central Fund of Israel (CFI), has also grown remarkably over the past several decades since its founding in 1979. In 2013, CFI brought in over $19 million, compared to only $350,000 in 1991.[47] In the early twenty-first century, additional pass-through organizations were established, including the online platform Israelgives.com. Collectively, these organizations are becoming a very important part of the overall picture of giving to Israel. By 2010, PEF, CFI, Israelgives, and a number of smaller pass-through organizations were facilitating tax-deductible American donations to over two thousand Israeli NGOs annually.[48]

### Organization Type 3: Ideological Umbrella Organizations

The third type of American fundraising organization is what this book terms the "ideological umbrella organization." Such an organization has a mission, raises money based on that mission, and then searches to build a portfolio of various NGOs in Israel that work on the goal issues. The most prominent is the New Israel Fund (NIF), an organization committed to promoting various progressive values in Israel.[49] Started in 1979, NIF distributed an average of approximately $25 million each year during the early 2010s to its portfolio of grantees.[50] By positioning themselves as the experts on certain issues, ideological umbrellas have become trusted voices in determining worthy causes and recipient NGOs for a pool of donors committed to the umbrella organization's ideology. Counterparts to NIF on the right include the Israel Independence Fund, an organization formed in 2009 that supports right-leaning Zionist NGOs working on either side of the Green Line. Though the growth of this segment has been notable, it represents only a small part of total American Jewish giving to Israel.

### Organization Type 4: Foundations

The fourth type of organization is the private grant-making foundation. Such foundations are asset-based organizations—meaning that they maintain large endowments and typically make their donations (grants) from the interest they accrue on that endowment.[51] Foundations enable an individual or family to incorporate their assets into an organization and gain all associated rights—meaning, in this case, that though their foundation they can give tax-deductible gifts *directly* to any charitable cause in Israel, without using another intermediary organizations, aside from the foundation itself. Families or individuals not associated with a foundation, on the other hand, cannot get tax deductions for giving to Israeli NGOs unless they do so through a federation, "friends of," pass-through, or ideological umbrella.

The scope of direct giving by foundations has yet to be documented in a comprehensive fashion. But evidence suggests that it is becoming an increasingly important part of the story of contemporary American Jewish giving to Israel.[52] Between 1995 and 2001 total assets and grant dollars of all U.S. foundations nearly doubled,[53] and Tobin's preliminary research on foundations suggests that Jewish foundations are at least keeping pace with the trend.[54] Though many of the foundations do not have an Israel agenda, many do. However, since the IRS holds foundations legally accountable for making equivalency determinations and exercising expenditure responsibility on donations they make to organizations overseas, most family foundations that want to support Israeli NGOs refrain from giving to them directly. They instead choose to give to Israeli NGOs via "friends of" organizations, pass-through organizations, ideological umbrellas, or federations, thereby reducing their legwork and potential risk. But still, risks aside, some do give directly to Israeli organizations. With only a cursory search, Fleisch and Sasson identified hundreds of Jewish family foundations with Israel portfolios, one hundred of which give grants directly to Israeli organizations.[55] This number is certainly only a fraction of the total, but there are several methodological challenges to getting clear, comprehensive data.[56] While the emerging importance of Jewish foundations—particularly larger, staffed family foundations—is not yet known, they stand to play an important role in reshaping much of the philanthropic landscape. This study does not devote specific attention to the growing foundation sector, but the conclusion will briefly touch upon its potential for impacting overall Israeli-diaspora power sharing in the future.

## INTRODUCTION TO THE CONTEMPORARY CASE STUDY

The processes of attitudinal and organizational changes outlined in this chapter and the last have yielded a vastly different technical structure of transnational giving than in the heyday of the UJA–Jewish Agency partnership. The new field of American Jewish philanthropy for Israel now involves hundreds of American organizations and thousands of Israeli organizations. But the question remains as to the extent and ways that relationship dynamics between Americans and Israelis—including power sharing, communication, and identity—have changed in this new environment. The next chapters focus on these questions. Yet there is a major methodological challenge in doing so. With such a large field of involved organizations on both sides of the ocean, it is not possible for a single study to adequately survey all of them. The approach this book has therefore taken for shedding light on the structures and dynamics of the relationships in the contemporary era has been to look closely at the interactions between a sample of sixteen Israeli NGOs and their American Jewish donors. Through comparative analysis of interviews with more than a hundred stakeholders, it has identified some of the most common attitudes and behaviors within donor-NGO relationships.

In preparation for the analysis discussed in the next chapters, the final sections of this chapter introduce the specifics of the case study—including research design and methods, an introduction to the Israeli NGOs in the research sample, and an overview of the role of American philanthropy in supporting the organizations.

### Organizational Selection and Methodological Approaches and Challenges

As explained in the book's introduction, it was determined that it would be easier to comparatively assess the behaviors of similarly focused organizations rather than organizations doing very different types of work from one another. The NGOs selected for this study's sample therefore all work on the same broad issue. They are all groups that focus on the settlement issue: either opposing or promoting/supporting the vitality of Jewish settlement in the West Bank and the traditionally majority-Arab neighborhoods in East Jerusalem.

On the one hand, the highly charged nature of the settlement debate may make the issue seem like an unexpected choice for a case study. NGOs working on the settlement issue are not typical of the larger Israeli nonprofit sector in all ways—principally that like many social change and advocacy groups, their agendas and solicitation efforts are targeted to the interests of a narrow constituency in Israel.

Yet, on the other hand, settlement NGOs are an almost ideal choice for a research sample for several reasons. First, these organizations work at the front lines of an issue regarded as deeply important to Israel's future by both Israelis and diaspora Jews. As a result, the NGOs in this study and their supporters demonstrate some of the most cutting-edge approaches to philanthropy and strategic collaboration precisely because of the high-stakes nature of the settlement debate that many involved stakeholders see as a battle for the future of Israel's character and long-term viability. In addition, because of the complicated nature of the settlement issue, a wide variety of groups covering many angles of the issue have been established. The selected NGOs in this case therefore represent a broad diversity from one another in a number of ways. They use a variety of strategies and approaches to address a divisive issue and collectively attempt to impact opinions about settlements at all levels of society. In addition to classic strategies used by advocacy organizations and pressure groups like lobbying and vying to win public opinion battles, these organizations work to change the popular narrative through targeted public education campaigns—largely abroad—and, in a traditionally Zionist manner, actually to "create facts on the ground." Taken together, this subset of NGOs illustrates the potential NGOs have in contemporary Israel for creating influence and therefore may present a blueprint to the broader Israeli nonprofit sector for its future development.

Beginning with a pool of thirty potential NGOs, this study identified the sixteen that would compose the best sample of NGOs operating in this area. Of the sixteen organizations, eight work to support settlement in some way and eight work to oppose it. In addition, the groups approach settlement from a variety of thematic vantage points (i.e., security, agriculture, legal issues, rights, etc.) as well as strategic approaches in their work. The NGOs are also a good mix of large- and small-budget groups, very established and relatively new organizations, and influential players in the field and less influential but innovative groups. Importantly, the common thread is that they all had some degree of focus on collaborating with potential donors abroad.

The data collected for each of the NGOs came from a variety of sources: over one hundred in-depth interviews with key organizational members and supporters (including leaders, visionaries, fundraisers, industry experts, and their American Jewish donors); firsthand observation of NGO staff and volunteers as they conducted their field work and/or guided tours given by NGO staff and volunteers to showcase and explain their activities; an extensive study of available written material, both produced by the NGOs (publications, promotional pieces, and, in some cases, internal documents and organizational archives) and publicly available material (documents, legal and financial records, websites, and coverage in the press).

### Additional Methodological Note

In writing about this issue, it is natural for the author to develop his own personal views on the subject. Because this work aims to be a neutral, fact-based scholarly inquiry, these materials are presented as free of the author's personal beliefs and biases as possible. The narratives of the NGOs are relayed from their own perspectives. The opinions of critics are provided, though those of the author are not.

Regarding language, it is important, for obvious reasons, to use common terminology while discussing the work of the various NGOs. However, as certain terms used to discuss West Bank settlement are considered loaded and partisan, this writing contains neutral terminology whenever possible—bearing in mind that it is impossible to do so in all cases. For example, settlers and their supporters typically refer to the "West Bank" as "Judea and Samaria" or "Yesha."[57] Likewise Palestinians and other opponents of settlement may call the West Bank the "OpT" (Occupied Palestinian Territories) or "Occupied Palestine." However, this book references only the "West Bank," even when writing from the perspectives of the various groups. Readers are presented a common language through which to examine these varied NGOs instead of being provided the more loaded language choices of particular groups.

In addition, since the NGOs in this study by and large approach their activity within the context of Israeli law (as opposed to other legal systems such as international law or religious law), the analysis intentionally uses terms and concepts that are consistent with Israel's own legal categorizations. For example, East Jerusalem is treated as part of Israel, since Israel unilaterally annexed it, but the West Bank is treated only as territory occupied and administered by Israel.[58] Likewise, the complicated issues of land ownership and land status in the West Bank are approached in accordance with the meanings defined by Israeli law.

## PROFILES OF CASE STUDY NGOs

The profiles that follow introduce the players highlighted in the analysis and findings detailed throughout the remaining chapters of this book. Each NGO profile includes the background of the issues the group was formed to address, the organization's history and development, and some of its biggest accomplishments. The issues of fundraising and donor relationships are not included here but will be covered extensively in the last three chapters.

### 1. Yesh Din

In the early 2000s, a group of left-wing Israeli activists observed what they regarded as a pattern of unchecked lawlessness and violence against Palestinian civilians carried out by Jewish settlers living in the West Bank. While there was Israeli law on the books designed to protect Palestinians and their property against aggressive settler activity, the activists believed the Israeli police and army too often were lax in their enforcement, not holding settlers accountable. In response, they founded an NGO in 2005 called Yesh Din (There Is Justice) for the purpose of advocating for a more dedicated culture of Israeli law enforcement throughout Area C of the West Bank. It would focus on two main goals: empowering Palestinians and motivating the Israeli police and army to more thoroughly fulfill their job duties.

Yesh Din believed that Palestinian farmers often do not stand up to settler violence and dispossession because they are both intimidated and likely unable to find their way in what one member of Yesh Din's Public Council called "the State of Israel's civil and military bureaucratic maze."[59] So it created a system to encourage Palestinians to report alleged crimes and then help guide them through the legal process. Yesh Din volunteers begin by collecting testimonies from Palestinians claiming they have been targeted by settlers. They then physically accompany claimants to police stations to file their reports. Afterward, Yesh Din follows up to help oversee that the claimants' investigations are being handled seriously and responsibly by police and ultimately compiles and publishes reports documenting its assessment of law enforcement.

In addition, Yesh Din runs a program called the Land Advocacy Project, which uses GIS technology and often difficult-to-locate land deeds in order to identify places in which Israeli settlers are building or planting without permission on privately owned Palestinian land. If it determines that such illegal activity is taking place, Yesh Din files court petitions to first legally verify Palestinian ownership and then call for the eviction of any settlers illegally using Palestinian land.

Yesh Din believes its work has raised awareness on the issue of inconsistent law enforcement to the Israeli power structure and the Israeli populace more generally, diaspora Jewry, and the international human rights community. In the group's estimation, the result of its work has been improved training for Israeli law enforcement, empowerment of Palestinians, and the establishment of increased (albeit still insufficient) legal accountability for illegal settler activity.

## 2. Mishmeret Yesha

In the opinion of Mishmeret Yesha (Guardians of Judea, Samaria, and Gaza), Jews living in settlements are under attack from all sides. While settlers have the option to live anywhere within Israel and be surrounded by all the comforts and amenities of modern life, they have instead chosen to forego mundane comforts in order to be holy patriots—pioneers on the front lines of Jewish history, living out biblical commandments and selflessly securing their country. Yet despite all of this, in Mishmeret Yesha's opinion, as settlers face relentless aggression from Palestinians, the Israeli government provides them only sporadic and insufficient support to defend their rights, livelihoods, and personal safety.

From the time of its creation in 1998, Mishmeret Yesha has taken a kitchen sink approach in its activities. It identifies a problem facing settlers and then creates programs to address it. Over time, this has included things like teaching self-defense techniques to settlers and providing legal aid to settlers claiming they have been falsely accused of illegal activities.

One of Mishmeret Yesha's more original initiatives is the trade and agricultural school it runs in the settlement of Nachliel. The purpose of the school, opened in 2010, is to help bolster the stagnant economies in a number of outlying settlements. It teaches unskilled and unemployed settler youth vocational and farming skills. Its hope is that its graduates will be able to operate their own small businesses within their settlements, providing for their families and helping their home communities to become more economically self-sustaining.

Mishmeret Yesha's greatest impact to date may be the training and equipping of volunteer Rapid Response Teams (RRTs) in settlements. Mishmeret Yesha explains that RRTs are the main line of defense against potential attacks by Palestinian militants in the crucial few minutes in between when an attack is launched and Israeli security forces arrive on the scene to respond. Mishmeret Yesha believes that RRTs have saved many lives over time and served as an effective deterrent saving untold others.[60]

Mishmeret Yesha sees its future as continuing to provide a variety of programs and services to support Jews living in the West Bank based on the changing needs of the settler communities.

### 3. Settlement Watch

The oldest and arguably most influential propeace advocacy organization in Israel is Shalom Achshav (Peace Now). Founded in 1978, the group made a name for itself in the 1980s organizing large rallies and pushing for dialogue between Israel and the Palestine Liberation Organization (PLO).[61] But when it achieved its main goal of helping to spur a high-level peace process, Peace Now shifted its focus to tackling more discrete challenges it believed were the main obstacles to peace. Its most impactful subproject, known as Settlement Watch (founded in 1996), monitors the expansion of Israeli settlements in the West Bank and East Jerusalem. Settlement Watch's field researchers regularly travel throughout the West Bank to collect information on new construction, which the organization then disseminates.

One of Settlement Watch's most significant achievements to date was bringing the issue of illegal outposts to light in the early 2000s.[62] Outposts are clusters of building erected outside of the state-delineated borders of a settlement community for the purpose of expanding the breadth of settler-held land. Because outposts are sometimes just a few modest (and often temporary) housing units built on otherwise vacant land, before Settlement Watch they tended to fly below the radar, popping up largely undetected all over the West Bank. Settlement Watch has argued the unwieldy, provocative, and unchecked growth of outposts has alienated Palestinians, entrenched settlers, and dealt a serious blow to prospects of Israeli-Palestinian peace.

Overall, Settlement Watch sees itself as less an advocacy body and more an information clearinghouse that can provide reliable data to decision makers and pressure groups. Indeed, Settlement Watch's research has made the organization a trusted voice on the state of settlement construction in the eyes of many. It has forged relationships with the press, NGO community, and foreign diplomats for the purpose of highlighting the reality of settlements and their role as obstacles to peace between Israelis and Palestinians.

### 4. Women in Green

Women in Green (officially Women for Israel's Tomorrow) was founded in 1994 as a women's movement to protest the Oslo Accords. The founders of Women in Green regarded Oslo's formula for granting autonomy over the West Bank and Gaza Strip to Palestinians as both a capitulation to terrorists and a foolish step that would ultimately lead to the complete undoing of Israel. Palestinians, they argued, would use their newfound control over rightful Jewish land as a staging ground to fight a guerrilla war that would not stop until all of Israel was eliminated.

In its first years, the group made a name for itself through its brazen rhetoric and demonstrations,[63] but following Israel's evacuation of settlements from Gaza in 2006, Women in Green's leaders had an epiphany. Since their activities had failed to stop the Israeli government from withdrawing from Gaza, they decided that for Women in Green to make a greater impact it would need to sharpen its approach. From then on, rather than focusing its opposition on the concept of Israeli withdrawal and compromise writ large, Women in Green would instead focus on targeted advocacy campaigns over discrete pieces of land that Israel was rumored to be considering handing over to the control of the Palestinian Authority. The campaigns would focus on a three-step approach of mobilizing grassroots support, hosting education and public relations events, and recruiting allies in the Israeli government.

In the years since, the NGO has organized countless marches, sit-ins, and cultural activities, hosted on tiny, disputed hilltops, roads, and abandoned army bases that have attracted a loyal contingent of volunteers. On multiple occasions, the upward pressure its activities helped to generate has, in Women in Green's opinion, compelled the Israeli government to change course and retain Israeli sovereignty over land it had planned to transfer to the jurisdiction of the Palestinian Authority.[64] Until and unless Israel annexes the entire West Bank and Gaza Strip, Women in Green believes that its work as a protest NGO will never be over as it fights a war of attrition inch by inch to secure the future of the Jewish people.

### 5. Rabbis for Human Rights

In the wake of the First Intifada, a small group of liberal Israeli rabbis identified a crucial void in the rabbinic leadership of the country. To them, the intifada raised pressing moral and ethical issues that Israeli society needed to reckon with. Yet, in their opinion, the rabbinic leadership of country, with its focus on ritualistic matters, all but ignored these issues. They decided, in response, to form an NGO called Rabbis for Human Rights (RHR) that could fill the gap and serve as Israel's "rabbinic voice of conscience."[65]

In the early 2000s RHR first became involved in work directly related to settlements. Its leaders witnessed what they believed was a rampant culture of settler violence and intimidation intentionally aimed at both the dispossession of Palestinian individuals and, more broadly, the gradual depopulation of Palestinians from parts of the West Bank. Settlers would harass Palestinians as they harvested olives or would, themselves, steal the olives from Palestinian groves. When physical clashes in the fields invariably broke out between Palestinians and settlers, the Israeli army would be called in to mediate. The army's standard protocol for dealing with such clashes would be to declare spots where violence had taken place as closed military zones, legally barring all parties from using the land, and thus preventing Palestinian landowners access to their crops. RHR believed that if this pattern continued, settlers could increasingly keep Palestinians from maintaining an economically sustainable existence and thereby trigger increased Palestinian migration from the countryside and improve the demographic balance in favor of settlers.

In response, RHR launched its Olive Tree Project in 2002 to organize groups of Israeli Jews to accompany Palestinians when they harvested their olives. In RHR's opinion, the simple presence of Israelis would significantly change the dynamics of how Palestinian farmers were treated by both settlers and soldiers. The RHR volunteers thus effectively became a counterlobby to the settlers. They could advocate for the perspective and needs of Palestinian farmers in a way that soldiers would more likely hear and take seriously. RHR cites many examples of this dynamic successfully in action.[66]

RHR also undertook a legal campaign, charging that as long as Israel maintained jurisdiction over the West Bank it had a responsibility to guarantee rights and justice for Palestinian inhabitants. In June 2006, an Israeli court issued a landmark decision in favor of this position.[67] It acknowledged in its decision "the criminal acts of violent individual [settlers], who violate the rights of the inhabitants to their property." It ruled that Israel had a legal responsibility henceforth to guarantee Palestinian farmers access to their lands.[68] Since the ruling, the Israeli army has been forced to overhaul its policies regarding the olive harvest. It not only refrained from whimsical land closures but instituted mandatory training on Palestinian rights, settler activities, and IDF responsibilities to uphold the law. Most importantly, from RHR's perspective, it began coordinating harvesting times and posting soldiers to protect harvesters. RHR reported that the new climate yielded many successes.[69] Still, as the problem persists, RHR continues to expand the Olive Tree Project—each harvest season, bringing in more volunteers, aiding more Palestinian farmers, and raising greater awareness around these issues.

## 6. Regavim

In 2007, a group of self-proclaimed right-wing Israeli lawyers created a watch-dog NGO called Regavim (clumps of earth) to counter a growing trend of illegal Palestinian construction throughout the Negev, Galilee, and West Bank. While Israeli authorities had been well aware of illegal constructions throughout Israel's sovereign and occupied territory, numbering in the tens of thousands, Regavim has contended that illegal building by Palestinians—both Israeli citizens and West Bank residents—was not random, as Israel has assumed. Rather, it was being carried out according to centrally coordinated Palestinian national plans that targeted strategic areas and then erected clusters of buildings as a way to better maintain Palestinian control (and simultaneously disrupt Israeli control) over high points, roads, and natural resources. Regavim believes that this process—which it calls "the illegal building *intifada*"—causes serious security problems and/or environmental issues that imperil numerous Israeli settlements in the West Bank.[70]

Regavim's focus has been chronicling building patterns, monitoring new constructions, and making the case in Israeli courts and with the public that the state needs to take a more active role in legislation and enforcement against illegal Palestinian building. It uses GIS technology to chronicle existing constructions and compares them to approved building plans. Once it identifies patterns, it focuses on what it views as the most problematic clusters of construction and then files lawsuits to halt construction or order demolition. One example that illustrates the types of cases Regavim initiates (and not infrequently wins) is a 2012 suit against an illegally constructed Palestinian quarry that Regavim alleged was contributing to problematic air quality in an adjacent Israeli settlement.[71] Regavim has litigated dozens of cases along similar lines.

Regavim hopes that with better laws and enforcement, Palestinians will be dissuaded from continuing to disregard Israeli law. It believes this is Israel's best chance to address the illegal land use underway that is so detrimental to the state's interests.

## 7. B'Tselem

In comparison to a number of antisettlement NGOs in this sample that focus on bringing to light/opposing discrete aspects of settlement (violence, land theft, illegal building, etc.), B'Tselem (In God's Image) takes a more holistic approach. In the opinion of B'Tselem, the entire settlement enterprise is illegal and immoral; and through ignorance, silence, and lack of action, the Israeli government and, to some extent, Israeli society have been complicit in what it sees as the crimes of settlement. B'Tselem, which does not work only on issues related to Israel's presence in the territories, has made it a chief goal to document, expose, and publicize the broad variety of violations of human rights associated with the settlement project and to build an international coalition to pressure Israel to adhere to its *own* stated moral and humanitarian principles.

B'Tselem seeks to dispel the perception that there is a dichotomy between Israel's legitimate security concerns, on the one hand, and Palestinians' basic rights on the other. It argues that the two are not mutually exclusive as they are often conceived to be, and to assume that they are allows for a perpetuation of human rights abuses by Israel.

B'Tselem is perhaps best known for its in-depth data gathering and reporting. Several times each year it releases meticulously detailed reports on some aspect of alleged Israeli human rights abuses in the territories (e.g., checkpoints, the separation barrier, policing tactics, settler intimidation, etc.). Through these, it has developed a reputation with influential non-Israeli actors (including UN agencies, international human rights NGOs, and foreign diplomats) as perhaps the foremost "expert" on these issues.[72] B'Tselem has failed to gain much traction within Israeli government circles and the Israeli public, arguably due to its blunt critique of Israeli policy.[73] But it believes the external pressure it helps initiate holds Israel accountable and pushes it to rein in the settlement enterprise—at least to some degree. While B'Tselem recognizes that its task is large, it believes the quality work it produces will continue to cement its reputation on the international stage as the authoritative voice on the realities of settlement.

### 8. One Israel Fund

Since its establishment in 1994, One Israel Fund (OIF) has gone through a number of incarnations. It was initially set up to be an advocacy organization focused on building American Jewish support for the idea of permanent Israeli settlement in the West Bank and Gaza Strip at a time when the *idea* was still considered more controversial.

After its first years, OIF felt it could be more helpful to the settlement enterprise in other ways. It transformed itself into a grant-making body—principally focusing on helping individual settlements shore up their security against Palestinian attackers by providing funding for items such as high-grade fencing for settlement perimeters, closed-circuit camera systems, and first aid supplies. In time, it has fanned out its portfolio beyond security alone to address a spectrum of social, educational, and other charitable projects in settlements.

OIF offers grants for various projects aimed at improving the quality of life in settlements, including building playgrounds, funding medical clinics and Jewish education facilities, and supporting cultural and recreational programming. It sees itself as building crucial bridges between settlers who may feel vulnerable and isolated living in enclaves in the heart of the Palestinian frontier and Jews abroad who support the sacrifices settlers are making and worry about their well-being. In this way, it hopes to bolster both the comfort and viability of settlements, while also building morale among settlers and helping their allies abroad to feel a part of the important work of the settlement enterprise.

### 9. The Rebuilders of the Jewish Community in Hebron ("The Rebuilders")

After Jerusalem, religious Jews view Hebron, with its cave of the patriarchs (Maarat Machpelah), as the holiest site in Judaism. Jews had lived there continually for centuries until a violent mob forced them out of the city in 1929.[74] It is little wonder that after Israel captured the West Bank in the 1967 War that religious Zionists set their sights on reestablishing a Jewish community in the shadow of the legendary final resting place of the biblical Jewish Patriarchs and Matriarchs.

Throughout the 1970s and 1980s, Hebron became a flashpoint for activist settler groups, with Jewish families squatting in abandoned formerly owned Jewish properties in the heart of the city[75]—in violation of Israeli law. The activists were playing a long game, hoping that over time their selfless acts of pilgrimage and Jewish patriotism in the face of violence and opposition would win sympathy with the Israeli public and broader Jewish world, who would in turn pressure Israel's government to soften its position and allow for permanent Jewish settlement in the heart of an otherwise Palestinian city.

In 1979, Hebron settler leader Rabbi Moshe Levinger established an NGO known as M'hadashei Ha-Yishuv Ha-Yehudi B'Hevron (Rebuilders of the Jewish Community in Hebron) to be a tool to aid the grassroots activity of the squatting settlers. While settlers were establishing a physical Jewish foothold in Hebron, the Rebuilders and its associated American "friends of" organization (the Hebron Fund) played indispensable roles in both enabling Jewish Hebron to develop into a community of over a thousand and establishing the infrastructure and political alliances necessary to make the notion of a permanent Jewish Hebron viable.

As an NGO, Rebuilders is not allowed to purchase physical buildings, but it has played an active role in identifying Palestinian landowners looking to sell their homes and Jews (mostly from the diaspora) willing to buy and remodel them into apartment buildings for settlers.

While the Hebron settlement effort has faced stiff opposition from the local Palestinian community and often from the Israeli government,[76] Rebuilders has worked to make the lives of settlers in Hebron as pleasant and comfortable as possible. It raises funds to renovate and refurbish what were often decrepit, abandoned properties into livable space and build out playgrounds and common community spaces in Jewish Hebron.[77]

In addition, Rebuilders has undergone a branding campaign to market the *idea* of a permanent Jewish settlement in Hebron to diaspora Jews and secular

Israelis through public relations work and hosting events, tours, and festivals. Collectively, they are designed to emphasize that the reestablishment of a Jewish community in the heart of Palestinian Hebron is indispensable in order to maintain guaranteed permanent Jewish access to an important historical and religious shrine, otherwise surrounded by a hostile population.

Over time, Rebuilders has helped fuel a major change in opinion within the Israeli mainstream and power circles. Whereas the enterprise was once considered a fringe perspective, increasing numbers of secular Jews throughout the world now support some kind of permanent Jewish presence in Hebron,[78] softening government opposition and possibly rendering the notions of a return to a purely Arab Hebron in the future increasingly unlikely.

### 10. Ariel Development Fund

One of the more remarkable stories in the history of the settlement enterprise is that of Ariel. Founded in 1978 by a small caravan of secular nationalist Zionists, Ariel has grown to a city of twenty thousand people, rife with amenities—including state-of-the-art athletic and performing arts centers, a downtown promenade, a university, and one of the few luxury hotels in the settlements. The real miracle of Ariel is that what should probably be regarded as one of the more outlying, vulnerable settlements—two-thirds of the way from the Green Line to the Jordanian border and connected to Israel by a thin strip of highway surrounded on both sides by Palestinian villages—has somehow come to be regarded as "consensus" (or that it is understood by both Israelis and Palestinians to be a settlement that would definitely be annexed to Israel in the event of a possible agreement for a two-state solution).[79] In contrast, most other settlements in Ariel's precarious geographic position have been assumed to be likely candidates for eventual Israeli withdrawal. But not Ariel.

The story of why Ariel has been an outlier is intimately tied to Ariel's late longtime mayor Ron Nachman. Nachman meticulously built the "brand" of Ariel through both his leadership as mayor and his tireless work running an NGO he founded called Ariel Development Fund. Nachman believed that if he could convince Israeli society and allies abroad—both American Jews and Evangelical Christians—of the indispensability of Ariel to Israel's, and indeed Judaism's, future, he would be able to mobilize the resources to make it so. So Nachman began "selling" Ariel as the "Capital of Samaria" (an important sounding moniker, especially for a community that by that point in no way warranted it) to anyone who would listen.

But over time and dozens of trips abroad, public speaking events, donor solicitation meetings, and personally guided tours, Nachman and the Ariel Development Fund brought his vision to fruition. The Ariel Development Fund garnered the funding, public support, and high-placed allies in Israel and abroad necessary to bring amenities, commerce, tourism, public funding, and waves of new immigrants to Ariel. By the time of Nachman's death in 2013, Nachman and the Ariel Development Fund had transformed Ariel. Since then, the NGO has continued with the work of tirelessly branding, raising funds, and building to cement Ariel as a permanent part of Israel, irrespective of whatever Palestinian state might eventually emerge in the West Bank.

### 11. Sheikh Jarrah Solidarity

In the middle of the night on August 1, 2009, Jerusalem police entered six apartments in Sheikh Jarrah, a traditionally Arab neighborhood of East Jerusalem. They came to forcibly evict the fifty-three Palestinians living there, whose families had resided in the spot since 1956. That same afternoon, police returned to the spot—this time to provide secure escort to eighteen Jewish settler families moving into the newly vacated units. Though the evictions and resettlement were deemed permissible by a variety of court orders,[80] a small group of Israeli activists who caught wind of the story regarded it, nonetheless, as an immoral and illegal dispossession of the properties' longtime residents.

The group, which was to become known by the name Sheikh Jarrah Solidarity (SJS), began holding a weekly protest vigil outside of the apartments. In their first weeks, the gatherings drew no more than twenty or thirty demonstrators. But as word of the story—and of the allegedly heavy-handed tactics used by Jerusalem police to put down the demonstrations—spread, several hundred Israelis, including prominent artists and political leaders, began attending the events.

SJS focused on two discrete issues: the repatriation of the evicted families and the prevention of similar eviction orders from being carried out in Sheikh Jarrah in the future. While the first proved an elusive goal, the second was not. After months of regular protests—replete with civil disobedience, arrests, and what appeared to be to some an Israeli state trampling on the freedom of assembly of nonviolent protesters—drawing substantial media and international attention, the evictions stopped—at least for the time being.[81] In SJS's view, its activity had collectively applied enough pressure to indefinitely halt the processing of more than fifty other standing eviction orders.

Hoping to build on their success, the leadership within the then still-volunteer movement registered SJS as an NGO in 2010 under the legal name Democracy Defense Fund. Over the next months, it successfully raised funds, while charting its vision as an organization.

Some in the group hoped to build on the energy SJS had generated in Sheikh Jarrah and to apply the same formula to oppose settler expansion into other East Jerusalem neighborhoods. However, the more influential wing within SJS leadership opted for a different course. They determined the group should instead turn its attention to countering the problems they believed underlay the evictions in the first place: namely, a deeper Israeli governmental and societal culture of injustice and privilege that emboldened settlers and denied equal rights to Arabs.[82]

SJS's attempt to parlay its successes into this larger agenda never really got off the ground. It is possible that its advocacy for systemic societal change appeared more ambitious or radical than the more moderate portion of its activist and donor bases were interested in or comfortable with. Regardless, SJS never recaptured the momentum or attention it had had in its earliest months. By 2014, it ceased to be an operating body. SJS is an example of the many NGOs in Israel that may have initial success but prove unable to sustain themselves longer term.

### 12. Ir Amim

Ir Amim (City of Peoples/Nations) is an NGO focused on ensuring that Jerusalem—the self-identified symbolic/spiritual capital for both Israelis and Palestinians—will also be the eventual political capital for both. Initially established in 2000 to be a small policy consulting outfit aimed at impacting decision makers, by 2004 Ir Amim had developed into more of a public outreach organization, focused on generating domestic and international support for its vision of Jerusalem.

While Ir Amim's focus is not settlements alone, it sees Israel's settlement policy as the chief issue undermining the prospect for a shared Jerusalem. In the NGO's opinion, Israel has continually worked to enshrine Jerusalem as the capital of Israel alone. Ir Amim sees Israel's long game in Jerusalem as multifaceted—supporting Jewish construction in East Jerusalem (which Ir Amim considers settlements, but Israel considers neighborhoods) while likewise denying Palestinians building permits, empowering settler groups, funneling municipal resources disproportionately to Jewish-majority neighborhoods and settlements, and using the separation barrier constructed in 2002 as a means for dividing and demoralizing Palestinian residents of Jerusalem. Ir Amim's principal activities are collecting and disseminating research. It leads public tours, produces publications, and maintains an active relationship with the press and international diplomatic community based in Israel and the West Bank.

### 13–16. NGOs Active in Silwan: Ateret Cohanim, El'ad, Madaa, and Emek Shaveh

Four of the organizations in this study conduct most or all of their work in Silwan, an Arab-majority neighborhood of East Jerusalem. Since the work of these organizations is so deeply entwined, it is best to discuss them together.

Silwan is located on the outskirts of the Old City of Jerusalem, directly abutting the Western Wall Plaza and the Temple Mount / Haram Al Sharif. During the Oslo peace process in the early 1990s, talk became more prevalent of a future political settlement in which Israeli and Palestinian states would each receive a portion of Jerusalem as their capital city. With the future of Jerusalem and its holy sites therefore possibly hanging in the balance, both Israelis and Palestinians understood the importance of controlling the areas contiguous to the Old City.[83] In addition, Silwan stands on the site believed to be the City of David—the original Jewish Jerusalem King David captured in 1000 BCE to serve as the capital of the Jewish commonwealth. Though evidence to support this was uncovered starting in the nineteenth century and further corroborated through a major archaeological expedition undertaken by the Israel Antiquities Authority from 1978 to 1985, for years the Israeli government appeared disinterested in further promoting Israel's historical connection to the City of David, as the archaeological dig lay abandoned and by some accounts, as of the early 1990s, in decrepit condition.[84]

While the Israeli government largely ignored Silwan, two NGOs founded in the 1980s, Ateret Cohanim and El'ad, laid out ambitious agendas for furthering Jewish interests in the neighborhood. The organizations believed that the land on which Silwan stood was not only an important historical site for Jews but, perhaps more importantly, crucial to the longer-term vision of keeping Jerusalem as the permanent undivided capital of the Jewish people.

Ateret Cohanim (Priestly Crowns) believes that the coming of the Messiah and the subsequent divine redemption of the Jewish people are imminent. But for this to transpire as soon as possible, Jews have important work to do. This includes the re-Judaizing of Jerusalem. In Ateret Cohanim's opinion, the natural and long-standing Jewish character of Jerusalem has become far too subsumed by Muslims and Christians over the past several generations. The NGO's goal, therefore, is to aid in the restoration of Jewish life into the area as much as possible. To do this, Ateret Cohanim plays the role of what it describes as "Holy Real Estate Agent." It explains that since Palestinian officials consider it a capital offense for Arabs to sell property to Jews,[85] any Arabs who want to do so (typically for economic reasons) must do so clandestinely. Ateret Cohanim seeks to identify such Arab property owners in Silwan and other areas in and around the Old City who are quietly looking to sell their homes. It then pairs them with donors (many from abroad) who want to acquire such properties, usually for the purpose of leasing them out to Jews or Jewish learning institutions like yeshivot and kollelim. Ateret Cohanim believes that once a critical mass of Jewish life has returned to this area—which it refers to as "the Holy Basin"—the messianic redemption is much more likely to take place.

The other prosettlement NGO active in Silwan is El'ad (a contraction translated as "to the City of David"). El'ad's stated mission is to "strengthen . . . the Jewish people's connection to the city of Jerusalem through archeological excavations, tourism development, and educational programming—at the actual location of Biblical Jerusalem, the City of David."[86] El'ad's approach of helping to facilitate Jewish settlement in Silwan has mirrored that of Ateret Cohanim's in some ways, but it has also undertaken a much more ambitious agenda of acquiring rights to conduct a large-scale archaeological dig. Like Ateret Cohanim, El'ad has identified both willing Arab sellers as well as some Jews with prestate deeds to land in Silwan. But it has also been granted rights by the Israeli government to administer large swaths of unoccupied public lands on which it has rehabilitated the abandoned archaeological site and constructed an elaborate tourist attraction around it.[87] In the late 1990s, El'ad began leading tours around the site, known as Ir David (City of David). Over time, the site has grown to become one of Israel's top tourist attractions. Some estimates say that tourism to Ir David grew from only 25,000 annual visitors in 2000,[88] to approximately 1.5 million visitors in 2012.[89] The tours and El'ad's other promotional work showcase the ongoing excavation and specifically reveal the Jewish people's deep historical connection to Silwan, and to Jerusalem more broadly.

From the perspective of the Arab residents living in Silwan, they believe a hostile takeover of their home community is underway. In some cases in which Ateret Cohanim and El'ad have been involved in acquiring property, the Arab residents living there hadn't known their homes had been sold until they found themselves forcibly evicted by Israeli police. It has become commonplace for the Arab residents and Jewish settlers in Silwan (along with the private security guards Jewish settlers have hired to protect themselves) to harass and attempt to intimidate one another. The simmering tension has not infrequently boiled over into violence between the groups.

In 2007, a Palestinian social worker named Jawad Siyam observed that the cumulative acrimony and violence in Silwan was having a corrosive effect on the community's youth. He decided, in response, to organize basic after-school recreational activities to provide some positive outlets for local children. Quickly realizing how high the demand was for such services, Siyam expanded the offerings. He also incorporated his programs into an NGO called Madaa (Horizons).

In the years since then, Madaa has expanded to provide a wide spectrum of arts, music, sports, and conflict resolution programs for its youth as well as women's empowerment programs and community training in nonviolent resistance and organizing. Madaa has come to believe that an investment in the personal and community growth of Silwan's residents is the best way under trying circumstances to oppose the encroachment into its neighborhood by El'ad and Ateret Cohanim. It believes that a happier, more aware, and better organized Arab grassroots population in Silwan stands to provide the best check and obstacle to the further expansion of Israeli settlement and unwanted archaeological activity in its neighborhood.

The fourth NGO active in Silwan is called Emek Shaveh (Equal Valley). While it, too, sees the work of El'ad as incredibly damaging, the basis for its critique is very different. The founders of Emek Shaveh—all archaeologists—concur that the excavation of the City of David area in Silwan is indeed a very important project. But they believe it has been conducted through deeply problematic methodologies anathema to ethical archaeological practice. Emek Shaveh believes El'ad has knowingly misused archaeology to advance its political/messianic vision for Jerusalem, intentionally employing sloppy and nontransparent methods, highlighting some findings and ignoring others.

Emek Shaveh sees the problem with the City of David site as much larger than El'ad's activity alone. It believes that due to the strong support and cover El'ad has received from the Israeli government, many credible archaeologists have been unhappily pressured into doing work in service of an endeavor they know is counter to their professional ethics.

Emek Shaveh's work consists of offering tours and producing literature to publicize El'ad's unsavory professional behavior and the complicity of the Israeli government. Emek Shaveh's hope is that by attacking the methodology of an organization that tries to position itself and its work as the paragon of Israeli archaeology, it will expose how wrong politicized archaeology is and ideally put an end to it.

## NGOs and American Jewish Philanthropic Support

The NGOs in this book's case study collectively receive overseas funding from a variety of sources. A number of the antisettlement organizations receive funds from European governments and foundations.[90] Some prosettlement organizations receive funding from Evangelical Christians.[91] However, the common denominator for the organizations is that they receive significant—and in many cases vital—support from diaspora Jews, most of which comes from the American Jewish community, the largest and wealthiest diaspora community.

### Methodological Challenges to Collecting Financial Information

When this study was first conceived of, it was hoped that it would be able to demystify the mythology surrounding foreign funding of settlement support and human rights NGOs in Israel. Articles and reports that have touched on this topic tend to be unconvincing and deeply partisan accounts that give the impression that the NGOs on "the other side" of this issue from the author's political perspective are swimming in seemingly unlimited amounts of foreign funding and well outspending the modest budgets of their adversaries.[92] It was hoped that through a study of the exact budget figures for each of the NGOs, the exact quantities and the relative portions coming from American Jewish sources could be reported.

After all, American 501(c)(3) organizations are required to file the IRS form 990 every year. By rule, they are required to disclose information about donations received, grants made, and other helpful information to a study like this, including specific organizational objectives and the names of board members. Not only are these forms publicly available, but thanks to the existence of several websites that publish 990s (including www.guidestar.org, www.found ationcenter.org, and www.eri-nonprofit-salaries.com), they are usually easy to access.

However, this turned out to be an unrealistic goal. While the use of 990s proved invaluable in piecing together the financial pictures for several of the most important American organizations in this study, due to organizations consistently omitting information and often using vague language in describing their activities, the 990s, in some cases, provided little more than basic information. In addition, the pass-through organizations that are so important for so many of the NGOs in this study (i.e., Central Fund of Israel, Israelgives, and the donor-advised giving option for the New Israel Fund) usually do not release information on how much money specific Israeli NGOs receive through them. When asked any specific questions about recipient organizations and amounts, pass-throughs typically responded that all information was private and would not be released without the permission of the recipient organizations.

So while there was adequate detailed information on the finances of some of the NGOs in this study available, the information on many NGOs was incomplete (missing forms, numbers reported without explanations, some numbers blacked out). Nonetheless, this study was able to gather enough information from public sources, annual reports, and information disclosed by some interviewees to paint a collective picture of just how important foreign funding—and specifically American Jewish funding—is to the NGOs in this case. This study primarily focused on the years 2010 to 2013.

### Significant Percentages of Budgets from American Jewish Donations

In most cases in which there was enough available information—through either what could be culled from Israeli and American tax documents or what NGOs, themselves, reported—it was apparent how dependent organizations are on the funding they receive from American Jewish donations. For example, Ateret Cohanim reported that about 60 percent of its budget came from American Jewish donors,[93] and Peace Now / Settlement Watch acknowledged that it brings in about 40 percent from its donors in the United States.[94] An examination of the few NGOs with fully available documentation revealed a consistently high portion of groups' funds came from the United States. For example, of the total 18.2 million NIS budget for the Rebuilders of the Jewish Community of Hebron over the five-year period from 2007 to 2011, 9.2 million (51 percent) was contributed by the Hebron Fund and another 4.99 million (27 percent) came from unattributed donations—a portion of which may very well have been from American Jews.[95] In addition, organizations like Rabbis for Human Rights and SJS, though also drawing from other sources, received very high percentages of their operating budgets from donations from American Jews.[96] For a few other NGOs, while the percentage of their budget from American Jews was smaller, it still represented significant portions. For example, B'Tselem reported that it receives 33 percent of its funds from American donors,[97] and Ir Amim brought in at least 17.2 percent of its budget from American Jewish donations in 2009–2010.[98]

### Large Sums Received from American Jewish Donations

In other examples in which there was less complete information on total budgets, it was impossible to determine the exact relative importance of funding from American Jews. However, in some cases a look at total amounts donated suggested the impact of these donations, nonetheless. For example, from 2002 to 2011, Friends of Ir David brought in $39.4 million in donations, $38.6 million (98 percent) of which it passed along to Israeli NGOs—presumably all or most going to its sister organization, El'ad.[99] In this case, no matter how large El'ad's budget may have been, it is probably safe to assume that the $38.6 million it received in donations from its supporters in the United States played a significant role in the development of its activities. On a smaller scale, Friends of Ariel raised $12.4 million from 2001 to 2011, granting over $10 million to the Ariel Development Fund. In this case, the impact of these funds is clearer. Leadership from the Ariel Development Fund directly credits the support received from American Jews (and Christians) for making possible the construction of Ariel's modern recreation and entertainment facilities—unparalleled among amenities available in West Bank settlements. When asked to evaluate the overall impact foreign support has played in the elevation of Ariel from midsized settlement to a city with twenty thousand residents, an executive at the Ariel Development Fund said that without all of the public facilities Ariel now offers, it would not have been able to grow and thrive as it has. Without this support, she explained, "I have a picture in my mind—a gray and black city—which is not a city—which is a poor town with [a] big backup in social services department. A couple of convenience stores, maybe a bank, and two small playgrounds. . . . [the] aliya program [which brought approximately 10,000 immigrants from the FSU to Ariel] never would have worked—all community life and culture would have been more dull. . . . I exaggerate, but it would've been very, very dull."

### Overall Impact

Leaders from all sixteen NGOs were asked what their organizations would look like without the support of American Jewish donors. A majority indicated that they would likely be out of business without this funding. Others, perhaps less reliant on funding from American Jews for their survival, confirmed the importance these contributions play in their ability to function effectively. One director of a prosettlement NGO indicated that though "the base [of our activities] doesn't depend on overseas gifts," in order to be able to have the kind of impact his organization hopes to have, it relies on the staff it can hire at this point only because of its support from American Jews. A leader from an antisettlement NGO similarly explained that without American Jewish support his organization would still be able to carry on the same advocacy activity it does, but would have far less funds for marketing—something that has been crucial to the ascendency of the organization as the issues it addresses came to the attention of the public and the press. For newer and smaller organizations, every dollar counts. Two of the newer, less established organizations in this study operating on low budgets and receiving smaller amounts from American Jewish donors still admit that at this stage the little extra they do or do not receive from communities abroad can make the difference between whether they have the funds for things like web designers, legal advisers, and other crucial tools for organizations just getting started.

In sum, even though a comprehensive financial picture of each of the NGOs in this study could not be constructed, research revealed that philanthropic support from American Jews plays somewhere between an important and a crucial role for all of the NGOs in this study. The next chapters look specifically at how the power dynamics of these key funding relationships have manifested.

CHAPTER 5

# Prospects for a New Era of Partnership?

Prevalent Zionist/Israeli attitudes about diaspora philanthropy in the prestate era and first decades of the state held that Jewish donors from abroad should not have a substantive role in deciding how to spend the money they contributed to Israel. Israelis' deep aversion to sharing power with diaspora Jews, on the one hand, had pragmatic justifications: they believed they were more knowledgeable about their own society and therefore better equipped to make decisions that would be in their best interest without having any interference from the necessarily less knowledgeable and less personally invested population of non-Israeli Jews. But the aversion was also rooted in the traditional derogatory Zionist conception of the diaspora (known as *shlilat ha-galut*, or "negation of the exile"), which said that in the era of a modern Israeli state, Jews should not live in other countries; or if small numbers of Jews still did choose to stay in diaspora, they should not have an equal voice in deciding important global Jewish matters and certainly not regarding the affairs of the Jewish state. And while more overt assertions of *shlilat ha-Galut* receded from Israeli public discourse over time, the attitude at its core remained, with Israelis largely continuing to see diaspora Jews as not entitled to play substantive roles in shaping the ongoing development of Israeli society.[1]

## CHANGING CONCEPTIONS OF PARTNERSHIP?

As previous chapters have discussed, the philanthropic environment has changed dramatically in the decades since the 1980s. But has the traditional Israeli conception of partnership developed as well?

On the surface, American Jewish giving to Israel in the twenty-first century is considerably different from what it was for most of the twentieth century. At the peak of Checkbook Zionism, American Jews gave more than 80 percent of the total dollars they contributed through centrally federated, largely deferential giving vehicles like the UJA. But the balance has shifted considerably since then. In 2007, for example, less than 7 percent of donations went as unrestricted donations through the traditional JFNA (successor to the UJA) or Jewish Agency channel, with the overwhelming majority of American Jews' donations to Israeli causes instead going to vehicles that allowed them some degree of choice and control: either to the general campaigns of organizations they handpicked themselves ("new federated giving") or to specific projects within such organizations ("direct giving").[2]

This substantial shift suggests that American Jews have become more interested in having input into the use of their donations in Israel. This idea would be consistent with the literature on directed giving (discussed in chapter 3). It speaks of a new generation of donors on the rise who are increasingly plugged into their philanthropy. They place a premium on being better informed on the issues they support as well as on evaluating the effectiveness and impact of their giving.

If these general observations hold true for at least some critical mass of American Jews engaging in directed giving, the classic Checkbook Zionism partnership framework would no longer work for them. A new breed of savvy, tuned-in donors would not stand for being sidelined as donors had in days of old. They would demand more input. For Israeli NGOs to be able to attract these donors, they would therefore theoretically need to make use of a new type of philanthropic engagement—that this chapter will refer to broadly as "enhanced partnership."

Broadly speaking, enhanced partnerships would have to give American Jews a greater role in deciding on use of funds than they previously had had. This could be as simple as Israelis seeking out or at the very least genuinely listening to the viewpoints offered (and possibly agendas proposed) by American Jewish donors. At a more involved level, enhanced partnerships might include American givers and Israeli recipients each valuing the unique perspective the other could bring to conversations about allocations. In an advanced form, enhanced partnerships could even mean Americans and Israelis striving toward a form of joint equal decision making over organizational priorities and expenditures.

But could any of these ideas about partnership truly be possible in the Israeli-diaspora philanthropic relationship—one that has long repudiated notions of equitable power sharing?

This chapter looks at the tension between these two ideas: still-held traditional Zionist and Israeli biases against diaspora participation in decision making, on the one hand, and the hypothesis, on the other, that American Jews, by nature of their dramatic move to directed giving, have ever-growing interest in playing a larger role through some type of an enhanced partnership model. For Israelis to comfortably move from classic relationship patterns to enhanced partnerships, they would have to view diaspora Jews as both capable of and entitled to having a greater voice. The chapter, therefore, focuses on the two core questions at the heart of traditional Israeli aversion to greater power sharing—the "could" question and the "should" question. Namely, in the opinion of Israeli fundraisers and NGO leaders, (1) *Could* American Jews theoretically be effective enhanced partners? Are they—or could they be—equipped with the necessary knowledge and understanding to competently exercise a greater voice in deciding how to allocate the money they contribute to Israeli causes? (2) *Should* they be enhanced partners? In contrast to the idea of *shlilat ha-galut*, how have Israeli attitudes developed on the question of whether it is acceptable for Americans to believe they are "entitled" to have some say in how their money is spent—as Brandeis had advocated for—even knowing that their decisions may affect Israel? In other words, are Israelis ready for the kind of partnership arrangements data suggest Americans may be seeking?

The ideas presented in this chapter highlight the range of Israeli opinions on the possibilities for and potential benefits and drawbacks of enhanced partnership with American Jewish donors. They are based on interviews with more than sixty Israeli leaders and fundraisers affiliated with the NGOs in this case study as well as a handful of Israeli scholars and veterans of diaspora fundraising. Unless otherwise stated, the opinions reflect the most common responses from interview subjects.

### Question 1: The Could Question
#### Could American Jews Be Competent, Contributing Partners in Decision Making?

To welcome a greater role for Americans in the philanthropic partnership, decision makers at Israeli NGOs would first have to feel confident that their American partners were capable of bringing informed, valuable perspectives to discussions. For their part, the limited number of American donors participating in this study mostly believed that they *were* up to the task. For example, one donor to a prosettlement NGO noted that he and his peers understood the realities of Israel very well. "I know the people living there," he said. "If I was living in Israel, I don't know that my information would be any better." Similar opinions were echoed by most of the donors.

However, the impressions of the much larger interview cohort of NGO fundraisers and leaders told a very different story. As the next pages reveal, nearly all Israelis interviewed in this case—whether from pro- or antisettlement groups, Israeli-born or born in the diaspora—did *not* believe that Americans were properly equipped to be meaningful contributors in discussions about allocations. Interviewees indicated that even many of their organizations' most involved donors simply did not understand the basics about Israel—its people, its culture, its issues, never mind the more complicated aspects of the NGOs' work.

### The Problem of a General Lack of Knowledge

Most interview subjects spoke in dramatic terms about how *little* the American Jews they encountered understood about Israel. One development director for a prosettlement NGO, for example, articulated just how uninformed he believed his donors to be even on issues related to settlement. "They have no idea . . . I'm not exaggerating if I tell you for the most part . . . to them, Samaria is somewhere between Albania and Macedonia."

He was far from alone in his assessment. Interviewee after interviewee made statements to the effect of the widespread misinformation and general lack of knowledge plaguing American Jews. Some examples include:

- "A lot of people don't know basic stuff."
- "American Jews know so little."
- "I don't think that they're at all really aware."
- "I think there's an illusion of knowledge."

In lieu of having an informed perspective, interviewees agreed, American Jews build a picture of Israel based on mythology that reflects less what Israel is and more what they want it to be. One Israeli academic who studies the nonprofit sector, for example, observed that American Jews "have a hard time letting the facts get in the way of their perceptions and ideas. . . . They have close ties with a narrow group of Israelis who take them to see things which reinforce the images [they have of Israel]." When compelling facts may emerge to the contrary, he explained, they can and do still maintain their positions.

Numerous interviewees echoed the idea of how deep a commitment American Jews have to their own version of Israel. For example, a fundraiser for anti-settlement initiatives in Jerusalem noted how the emotional gravity of American Jews' relationship with Israel overwhelms their abilities to discern. She believes her organization's American donors—even those visiting and seeing Jerusalem firsthand—simply do not engage seriously with trying to understand the realities facing the city. "For the people that come here," she explained, "they only see Jerusalem of heaven, not Jerusalem of earth." In her opinion, the minds of American donors have been skewed by their own mythic understandings so much that it is hard for them to really understand key aspects of Israel even when they are staring them in the face. The head of development for an antisettlement NGO similarly noted that the majority of her organization's most actively involved donors almost exclusively advise from afar without understanding how things in Israel really are. "They have some fantasy of what it should be like here" that does not reflect realities, she explained. "Coexistence. And why can't we all get along?"

Almost all of the Israelis interviewed shared similar viewpoints. Most regarded American Jewish donors as having a substantial gap in their understanding of Israel that would hamper their ability to offer respect worthy input.

### Are Donors Seeking to Be Better Informed?

Based on their perception of an American knowledge gap in their understanding of Israel, interviewees were asked whether they believed the situation of uninformed donors might be changing or could change in the future. They were referred to the theory, common in direct giving literature, that the increasing number of those giving directly likely suggests a new breed of donors interested in having a better understanding of their giving and seeking information and data as a way to drive and evaluate their giving decisions.[3] If American Jewish donors were regarded as not having an adequate understanding of Israel, therefore, did interviewees believe that they were trying to actively close that knowledge gap, as the literature suggested they would be doing?

One Israeli fundraising professional working for a charitable foundation in the early 2000s, who will be referred to as Jacob, explained how he observed the growing trend of more American Jews choosing to give to Israel outside of umbrella organizations like federations. In his estimation, this new group of more "entrepreneurial" donors would likely be hungry to obtain the information necessary to inform their specific giving choices. He reasoned that many of them would appreciate having someone on the ground in Israel to help them sort through the thousands of giving options as well as monitor that the organizations they were supporting were actually doing work they claimed to be doing.

With this in mind, Jacob started an organization in 2001 to provide such services to American donors supporting work in Israel. In short time he attracted numerous American Jewish clients. He later recalled that at least half a dozen similar donor service firms were established in these same years to meet American donors' presumed growing demand for better information.

Yet he soon found that regardless of what his clients may have said on the surface, most seemed to care very little about specific information on the actual activities of the organizations they were supporting. He routinely gathered information and conducted site visits at the request of his donors, but as far as he could tell they would rarely read the reports he generated. He explained that his counterparts at the other donor services organizations reported similar experiences. Donors would have their donor services organizations ask Israeli NGOs "a million questions on applications or evaluation forms and then . . . [not] even read [their answers]," he explained. "It's almost like [they felt that] 'if we ask the questions, then we're done.'"

Jacob did not understand why so many donors insisted on directing the donations and selecting the organizations to support, rather than giving to general federated campaigns and organizations, but then cared so little to know whether the promises being made to them by the NGOs they supported were being kept. "We thought we wanted to protect them [donors] from getting screwed over by the organizations, but in the end, I guess, despite all the talk, as long as there was nothing really crazy or corrupt [going on with the NGOs they supported], it was good enough [for donors]." This group of donors was arguably among those who most cared about being informed givers by virtue of them employing a donor services firm. Yet they apparently placed a relatively low priority on vetting and due diligence in their giving, despite pronouncements to the contrary.

The majority of interviewed fundraisers reported similar experiences: though donors, themselves, might indicate—and may have truly *believed*—that they wanted to better understand Israel, what they *actually* wanted was much different. Interviewees reported that donors were most often concerned with receiving tangible benefits or recognition or just feeling good about themselves.[4] This stands in contrast to the assumption in the literature that the spike in donor-directed giving to Israel reflects donors' desire to have the necessary information to make smart, informed choices. On face value, this seems puzzling. Why would donors, on the one hand, insist on picking the destination of their gift to such a great degree (93 percent in 2007) but, on the other, not want to know too many details about the organizations they are supporting?

Jacob's take on this apparent contradiction was that the donors he encountered really wanted to "feel good" above all else. "If you start to tell them the nitty gritty of what goes on and all the little things, it's not going to be pretty." Their passion for giving, he explained, "very often goes against the idea of wanting to know what goes on." From Jacob's perspective, in other words, American donors did not want too much information because it would force them to encounter certain realities in Israel that they preferred to avoid.

An executive of another donor services organization called Midot shared similar impressions. Midot's mission was to rate Israeli NGOs on their efficiency so donors could have metrics by which to sort through the thousands of organizations. At first, we assumed that it would be "simple or obvious that the [American] donors want their donations [to Israeli organizations] to be effective and high impact." But he and his colleagues learned this was not the case. "Donors don't want to be confused with information. They want to give from their heart. . . . There's research about it. The more information you give, they give less. When you show a donor a picture of a girl from Africa in starvation, they give 'x' amount of money. If you show her as part of a group of children, they give less. . . . If you give them information about her village, and the problem of food in the area . . . they give even less."[5] For this reason, he explained, even the most savvy philanthropists he worked with—who theoretically recognized the importance of having their giving be effective and impactful—barely read the evaluation reports Midot produced for them.

Most fundraisers from the case study NGOs echoed these perspectives. One who worked for an antisettlement organization, for example, said that the American Jewish donors she works with do not want to know too much about Israel's human rights record in the West Bank. "There is a large dissonance between the gruesome facts on the ground and what most people would want to know." Therefore donors choose to live, as she put it, in "blissful ignorance," pretending that realities in Israel match their ideals, despite any facts to the contrary.

A former fundraiser for one of the prosettlement NGOs recounted how almost all of their American supporters only partially tuned into the work of her organization, as much as they may have expressed support for the NGO's work. From her perspective, there may have almost been a willful ignorance at play. If they looked *too* closely at what they were supporting, she mused, donors would have to be honest with themselves and realize that if they truly cared about the struggles of settlers and wanted to help, as they claimed, the only conclusion they could reach is that "their place was in Israel." In a sense, an intentional lack of honest inquiry was the only way they could justify, as she put it, "maintain[ing] their comfortable diaspora existences" and not making *aliya*.

The director of one of the prosettlement NGOs offered a more damning perspective, noting how detrimental it was to his organization that some of its most active donors wanted to have some say in the organization's activities. In his opinion, their combination of lack of knowledge and disinterest in better understanding the specifics of the NGO's work sometimes actually got in the way of his organization's ability to do productive work. He explained that he would be open to truly hearing and considering their input if they took the time to be more properly informed. He urged them, he continued, that if "they want to suggest . . . ways to do things, perhaps they should come out to the field [to observe the environment in which we do our work]," but noted, "they never do." Instead, he said, they remain uninformed but still insist on sharing their opinions: "They love to drink coffee, eat cake, and tell you what you have to do . . . any time there's a meeting [with them], it's a fight—nothing else."

A fundraiser for another prosettlement NGO expressed in more emphatic terms his organization's frustration with their donors having neither adequate knowledge nor interest in learning, yet still wanting to push their opinions. As much as his organization tried to offer their more activist donors—including board members—a more lucid portrayal of the background issues surrounding their work, he explained, their donors don't seem interested in really learning. "It's not just the knowledge problem," he explained. "There's a much bigger problem besides that. . . . If I was to sum it up in once sentence about the Americans [we work with]: The only thing that supersedes their ignorance is their arrogance."

While not all interviewees shared such a scathing impression of working with donors, most concurred that it was a rare case in which they witnessed donors who wanted to be more involved actually doing the necessary legwork to inform themselves. Irrespective of opportunities NGOs offered donors to learn about the complex realities facing their organization's work, interviewees observed that the vast majority of donors showed little interest in truly learning, regardless of what they may have otherwise said.

### Potential for an Informed Donor Class?

Many Israeli interview subjects indicated there was an even bigger barrier to potential American Jewish understanding of Israel than donors' lack of knowledge and their disinterest in learning: Israeli subjects wondered whether Americans even theoretically *could* come to understand the crucial nuances of Israeli society if they tried. Perhaps such nuance about Israel could be understood only by the people who physically lived there.

The development director for one of the prosettlement organizations articulated this perspective. "Nobody can really know . . . about a place they don't live in. So I'm in the States eight to nine times per year. Could I tell you the ins and outs about Teaneck [New Jersey]? The ins and outs about Woodmere [New York]? To a certain degree [only]. . . . Unless you live in a place. And you work there. And you live it, you can't [really know]." One former federation representative in Israel argued how difficult it would be for someone not living there to truly understand Israel. "Unless it's somebody who has an apartment here and comes here and sees Israel as not through hotel rooms and through taxis, but goes to the *makolet* [grocery store] and keeps the appointment and deals with electricians," he said, they cannot fully understand Israeli people, culture, and society. An Israeli board member of a pass-through organization that funds NGOs in this study who was born in the United States and made *aliya* in the 1980s shared a similar sentiment: "Ultimately, there is no substitute for existing, living, and breathing the experience of being in Israel. . . . If you live here, you're just more in touch with what it's all about. . . . It has an impact on your thinking." Another likened the unique life one experiences in Israel as understandable only by those who live there. "It's like other unique life experiences," he explained. "If you haven't been to war, you don't know what it's like. If you don't have children, you don't know what that's like."

The takeaway from these perspectives is that the context and nuance one needs to understand Israel in order to be a valuable contributor to conversations can be acquired only by living there. The problem with misunderstanding context and nuance, interview subjects emphasized, is that it can lead well-meaning donors to make incorrect assumptions about whatever agendas they may be advocating for. An officer at the JDC and a veteran of fundraising in the diaspora explained the challenge one has in seeking to understand a place when not living there. "If you're sitting in Boston, and you look out at the community in Bucharest, you will tend to understand what is happening in Bucharest using your understanding of what is Boston. . . . You'll mostly use a different paradigm for understanding what is happening in Bucharest—the stage of communal development it is at, the local strengths and local weaknesses." Numerous interviewees likewise explained that when American donors try to understand Israel within the context of their own experiences, they often make fundamental misappraisals of what would be beneficial for or even possible in Israel.

Gerald Steinberg, founder of the Israeli think tank / watchdog organization NGO Monitor, has become a vocal critic of uninformed donors from abroad who—sometimes knowingly, but often unknowingly—promote misguided agendas in Israel that do not align with locally perceived needs. He gave the example of young donors who after "clicking with Israel on a personal basis" then attempt to promote certain value systems in Israel that are important to them in their own domestic political agendas, but make the mistake of pushing them in Israel without understanding necessary context. They may like human rights, he explained, but they don't understand the political currents underneath, like "how this plays out in Israeli politics or how it plays out with the UN."[6]

A development director for an antisettlement NGO offered an example of how the lack of sensitivity to the realities in Israel of the American board of his NGO's "friends of" organization nearly played out in a public relations debacle for his NGO. At one point, the "friends of" organization wanted to put a full-page ad in the *New York Times* condemning the Israeli policy of demolishing the homes of Palestinian who had committed terrorist attacks. Although the leaders of the Israeli NGO were in agreement with the American "friends of" organization on the issue of home demolitions generally, they argued that it was not the right time to place the ad. A major terrorist attack had taken place in Israel only a few days before. As Israelis, they understood that such an ad would, at that time, be considered in poor taste by segments of the Israeli public otherwise sympathetic to their cause and resultantly reflect badly on their organization. Though the "friends of" organization knew about the attack, it saw the two issues as unrelated and thus remained adamant about running the ad. It was only through concerted pressure by the Israeli NGO that the "friends of" organization grudgingly relented. Such an example, he explained, is "very emblematic" of the gaps between Israeli NGOs and their American supporters.

An interesting wrinkle on this issue was shared by a former director of the American-based fundraising branch of one of the prosettlement NGOs in this study, who had made *aliya* in 2006. She explained that for all the years she lived in the United States, passionately engaged with Israel, personally and professionally, she was certain that she understood Israel as fully as she would have if she lived there. But upon immigrating, she "immediately" realized just how much less she understood about Israel than she thought she had. She too now believes that "unless you're here, you can't get it." In this example, before moving to Israel, she presumably knew about Israel but had a different perspective on Israel than

Israelis *specifically because* she was an American and she did not live in Israel. When she made *aliya*, while she acquired an Israeli perspective, she simultaneously also lost or diluted part of her previous American perspective. This raises the question of whether there may be a unique value that *only* a non-Israeli can bring that may enrich allocations and policy conversations.

### Disparate Perspectives

Despite the overwhelming majority of interviewees sharing similar opinions, there were a handful who believed the opposite. One fundraiser for an NGO supporting settlement, for example, explained that though it might be hard for Americans to have a good overall understanding of Israel, they are able to do so regarding very discrete issues. He believes that his organization's most involved donors from the United States have a good feel for the realities of the issues his organization addresses. A few others noted that they believed that available information on the internet was enough for American Jews to make adequately informed evaluations of issues in Israel and then locate the Israeli NGOs who can best address them. As one veteran Israeli fundraiser commented, "People are very confident running businesses in China and India and Mexico and Wisconsin, so why wouldn't they be able to—without perfect data—also run their philanthropy in these places?"

Maybe these ideas are correct and it is possible for Americans to adequately understand Israel using accessible online resources and making periodic visits. But the important point to understand here is that almost all *Israelis* working for the case study NGOs do not think so. So the issue of what an American's *actual* capability or potential would be in bringing an adequately informed perspective into an allocations or policy setting conversation aside, it is clear within the NGOs in this case that Israelis believe that American Jews bring an inferior ability to make such judgments. This may speak more to the remnants of Zionism's latent disrespect for diaspora existence than it does to an actual honest evaluation of American Jews and their abilities. Nonetheless, the vast majority of Israelis in this case do not feel Americans are adequately informed, do not care to be adequately informed, and perhaps are not even capable of becoming adequately informed.

### QUESTION 2: THE "SHOULD QUESTION"
### *SHOULD AMERICAN JEWS HAVE AN INCREASED ROLE IN DECIDING HOW THEIR DONATIONS ARE USED?*

The second question at the heart of traditional Zionist/Israeli unwillingness to further involve diaspora Jews in consequential decision making is this: *Should Israelis accept American requests for a greater role?* If diaspora Jews want more involvement in shaping influential allocation decisions in Israel—as both the literature and the major shift toward directed giving suggests—issues of qualifications aside, do Israelis believe such diaspora participation is even valid? Traditional Zionist philosophy, as discussed earlier, rejected out of hand the idea that diaspora Jews might be entitled to have a say in what went on in Israel. But has Israeli opposition to diaspora involvement softened in the modern era just as many of the other founding ideas of Zionism are no longer as resonant? And if it has, how much and in what ways? Interviews revealed a much more variegated range of responses to this question than to questions about American Jewish knowledge level. Though almost half of the sixty-plus interview subjects held to the traditional repudiation of substantive diaspora involvement in decision making under any circumstances, a majority did believe that diaspora participation in influential decision making actually could theoretically be valid—but only under certain circumstances. Most focused their criteria on two core issues: (1) Whom Israel principally "belongs" to—Israelis or all Jews? and (2) Which types of issues are legitimate for diaspora involvement and which are off-limits? The remainder of this chapter explains the range of perspectives for each.

### Does Israel "Belong" to Israelis Only or to All Jews?

Traditional Jewish thought views the entirety of Eretz Yisrael (Land of Israel) as the eternal possession of the Jewish people—the land promised by God to the descendants of Abraham. Although Jews went into exile in the first century CE following the destruction of the biblical temples, they understood their diaspora status as only a temporary period of being away from home. Eretz Yisrael had been theirs in the past and would be again in the future even if their present circumstances had them living outside of the Promised Land.

This conception of an eternal ethno-religious-based patrimony over a specific piece of land stands in stark contrast to modern conceptions of sovereignty and citizenship—in which (in open societies) the legal citizens of a state are the ones deemed to have a legitimate voice in shaping that state. Citizenship is not the automatic domain of a certain global ethnic or religious group but rather belongs to people either who are born in that state or who undergo a legally stipulated process of naturalization. Along these lines, the traditional Zionist conception was that since diaspora Jews had willingly chosen to live outside of Israel—in a sense forfeiting their birthright—they were therefore not entitled to be involved in the matters of a sovereign society not their own unless they immigrated to Israel.

How then do these differing perspectives of people and place bear out in a society that seems to inherently value both ideas of citizenship, epitomized by how it simultaneously identifies its core character as Jewish and democratic?[7]

The biggest issue that shaped interview subjects' perspectives on the validity of diaspora Jews assuming an enhanced role in allocations and agenda-setting conversations was tied to the question of whether Israel should principally be understood as the common domain of the Jewish people or as a separate entity. Interestingly, the divide on the issue among interviewees had little to do with who was affiliated with prosettlement NGOs and who was affiliated with antisettlement NGOs. Rather, nearly all interview subjects affiliated with NGOs purporting to speak for "Jewish values" or "Jewish issues"—be they pro- or antisettlement—tended to come down on the same side of the debate. They believed that *all* Jews—irrespective of whether they lived in Israel or the diaspora—were entitled to have some stake in shaping the future of Eretz Yisrael.

On the other hand, those affiliated with NGOs not specifically purporting to be concerned with Jewish matters, believed that non-Israelis were simply not entitled to have a voice in consequential matters of Israeli society. For example, one interviewee offering a perspective emblematic within this cohort explained that they regard issues taking place in Israel as *"our* own local issues." Regardless of what diaspora Jews think, the notion of *K'lal Yisrael* (the idea that espouses universal Jewish participation in the common destiny of the Jewish people) does not apply. By the same token, he added, Israelis should also not get involved in the internal issues of diaspora Jewish communities, which he referred to as *"their* issues."

Among those supporting the rights of diaspora Jews to have greater involvement, their conception of why this was valid varied. As one development director for an antisettlement organization argued, diaspora Jews are entitled to have their perspective listened to on all important matters because, as he explained, in contemporary times "Israel is possibly the most positive force for creating Jewish identity / Jewish continuity." Israel, he continued, is therefore a *Jewish* issue more broadly rather than a particularly *Israeli* one. While he admitted that how he, as an Israeli, sometimes found it difficult to hear out diaspora Jews because they may push "for a different vision of Zionism than I hold," he still believed that their rights as Jews superseded the citizenship status/place of residence of either them or him.

A founder of one of the antisettlement organizations argued that those wanting to weigh in on Israel out of their love for the Jewish people and Jewish values are entitled to be included players irrespective of where they lived. "It's about opening up the discourse and thinking about the place we want Israel to be," she said. "And in that way, the diaspora has always had and still has an important role." It is to Israel's benefit, she continued, if "at some point, they . . . say, 'this is not the kind of state that we [as Jews] imagined as a Jewish state. We don't imagine a repressive state. We don't imagine a state that discriminates against people,'" and then they partner to make it a better place. In addition, she noted there is unique benefit to Israelis in including diaspora Jews in important conversations *specifically* because they may bring a more clearheaded vantage point than those living their lives in the midst of a complicated Israeli society. Their love for Israel, alone, according to this perspective, gives them a credible seat at the table.

A number of more religiously observant interview subjects felt that this issue should be understood based on religious, rather than Jewish identity criteria. One leader for a prosettlement NGO and a self-identified "Torah-observant Jew," for example, explained that since the Torah articulated that the land was given to the entirety of the people, that alone—and not modern notions of state and citizenship or identity—was the final arbiter of who had a say in Israel's development. In fact, he continued, "*any* Jew has full rights . . . to determine issues related to Eretz Yisrael." Conversely, he argued, non-Jewish Israelis—including Israel's sizable Arab population—do not, irrespective of whether they are citizens of the state.

A fundraiser for a prosettlement NGO similarly argued that the location of where Jews lived should not be a determinant in who was involved, but for very different reasons. Hinting at the messianic prediction, she argued that there is no contradiction between modern conceptions of citizenship and Jewish birthright because all Jews should be understood as eventually making *aliya*. As future legal citizens of the state of Israel, therefore, diaspora Jews are as entitled as any Israeli citizens to have a voice in the current affairs of the state.

Some interview subjects, while supporting the notion of all Jews having a say in the destiny of Israel, took a more middle-of-the-road approach, making the point that religious sources and Jewish identity needed to be balanced with present realities. A few argued that there was a distinction between core pieces of the Promised Land and other areas of the modern state of Israel that were not necessarily part of the biblically delineated Land of Israel.

A fundraiser for social service work in both Israeli communities and West Bank settlements, for example, argued that Jerusalem had a unique status in regard to this question. "Jerusalem is yours as much as it's mine—and it's obvious to both of us," she contended. "Tel Aviv is not. Tel Aviv is mine more than it's yours . . . or, I don't know if it's yours. I mean . . . it is, but do you feel it's yours? Do the people in Tel Aviv feel it's yours? Not necessarily. But Jerusalem, that's the roots of all of us." The executive director of a prosettlement NGO articulated a similar distinction: "When it comes to *Yerushalyim*, I think that every . . . [Jew] in the world, should have a vote on what should happen," he contended, citing the biblical verse that Jerusalem should not be divided between the tribes of Israel. But, he explained, like most Israelis, he makes certain sacrifices in the name of defending the sovereignty of his country that diaspora Jews would never have to make: "I have six boys. . . . [They] will all be going to the army. They will all be risking their lives. I went to the army. I risked my life. I got injured in the army and I'm suffering for the rest of my life from my injury in the army. I pay taxes here. I drive the roads here. I've lost over sixty friends." Therefore, he argued, "in terms of the rest of [what happens in] the country: No [diaspora Jews should] not have a vote."

In sum, more than half of interviewees indicated they believed some subpopulations of diaspora Jews are entitled to be included in NGOs' influential allocations and policy decisions about Israel due to issues of either Jewish law or religiosity, or self-identity. Their opinions represent a major shift from the traditional Zionist conception that denied the legitimacy of enhanced diaspora donor involvement in Israel.

### Which Agendas Are Legitimate to Support and Which Are Not?

Beyond the question of which diaspora Jews might be entitled to be included in some enhanced partnership role, nearly all interview subjects supporting greater diaspora inclusion believed it was acceptable for donors to be included in conversations related to some issues, but not others. Their criteria were mostly based on two factors: that diaspora Jews push only for agendas that would be considered "authentically Israeli" and that whatever they supported could not be overtly political.

———

*"Authentically Israeli ideas."* Most Israeli interviewees comfortable with greater involvement from donors indicated that they did not want diaspora Jews to inject what were described as "foreign values" into Israel. The head of an umbrella fund that supports two of the prosettlement NGOs in this study, for example, argued how problematic it was for diaspora Jews (or any non-Israelis) to "partner" with fringe politicized Israeli NGOs that had limited support from the Israeli populace. Doing so, he argued, effectively allowed non-Israelis to use financial influence in organizations to push foreign agendas that could effect a "cultural and social shift" in Israel, which, in a country as small as Israel, could be "very strongly felt." In this case, he believed the work non-Israelis were doing to advocate for vehement antisettlement agendas could, if successful, gradually "denude Israel of not only its de jure connection to Zionism . . . [and] in effect create something that's closer to their . . . dream of a unicameral Palestine than anything." Changes like that, he argued, are neither asked for nor wanted by a critical mass of Israelis, and therefore diaspora Jews supporting such agendas should not be allowed to wield influence at NGOs operating in Israel.

With similar concerns in mind, a number of interviewees suggested that perhaps a proven commitment to Zionism should be a purity test for evaluating the legitimacy of diaspora Jewish involvement in NGO allocation decisions. Short of that, a fundraiser for one of the prosettlement NGO, making this case rhetorically, asked, "Would America tolerate supporters of al-Qaeda's ideology pushing for a social change agenda in American NGOs? Of course not!" Likewise, she argued, Israel should not tolerate input from people who, in her opinion, "want to destroy the state."

Two fundraisers for umbrella groups that support socially oriented work in settlements argued for this perspective in more neutral terms. According to one, as long as agendas pushed by non-Israeli Jews do not "endanger . . . the core" of Israel, they are okay. Another noted that foreign influence in decision making is okay as long as their ideas and proposals are within "a broad Zionist discourse." If diaspora Jews do not have a baseline commitment to Zionism, she argued, they should not be included.

Some interview subjects argued the same issue about what is "authentically Israeli," but from the opposite perspective: that there is unique value in having non-Israeli voices in allocations and policy conversations at NGOs precisely so that they could identify ways that some of the "authentically Israeli" positions held by the majority of society may not be in Israel's best interest and/or not commensurate with Zionism's core values. They argued that as long as the agendas advocated for by diaspora Jews were within the framework of Israel's Zionist and democratic identity, they should be considered as acceptably authentically Israeli, irrespective of their current level of popular support in Israel. An Israeli board member for one of the antisettlement organizations also argued this position, making the point that "if we went by what Israeli society is calling for—[some of] . . . the antidemocratic trends—Israel would be finished in no time, morally, and I think also physically." Another added that a locally supportive population "doesn't have to be a majority," but rather the mere existence of Israel-created and Israel-run programs and NGOs is a statement of a legitimate Israeli constituency regardless of how large it is. The executive director for one antisettlement organization argued that the issue of needing a locally supportive population is overblown. "If Chinese are not supporting human rights and the initiative has to come from elsewhere, should they then not exist?" he asked. "Of course not."

As the variety of interviewee perspectives confirmed, the challenge of using these criteria of "authentically Israeli" or "authentically Zionist" for evaluating legitimate diaspora participation, naturally, is that they are subjective concepts. There is a broad range of perspectives on what constitutes Zionist or even democratic values.

————

*Overtly Politicized Ideas.* Almost all interview subjects, believing a greater role for interested diaspora Jews could be valid, indicated that politics was a red line for the involvement of non-Israelis. In other words, it was okay for diaspora Jews to weigh in on social or other charitable issues in Israel, but not anything with political implications. But, like with other definitions, what "political" meant also varied widely. The way an interview subject identified what was "political" about the work of NGOs in this case was usually based on the personal/organizational politics of each individual interviewee. To put it simply, most viewed what their NGOs were doing as apolitical, but those doing work diametrically opposed to their organizational missions as political.

A fundraiser for an umbrella organization that solicits funds for social and recreational programs in settlements, for example, chafed at the critiques his organization receives for being political. Their critics claim their work is political, he explained, but how can American support for the erection of a "playground in the West Bank . . . be viewed as political? [It] should not." He explained that their donors pushing for the construction of playgrounds are not actively trying to deny Palestinians a state; they are just trying to make lives better for Israeli children. Playgrounds are playgrounds, he said. This is not a political issue.

Likewise, several interviewees affiliated with antisettlement NGOs explained that their critics complained of diaspora Jews pushing for certain agendas in their activities. As one executive director explained, for instance, to their critics, human rights advocacy is deemed inappropriate because it is "considered political." "But how can that be?" Another fundraiser argued if there are actual human rights abuses going on, opposing them is simply not political. She wondered why in an open, liberal society like Israel the validity of promoting basic rights could even be called into question—irrespective of who was calling for them and regardless of whether they offended the culture of a more illiberal segment of the Israeli population. "Why is human rights considered political?" she asked. "Is women's rights then also political? To Haredim it is," but that does not make it so.

While most interviewees held to the idea that diaspora Jews should stay out of political issues (as they, themselves, defined them), a few did not. Two American-born Israeli fundraisers supporting prosettlement NGOs, for example, articulated the tension they felt over the issue. They both acknowledged that while allowing non-Israeli voices into politicized decisions like the fate of the settlement project was frustrating, preventing them from doing so because it was overtly "political" would be antithetical to Israeli values. One explained that as long as initiatives supported by diaspora Jews are not calling for things "that break the law, then my perspective is that's okay." He suggested that Israelis frustrated with foreign donors supporting antisettlement initiatives should, themselves, donate to prosettlement organizations to counter the influence coming from abroad. Suggesting that agendas coming from supporters from abroad that "we don't like" are not valid, he argued, "is akin to behavior of theocratic/ideological state, rather than democratic state." The second fundraiser, still a dual American-Israeli citizen, shared his conflicted perspective about antisettlement organizations that he called "leftist self-hating Jewish institutions": "As an American, I'm supportive of people having free, democratic organizations to do what they wish with them. The bottom line is it's a philanthropist's right [to do what he wishes]." But, he continued, "as a traditional Jew, I'm not happy with foreigners pushing for [antisettlement activity in Israel]," noting wistfully, "personally, if there was any way I could stop it, [I would.]"

A leading figure in the study of the Israeli nonprofit sector observed that this social/political debate was rather foolish. "What is 'nonpolitical'?," he asked. "I don't know of almost any NGO from the smallest one-man show to the largest organization that doesn't think or try to influence government policy. That's almost the purpose of being an NGO. Not only to deal with the situation, but trying to change the situation on a policy level." Therefore, he argued, by virtue of allowing foreign funding for NGOs at all, the Israeli state has made the statement that it has little problem with non-Israelis—Jews or non-Jews—having influence over political issues in Israel. The executive director of an antisettlement organization echoed a similar point when it came to any work related to the settlement question: "Nothing on this issue is apolitical. Not taking a side is taking a side."

Like the issue of determining what is "authentically Israeli," the question of what makes something "political" varies greatly depending on one's own political perspective. So while there was broad support for disallowing politicized involvement of diaspora Jews in the affairs of Israeli NGOs, there was no agreement on what that meant exactly.


## CONCLUSION

The overwhelming message from Israeli interviewees in this study is that while there has been some increased openness to the idea of enhanced partnership arrangements between themselves and their diaspora donors, most still hold at least aspects of the traditionally intransigent antidiaspora Zionist positions. Almost half still see no valid role for diaspora Jews in making decisions about NGOs' allocations and policy priorities. And though more than half do believe that diaspora donors, as Jews, have a right to weigh in on issues of consequence in the Jewish state—a major break from the classic Zionist perspective—even they have articulated stringent conditions for diaspora participation based on specific and subjective criteria regarding what ideas they espouse and what issues they get involved with. All this said, the opinions on whether diaspora Jews should play a greater role are almost moot because the Israelis interviewed nearly universally demonstrated that they do not respect their American counterparts' knowledge levels and judgments, rendering unlikely the prospect that they would enthusiastically embrace an enhanced partnership with diaspora Jews.

To more fully understand the contemporary state of power sharing, it would be helpful to have a corollary study of contemporary American donors' opinions. But even without these data about American attitudes, a great deal can be inferred by looking at how the relationships between the two sides are actually manifesting. The next two chapters do just this. They look specifically at power sharing in direct giving and new federated relationships to examine how Israeli NGOs are or are not, willingly or unwillingly, including their donors in decision making, as well as steps Americans are making to seek greater roles in the relationships.

# CHAPTER 6

# Power Sharing in the Twenty-First Century in Direct Giving Arrangements

Recent decades have seen a rapid transformation in how Americans—Jews and non-Jews alike—donate charitably, with the ideal of the collective federated pot giving way to more donor-directed forms of giving. Some have credited direct giving with revolutionizing power relationships in philanthropy and democratizing the field of giving, vesting donors with power they had never had.[1] Noted scholar of civil society and philanthropy Susan Ostrander has even gone so far as to say that direct giving relationships have given donors perhaps even *more* power than the organizations they support.[2]

The emergence of direct giving has had a significant impact on how American Jews give to Israel. By 2014, direct giving collectively accounted for between 25 and 35 percent of all American Jewish giving to Israel.[3] Direct giving appears, at the very least, to be a massive departure from the deference of Weizmannian giving. Largely eliminating the role of intermediary organizations, it creates an uninterrupted "straight-line" relationship between American Jewish donors and the Israeli NGOs they support (see figure 6.1). The mediating bodies facilitating the passage of donations—pass-throughs, umbrellas, etc.—are usually there only to connect donors and organizations and to provide opportunities for the tax deductions donors want.[4]

Yet, it is no easy task to study how power is negotiated in direct giving arrangements. Unlike studying power sharing in the era of UJA–Jewish Agency dominance or within contemporary new federated relationships (as will be discussed in chapter 7), in direct giving relationships there are no large organizations with paper trails detailing recorded internal debates. The only principals in the relationships are individual American Jewish donors and the Israeli NGOs receiving their donations. There are hundreds of thousands or more of small-scale donor-NGO interactions, and most of their communication is done privately.

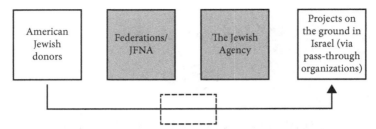

Figure 6.1. Flow of direct giving to Israeli NGOs (via pass-through bodies or other organizations acting as pass-throughs).

Organizations are not required to disclose the identities of their donors, so beyond the aggregate numbers raised, it is impossible to know much about the attitudes of donors, writ large. Therefore, the degree to which American donors giving directly to NGOs even view their relationships through a frame of influence is not known. If classic American attitudes still hold to some degree, it is likely that many do not conceive of their giving in these terms,[5] viewing their direct giving much more casually. They may simply find it appealing to support the causes and organizations they are personally drawn to, rather than putting their money into a common pot.

On the other hand, however, as was consistently borne out by interviewees in this study, Israeli NGOs often *do* view their direct giving relationships within the prisms of power and control. Israeli interviewees mostly looked fondly at the past of classical American Jewish donor deference and wished, in their current relationships with American donors, to preserve those dynamics and retain allocations powers as much as they possibly could. This is in part because, as discussed in the last chapter, most believed that Americans are neither entitled nor qualified to exercise a meaningful voice in serious conversations about allocations.

The confluence of these factors creates a complex background for understanding power-sharing dynamics in direct giving relationships. As this chapter will lay out, direct giving arrangements create various opportunities for donors to exercise substantial power in the relationship, if they so choose. Any donors intent on asserting their own power and truly determining how their money is spent, for example, are likely going to be successful. And though, as indicated, many donors may not see it this way, it is important to note that by opting to give directly rather than through classic vehicles or new federated options, American Jewish donors, by definition, are expressing a desire to exercise at least *some* choice in their giving.

From the perspective of NGOs, this creates both an imperative and an opportunity to find a way to retain the power in direct giving relationships that they so value. To that end, the study of the NGOs in this case indicates that most proactively search for a balance. They attempt to give donors the basic latitude they want. But at the same time, their fundraising and donor relations strategies are designed, in large part, for the purpose of preserving the NGOs' own decision-making powers.

This chapter explores the ways each side can theoretically exercise influence and control in direct giving relationships. It is broken down into what were identified as the three main opportunities in the relationship for donors to make their voices heard—picking organizations, designating their gifts to specific projects, and remaining with or leaving the organization longer-term. For each of the three, it looks at the approach the Israeli NGOs in this case study take in response, which is typically intended to minimize donor assertions of power in ways that are effective, while also not making donors feel that they are being shut out.[6] The chapter is divided into power-sharing issues related to the NGOs' efforts to (1) attract donors, (2) appear to adequately empower donors, and (3) retain donors.

## The Challenge of Attracting Donors

The first way that donors in direct giving relationships can exercise power is simply by selecting the organizations they want to support. Donors have a vast array of choices. Each year American Jews support thousands of different Israeli NGOs, and there are new options appearing all the time. In fact, approximately fifty new American 501(c)(3) organizations are created every year for the purpose of supporting various NGOs and charitable activities in Israel—and most of the organizations allow for direct giving options.[7] In this wide-open field, it is fully up to donors to determine where they want to give and what criteria they will use to make that decision.

If those individual Israeli NGOs that count on diaspora support—of which there are many—are not successful at breaking through the multiplicity and distinguishing themselves as worthwhile charitable destinations, they are likely to go out of business. At least a few dozen organizations do each year.[8] Therefore, the first challenge that NGOs face in retaining their power to execute their chosen agenda in Israel is simply figuring out how to survive. They have to make a compelling case to convince often independent-minded donors that their organization does good work and would be a good partner organization for donors to support.

According to interviews, Israeli NGOs looking to make a pitch to American Jewish donors start from the premise that most Americans looking to support something in Israel are not necessarily wed to a specific organization or even a specific cause. The NGOs in this case believe that American Jews are, in a sense, free agents, susceptible to whoever can make the most compelling case for their support. One scholar and longtime observer of diaspora philanthropy remarked that Israelis rightfully view that many American Jews "are people of wealth and heart that bring their hearts to the issue more than their minds . . . acting out of a 'desire to do best for Israel.'" In addition, the organizations recognize that due to the enormity of the field of giving options, even the most astute donor is not immune from the inevitable sense of overwhelm. As one interviewee affiliated with an umbrella group in the study quipped, "There are 26,000 [charitable] organizations [in Israel]. Who can sort through that?" Dealing with the volume of possible organizations to support is a problem even for the most savvy, knowledgeable American donors. One American supporter of prosettlement organizations who is part of a donor collective explained how much of a problem he and his colleagues—all of whom consider themselves very knowledgeable about Israel—have in choosing organizations to support. He said that if someone from Hebron approaches him "and says, 'Look, we are in need of this shelter.' How the heck do I know? I have no way of assessing that." His sentiment was echoed by numerous interview subjects.

The NGOs in this case study all recognize the need to actively attract donors and, as expected, devote considerable resources to doing so. For the more established organizations, this usually includes opening U.S. fundraising offices, hiring English-speaking development officers, forming strategic partnerships with Jewish organizations in the United States, and building a robust online presence. But beyond building a professional fundraising infrastructure, they face the ongoing, inherent challenge, as one Israeli grants officer articulated, that American donors "can easily be manipulated and led astray" by other persuasive Israeli fundraising campaigns. The antidote to that, she argued, is to make a more believable and compelling pitch. To do so, the most successful NGOs in this case reported having to hustle for every dollar, in a way that the Jewish Agency did not have to during the previous era. They use a variety of methods that warrant closer exploration.

### Cultivating a Grassroots Fundraising Base

At whatever their stage of development, the NGOs in this case all recognized the importance of building a grassroots fundraising base. Though a number indicated they would prefer to find a handful of megadonors who could provide millions of dollars annually, as they admitted, and has been documented elsewhere, such benefactors are, indeed, few and nearly impossible to attract.[9] The only alternative then is to methodically and gradually find and woo individual donors and small foundations and then hopefully retain their support.

Ron Nachman, the late five-term mayor of Ariel, was a pioneer in this work starting in the 1980s. He built the Ariel Development Fund's loyal grassroots donor base in this way, for years traveling to the United States for as much as one to two months per year. Nachman realized early on that as a community over the Green Line, Ariel would not benefit from UJA support, which, at the time, exclusively went to communities within the Green Line.[10] He decided that his best chance to raise funds to bolster the social and recreational infrastructure he believed would be necessary to convert Ariel in thought and practice from small settlement to viable, attractive city was to start aggressively fundraising in the United States: "I said to myself: . . . 'What will you do?' . . . 'I [will] go to America and start to find people.' That's exactly what I've done. . . . So I schlepped around the United States from place to place. . . . It's a very difficult and very tough work, but each one of the people that I met became a friend, and each one of them started to know what was [Ariel]."[11] As a testament to the degree of legwork necessary for an Israeli NGO to successfully cultivate a grassroots base, Nachman was proud to show interested visitors to his office the stack of spiral notebooks he collected—each one packed with the names of the people he met and notes on his conversations with them.[12]

In a similar fashion, leaders of Israeli NGOs in this case study take anywhere from occasional to regular fundraising trips to the United States. As a result, regardless of how instrumental Arik Ascherman (Rabbis for Human Rights),[13] Nadia Matar (Women in Green),[14] Hagit Ofran (Settlement Watch),[15] Israel Danziger (Mishmeret Yesha),[16] and others are in leading their organizations and in personally conducting their time-intensive advocacy work, each recognizes the importance of finding time in their packed schedules to travel to the United States to work on building their donor bases through parlor meetings, speaking engagements, and individual meetings with donors and prospective donors. One longtime American board member for a "friends of" organization affiliated with a prosettlement NGO that he requested not be mentioned in his quote explained the importance of bringing the NGO's visionaries to meet with donors in the United States: "There's so much competition for that American dollar that if you're [the founder of the NGO], who's the most powerful person to speak for [the NGO]? It's you. It's not something that you're going to delegate. . . . I can't speak for other Israeli organizations. I've met some of them and I've met some of their fundraisers, but I really don't want to listen to them, because I know— eh—it's just another job for them. The more they raise, the more their incentive bonus and all this sort of stuff."

Even the organizations with bigger budgets still do the grassroots circuit, but have a greater number of U.S.-based lay leaders and professionals to help do the work. Some organizations have had the advantage of having the sponsorship of Israeli notables. During their first years in the 1980s and 1990s, El'ad, Ateret Cohanim, and One Israel Fund, for example, all had former general and defense minister (and eventual prime minister) Ariel Sharon personally conducting fundraising trips on their behalf.[17] Even in such cases, while Sharon's presence helped open doors to wealthier donors, it still required tireless travel and relationship-building campaigns to attract and retain the support of donors.

### Communication and Branding

Another way NGOs compete to persuade a critical mass of overseas donors to select them as an organization of choice is through careful, targeted branding. In all communications, the NGOs pay close attention to how they brand themselves. Even the names many have chosen for themselves do more than simply capture the nature of their work; they make use of emotionally evocative language they hope will resonate with potential supporters who care about the future of Israel. Thus words emphasizing values, concerns, and aspirations form the foundations of many of their names (italics added for emphasis): Emek Shaveh (*Equal* Valley), Mishmeret Yesha (*Guardians* of Judea, Samaria, and Gaza), B'Tselem (In *G-d's Image*), Yesh Din (There Is *Justice*), Women in Green (whose official name is "Women for Israel's *Tomorrow*"), Madaa (*Horizons*), Ir Amim (City of *Peoples*/City of Nations), Sheikh Jarrah Solidarity (whose original name was the "Struggle for a *Just Jerusalem*").

The NGOs create tag lines and slogans that they hope will penetrate the emotional core of supporters,[18] not unlike classic propaganda pieces from the early days of the Zionist movement through the promotional materials of the UJA, JNF, and other major organizations.[19] One of the most striking examples of this phenomenon is the Ariel Development Fund. In conjunction with the municipality of Ariel, it has long trumpeted Ariel as the "Capital of Samaria."[20] The moniker alone lends importance to the centrality of the Ariel settlement to the whole settlement enterprise. Though Ariel is presently among the largest settlements,[21] at the time when Mayor Nachman first started using this slogan, Ariel was just another of many small Israeli outposts in the West Bank. Nachman explained, "This was my slogan. Ariel, the Capital of Samaria. . . . In order to create a brand name, . . . I wrote it when we only had 15 people here. . . . When you position a project, a company, a city—positioning, you need to be very accurate to penetrate the mind, and the soul, and the heart of the people. So that was my understanding—not to say, Ariel—a settlement. No one is taking care of settlements. The Capital of Samaria. It's a brand name."[22] Throughout his grassroots promotion of Ariel in the United States, Nachman consistently clung to the brand. He believed that the consistent messaging of Ariel as a capital city permeated the imagination of supporters over time, ultimately making this aspirational vision a reality.[23]

Such attention to marketing and branding appear all over among the NGOs in this study. The Hebron Fund, the American group linked to the Rebuilders of Hebron, for example, in its outreach materials emphasizes the deep-rooted familial connections all Jews have with Hebron. They often pose the question, "Isn't it about time you took your children to visit your great-grandparents in Hebron?"[24] Emek Shaveh attempts to position itself as a voice of nonpartisan expertise that rises above the usual shrill, "archaeology in the shadow of the conflict."[25] By framing their work in glorious, emotional, or historically significant terms, NGOs hope their branding helps bring ample donor attention to their organization.

### Intentionally Promoting to Niche Interests

Numerous NGO activists interviewed for this study admitted to intentionally propagating mythology or half-truths in the name of drawing in American supporters. One veteran of several antisettlement NGOs explained how every organization working on the issues in this case lies and distorts information to draw on the heartstrings of potential supporters: "Everybody lies about Jerusalem—Jews, Christians, Muslims, Israelis, and Palestinians. . . . If you're a public outreach organization that wants to establish a name and things like that, you can take certain liberties with factual accuracy." Whether this is basic salesmanship or specifically intended to play on what they perceive as American Jews' emotionally based understanding of Israel, they tended to pitch Israel in mythic terms. In the opinion of fundraisers, the consequences of this gap in understanding is that American Jewish donors are often inclined to be swayed in their giving by whoever can most effectively project and perpetuate whatever mythic conception of Israel is most important to them. Such a phenomenon is not unique to the Israel-diaspora relationship, but it is prominent.[26]

This tactic did not apply to Jerusalem alone. For example, a former director of one of the antisettlement NGOs explained that he shifted his organization's message when speaking to American Jews. "There is an ultra-American sensitivity to the phenomenon of a state robbing individuals," he said. Once he realized that this feeling was, as he noted, "deeply imbedded in American history and political culture," he started emphasizing the issue of how Israelis use Palestinian-owned land illegally. Though his organization's own perspective might have evaluated the issue of land "theft" as a secondary or tertiary issue to the larger problem it addressed, it was willing to emphasize it as the paramount issue in its dealings with Americans.

In a more overt case of deception, a former fundraiser for a prosettlement NGO offered a firsthand example he witnessed of Ariel Sharon consistently *lying outright* in his fundraising meetings with wealthy American donors in order to better tap into the imagination of his audience. Sharon traveled around the United States with the fundraiser and the Israeli-born founder of the NGO, who will be referred to here as Avner. As the fundraiser noted, Avner typified the myth of the irreverent but lovable Israeli pioneer. The fundraiser explained that Sharon would speak, while Avner, who "wears only sandals and doesn't tuck in his shirt" and who did not speak English, "would nod his head. Arik Sharon would introduce [Avner] as someone who was part of the raid on Entebbe," he said, "even though [Avner] was never in Entebbe." By using his own stature as a war hero and linking Avner's NGO by association with Israeli heroism, Sharon, as the fundraiser recounted, successfully compelled crowd after crowd to open their wallets. The people they met with, he explained, "were not aware of the nuances and if Sharon is there, that's all they need[ed]" to believe that the cause was worthy.

*Tours*

One of the most important ways the NGOs in this study work to distinguish their organizations to donors is through intensive firsthand tour experiences that they offer to diaspora Jews visiting Israel. The central mood each NGO tries to project in its tours is that the settlement debate is a living and constantly changing issue and core to Israel's character and very existence. As such, they insist that one can really understand it only by seeing it up close.[27] One founder of a pass-through organization that, among other things, supports humanitarian work in settlements, explained how many from their loyal donor base first started giving through his organization after he led them on a private tour. "You're on location. You see it happen. People explain it to you." This, he explained, is more convincing and more appealing to many than what comes in the mail. He added that seeing people on the ground directly affected by the situation tends to be a great selling point—especially if they do not speak English, which, in his experience, somehow makes them seem more authentic to donors. This is also true for tours by Madaa, RHR, and other antisettlement organizations, which admittedly give prospective donors often what is their first chance to see Palestinian society and meet Palestinians and develop firsthand impressions of what like is life in the shadow of the settlement movement.

Many of the organizations in this study, including El'ad, Emek Shaveh, Ir Amim, Ateret Cohanim, and the Rebuilders of Hebron, offer regular public tours. Some of the more participatory experiential trips offer visitors opportunities like visiting a firing range where they can practice shooting (Mishmeret Yesha), assisting Palestinian farmers in their olive harvests (Rabbis for Human Rights), or working to preserve Jewish land usage rights through planting grapevines and trees (Women in Green). Some of the other organizations that do not offer public tours regularly take donors and prospective donors as well as foreign journalists and diplomats on private tours, including Settlement Watch, Yesh Din, and Regavim. In the estimation of all sixteen NGOs in this study, the tours they offer make great impact in solidifying the opinions of their supporters and converting skeptics and apathetics into new allies—consistent with literature on the impact tours can have on American Jewish opinions on Israel.[28] Regavim's tour, for example, includes three hours in a car and another in a plane. One of its guides explained the power the aerial tour has. "Once they see it with their own eyes," he said, "they understand the problem: Right. Left. Everywhere. You can't stop seeing illegal [Palestinian] building. . . . People go into the plane one person and come out a different person."

———

The NGOs in this case each understand how competitive the marketplace is for wooing American Jewish donors. They know that donors have myriad options of whom to support in Israel. They, therefore, have to execute intricate, multifaceted strategies in order to distinguish themselves from the field and draw in donors. In some ways, this is the most delicate part of power sharing from the perspective of NGOs. Most believe once they have "sold" donors on their organization for the first time, that the quality of their work and attention to cultivating relationships will enable them to retain donors. This process begins for most with an effort to make donors feel empowered.

## APPEARING TO ADEQUATELY EMPOWER DONORS

Aside from picking the organizations to support, donors giving directly theoretically wield enormous power through their ability to designate how their donations are to be specifically used by recipient NGOs. Israeli organizations have increasingly invited donors to choose how they want their donations to be spent. By their calculation, if they did not do so in the current environment, they would have difficulty competing for donors with the many organizations that emphasize project designation options.[29] While the development staff at most NGOs indicated that they would much prefer donors not designating their gifts and that they try to steer donors to instead give to their campaign's general fund, they also understand that to close sales with donors and build long-term loyalty to their organizations, they need to make use of designated giving options. The development director for a prosettlement "friends of" organization explained that once he builds an initial relationship with donors, he works to deepen their interest in the organization by approaching them with new projects he believes might interest them. One donor explained how the prosettlement ideological umbrella organization Israel Independence Fund (IIF) has helped secure his ongoing interest and that of his friends. The donor explained that after finding some issues that sparked their passion, the IIF professional "said to us . . . I will go look for interesting organizations that are doing good grassroots things in Israel. And that," he continued, "is exactly what [the organization] has done," explaining that being included in new and interesting projects of his choosing has helped deepen his long-term commitment to IIF.

In this study, seven of the sixteen NGOs actively advertised menus of giving options to their prospective donors at the time of data collection (2010–2013),[30] and several others allow for earmarking. For example, donors giving to One Israel Fund in 2013 could determine whether they want to support a horseback riding ranch near Shiloh that provides therapy to children, a computer center in Eli, perimeter surveillance camera systems in some of the smaller settlements that might have older equipment, or any one of the twenty or so projects promoted on its website.[31]

If organizations want to keep their donors happy, they theoretically might feel compelled to shift their agenda based on what donors seem most interested in. In a sense, by designating how their money is used, donors are essentially telling an NGO what they feel its biggest priority should be and, as a collective group, can indicate which projects they see as *not important* on the NGO's agenda. One director of development at a prosettlement NGO expressed his organization's sensitivity to this view, explaining that his organization decides some of the projects it will fund based on its calculation of what it believes will "sell" to its donors. A former head at the same organization gave an example: "Buying bullet proof vests was very sexy for American Jews during the *intifada*." The development director added that even in times of relative calm, "It's not as easy to raise money for a playground as it is a bulletproof vest for a child." So even if the group wanted to spend more on building recreational programs, if security was what was selling, in large measure, the organization would go with it. A number of both pro- and antisettlement NGOs shared a similar perspective.

Indeed, giving donors the opportunity to pick how their money is spent seems to grant them great responsibility in deciding what they believe should be the organization's priorities. However, on closer look, this is more illusion than reality for two reasons.

First, donor-advised giving options are typically within channels selected by the NGOs—not the donors. While it appears that donors are deciding how the organization spends its funds, a few things are important to point out. For one, they are offering a finite number of choices. So, for example, if a donor to One Israel Fund wanted to support the creation of a youth center inside a settlement, she could earmark her donation in that way, but it would be up to One Israel Fund to decide which of the many communities would receive the center, what the youth center would look like, and when it would be built. The donor would have no impact over these critical details. Additionally, if a donor wanted to support something not listed on giving menus, they could ask the NGO, but as interviews confirmed, in most cases, NGOs turn such requests down. So while they appear to leave crucial aspects of decision making open to individual donors, to a large degree NGOs have and stick to definite ideas about the range of possible destinations for giving that they will allow.

Second, the budgets of the NGOs are fungible, which means that it is up to each of the organizations to decide how to spend all non-earmarked funds.[32] So for example, if Ir Amim hypothetically planned to spend $100,000 of its unrestricted funds in a given year to help build civil society organizations in East

Jerusalem, and a new donor decided to donate $50,000 to additionally help the cause, though Ir Amim would honor the donor's request to direct her gift to the project, it could and (based on the accounts from interviewees throughout organizations in this study) very likely would redirect $50,000 of its general funds that it was intending to spend on the civil society project to anything it wished. Thus, the net effect of the $50,000 earmarked donation would be $50,000 for Ir Amim to allocate to anything it chose. This is a common phenomenon. But, as one retired executive from the federation system, who worked with the federations' donor-advised giving vehicles, explained, "In the donor's eyes, it doesn't make any difference. The donor doesn't think that way." Donors view the experience as them having spent their money on what they wanted to spend it on. And while they are not wrong per se, in the end, in most situations, designated giving does not take any real power over expenditure decisions away from the NGOs.

So while donor designation is a widespread phenomenon, does it really move the agendas of NGOs in any meaningful way? The interviews in this case study suggest that while offering direct giving options is effective in allowing donors to *feel* they are exercising choice—which many feel an interest in doing—and in building donor loyalty to organizations, it does not represent a major change in power relations. Rather, organizations still appear to pick their priorities, are not typically open to donor initiatives outside of their portfolios, and often have the flexibility to play with their budgets to make sure that designated donations do not meaningfully tilt their own allocations plans.

## Retaining Donors

From a big picture perspective, the state of American Jewish philanthropy to Israel is very healthy. From 2010 to 2014, the amount of total American Jewish donations to Israel grew by 34.1 percent (25.4 percent when adjusted for inflation).[33] This growth in receipts suggests that there are more donors, larger donations, more commitments to the cause of supporting Israeli society, or some combination of these factors.[34] It is the latest upward movement in a continued trend over the past decade-plus in charitable money coming into Israel in ever larger sums from American Jews, and it suggests that perhaps there may be enough American support to go around for all Israeli NGOs actively fundraising in the United States. But, as a closer look at the numbers reveals, that is not the case. Over the same period that saw substantial total growth, only slightly more than half of the organizations (53 percent) increased the amount of money they raised in the United States. In addition, 37 percent dropped in fundraising revenue, and another 10 percent entirely went out of business.[35] NGOs are aware of both sides of this story. They know that as much as raising money from supportive diaspora Jews is a lucrative opportunity for them, there is a very real risk that even successful organizations can eventually fail if they are not diligently working to retain their donors.

NGOs face great pressure to retain their donors in a competitive environment, with so many choices for how American Jews can give to Israel. In addition to the already thousands of NGOs American Jews can support, the field continues to expand all the time. Each year, approximately forty to fifty new American funding organizations are established to support specific Israeli NGOs, and dozens of additional Israeli NGOs affiliate for the first time with pass-through organizations, allowing for Americans to support them and receive their ever-important tax deductions.[36]

Compared to former days, in which Jews would be blacklisted from their communities if they diverted their giving away from their federation,[37] they can now stop funding the organizations they are supporting for whatever reason, at any point, and switch their support to a different organization or none at all, with likely no rebuke. Once a donor decides to stop funding an NGO, the recipient NGO has no recourse. With this in mind, NGOs, therefore, take pains to earn the ongoing support of their donors. There is no place for organizations to rest on their laurels. No support can be taken for granted. NGOs have to treat their supporters with adequate respect and appreciation, be amply transparent in their use of funds, and be able to demonstrate success, as well as having a compelling enough ongoing vision for future success.

Though this makes for a challenging environment, NGOs have one key advantage in their favor. As economist and scholar of philanthropy Lise Vesterlund argues, donor tendency, generally speaking, is to want to find organizations they like and stick with them. According to Vesterlund, "Donating to charity is rarely a one-time event." Rather, she contends, "people contribute to the same charity year after year."[38] This creates something like a home-field advantage for NGOs. If they find the right formula for keeping their donors happy, they are likely to retain many of their donors over the long term and perhaps deepen their connection along the way.

The challenges and opportunities around retaining donors apply to donors giving in all ways—traditional federated, new federated, and direct giving. But by the experience of the NGOs in this study, it is more difficult to retain donors who give directly than others. Since, by definition, donors giving directly are already voicing a greater desire for input than those giving to traditional or new federated options, perhaps this is not surprising. The NGOs in this study, therefore, invest considerably in donor retention, with special emphasis on their potentially more fickle direct givers

The organizations in the case that are most successful at retaining donors follow similar behavior patterns. This study has observed that the common denominator is that they all invest in a long-term strategy and specifically at cementing donor trust. They base this on what was a widely held opinion by interviewees: that American Jewish donors are looking for more hand-holding than is suggested by the triumphalist narrative of how direct giving has leveled the power-sharing playing field between donors and NGOs.

### The Question of the Middleman: No Middleman or "New Middleman"?

The removal of the middleman—the intermediary bodies separating donors and impact-creating causes—has been celebrated as a major accomplishment of direct giving. For example, one donor, who claims to have been giving directly via prosettlement pass-through organizations since the 1980s, emphasized how healthy it has been for American Jewish giving to Israel that what she describes as corrupt middleman organizations have gradually been sidelined. She explained that although federations and other umbrella organizations are good ideas in theory, such collective giving in her opinion is deeply flawed because it "cannot be done honestly." There is "too much money involved," she said. "You can't keep track of it."

As discussed earlier, proponents of direct giving see its rise as an indication that donors have become more engaged and prudent. A director of one of the pass-through organizations in this study argues that direct giving is on the rise over other types of giving because people are "getting smarter" and do not want "to see the money get lost." He continued, "They are tired of getting cheated by the middleman [and have decided] that it is better to have money go where they want it to go."

Yet, in such an open market, how do typical American Jewish donors cut through the multiplicity and figure out which organizations to support without a middleman—an intermediary organization to help them? Where do they get their information about realities on the ground in Israel and how various NGOs are working to impact them? If, for example, a donor wants to donate to help disadvantaged children in Israel, without the help of a centralized organization to steer the money to needy recipients, she is left to determine which populations she should support, which issues are most pressing for them, and which Israeli NGOs are the ones doing the best work to address these issues.

As individual donors try to make sense of Israeli NGOs thousands of miles away, are they actually less likely to be deceived, as has been argued, than they were by the UJA and Jewish Agency during the heyday of classic Weizmannian Checkbook Zionism?[39] Political scientist Gerald Steinberg, founder and director of NGO Monitor, an Israeli nonprofit sector watchdog and think tank, contends that American Jewish donors—including those who give directly—do not always *really* know what happens to the money they donate to Israeli organizations. He says this is "partly because they're very busy . . . partly because they don't have the resources to independently verify."[40] The interview subjects in this case would add that this is because donors do not know enough about Israel to really be aware what they are doing, and do not seem interested enough to learn. So unless donors are experts in the chosen areas they support, it seems likely that they will need to rely on *some* source of information to interpret realities in Israel. But without the traditional middleman to spoon-feed them narratives about how things really are in Israel, how do they get their information?

This book would like to put forward the hypothesis that it is because of this dilemma that in the new era of direct giving and the decline of centralized philanthropy many American Jews want not "no middleman," as is argued, but rather a "new middleman." While observers are correct that donors want neither what they regard as the same tired institutional voices of the JFNA and the Jewish Agency nor any middleman that will "make decisions" with their money, the observations of interviewees in this study suggest that American Jewish donors still want a trusted voice that can help them understand "realities" in Israel, just as they had in the past. This voice can present them with information on the groups doing work commensurate with their own interests.

### NGOs as the "New Middleman"

This is precisely where the Israeli NGOs come in. The NGOs in this study acknowledged that with thousands of Israeli NGOs seeking foreign philanthropy, Americans can be overwhelmed with possibilities and thus crave what they perceive to be good, reliable sources of information. If the NGOs can position themselves to be the purveyors of information or perspective that American donors are longing for, the organizations believe they have their best chance to build the trust needed for long-term donor retention. The NGOs in this study—and likely in the broader Israeli NGO sector—therefore, compete with one another to be *the* source of information on discrete issues that can help well-meaning but underinformed donors cut through the confusion—the voice explaining how things *really* are in Israel. Since, by their own admission, most leaders of NGOs in this study do not especially respect the knowledge base and discernment level of their donor bases, they view their relationships with their diaspora Jewish donors as deeply susceptible to their framing. They are keenly aware that for each of the core issues they work on (i.e., human rights, security, agriculture, quality of life issues for Palestinians and settlers, and the political destiny of Jerusalem and the West Bank), many voices—including the media, online forums, personal relationships, etc.—are speaking out, espousing a very wide range of opinions on the issues. The idea among NGOs in this study is that if they get potential American donors to buy into their version of realities and vision for affecting them in the future, they will become donors who (1) support the NGO's work, (2) increasingly defer to its expertise, and (3) exercise "control" only within the parameters the NGO sets.

Most of the organizations in this study—especially those that have existed for several decades—recognize their success to date in establishing themselves as "new middleman" for a subset of their supporters. A fundraiser for one of the antisettlement NGOs described how well his organization has developed clout with its most devoted supporters. For them, the organization has become their trusted destination for interpreting Israeli news and events on "a range of issues." He explained, "[When] it's not clear what's happening, they'll call us . . . to provide them some insight about what's happening. . . . They don't always need that [specific information] from us because most of that type of information [is available]. . . . We will provide the back story." The development director of another antisettlement organization relayed a similar experience, noting that her organization and its supporters have developed "excellent working connections. We feed them with a lot of information," she explained. "We update them regularly about what's going on. And also, it's not just giving the information itself, it's analyzing it."

Most of the more established NGOs in this study facilitate this kind of trust-building activity, be it through regular personal contact, private tours, or sharing of information and commentary. The New Israel Fund, an ideological umbrella organization that supports hundreds of progressive NGOs in Israel including several in this study, for example, has an entire department dedicated to organizing tours and study programs for its visiting donors, aimed at cementing donor faith in the organization's unique credibility and expertise.

This kind of trust-building activity aimed at positioning themselves as "new middlemen" not only helps NGOs with donor retention but also helps them over time to encourage their direct givers to increase their contributions to the organizations' general funds (which most organizations prefer). As one development director of a prosettlement NGO explained, by demonstrating knowledge and trustworthiness to donors over time, the NGO has seen its donors increasingly showing faith in project suggestions the NGO makes to them. The attitude, as he explained, is we trust your judgment because "we know what you do."

Steinberg sees this phenomenon as simultaneously growing and problematic. In his opinion, American Jews have become overly reliant to a fault on drawing on a small subset of often similarly minded Israelis to frame realities for them.

A founder of one of the antisettlement NGOs echoed this perspective. She described how much, for better or worse, she believed that American Jews look to Israelis like her to play the role of the "new middleman" in interpreting realities: "Diaspora Jews," she said, "feel like they need an Israeli to come and tell them what's going on, which I think is a good idea—not to think you always know better for a place you don't live in." But the result, she explains, is that they get their information and solidify their opinions and ultimately their giving choices from sources they grow to trust, but who may present them with an often very slanted view on realities.

When asked about this phenomenon of American Jews being possibly too dependent on NGOs for providing an authoritative picture of Israel, a development director from a prosettlement NGO agreed that he has observed this to be the case and wryly added that the issue for American Jewish donors is that "whatever bullshit they hear, they listen."

## Conclusion

As discussed, many observers of philanthropy have extoled the merits of direct giving as revolutionizing the field by giving donors a much greater voice in deciding how their donations are used than they had ever previously had. In the case of the Israel-diaspora relationship specifically, some have pointed to the growth of direct giving as a sign that American Jews have become more comfortable asserting that they have a rightful place in the discussion over the trajectory of Israeli society. One executive for an organization that facilitates direct giving to a number of NGOs in this study affirmed this idea, proudly noting that by providing American donors with so many choices of where to give, her organization is "letting them express their values in their philanthropy," in a way they never could before.

One of the biggest proponents of this idea was the late esteemed scholar of Israeli philanthropy and NGOs Eliezer Jaffe. In 2000, Jaffe praised what he identified as a sea change underway in how diaspora Jews were giving to Israel in which what he called the "give-and-run" philanthropic style of the old system was being replaced by a cadre of dedicated, engaged givers.

> The persistent appeal primarily to emotions rather than to intellect and the "give-and-run" philanthropic style ... [is] simply not enough for a growing number of educated, committed, sophisticated philanthropists. These young leaders want to move beyond their regular involvement with the mainstream Jewish fund-raising apparatus and want a personal stake in Israel, a partnership relationship. They want to see how their philanthropy is spent, they want more control over it, and more accountability for its use in Israel. They want to deal with real people in Israel, counterparts whom they can trust and whose energies they can cultivate for a better Israel.[41]

In addition to the notion that direct giving provide donors opportunities to be more involved or personally connected to their giving, another pass-through organization's director argued that direct giving was perhaps even a more "responsible" mode of giving. "Having options ... forces people to be smarter," he explained. A donor looking to give to Israel has to "do his investigation independently." For an organization to be able to compete in a field of donor-consumers with a lot of choices, he contended, it has to perform well because "the market tends to be the best judge of the quality of an organization." By taking part in this process of being consumers and allowing the market to work, he argued donors are ensuring that the best organizations thrive. To him, this is therefore the most responsible way for donors to give and brings the most benefit to the overall system.

There certainly could be an argument for this perspective that direct giving may be the most responsible way for donors to give to Israel. However, for this to be true, it would assume that donors were informed, knew what they wanted to support, thoroughly researched the organizations working on their chosen issues, handpicked their destination, and then designated their donation to something specific within that organization. They would be not only making sound donating choices but also holding the organizations accountable for delivering on their promises through an implied threat that at any time they could pull their funding and contribute it elsewhere. In this way, every individual donor would be like a small foundation and NGOs would be compelled to work hard to maximize their effectiveness in order to best compete with other NGOs to retain the support of their funders.

However, if the opinions held by the Israelis interviewed in this study are true, the fact is more likely that typical donors giving directly are not nearly that informed, focused, or hands-on with their Israel giving as the loudest advocates for direct giving seem to assume. Indeed, cursory observations of the limited number of American Jewish donors participating in this study seem to support these assessments. But more research on donor behavior awaits.

Though almost all of the NGOs in this study recognize to their displeasure that they cannot expect the automatic donor deference of old, they also understand how vulnerable they are to losing funding and being dictated to by what, for the most part, is only a moderately engaged American Jewish donor base. The solution that most of the NGOs in this study pursue is to try to capitalize on what they consider an American Jewish donor base that, they believe, does not know much and that, whether or not it realizes it, wants a "new middleman" to help guide them. By the reads of the organizations, donors giving to them directly are vulnerable to persuasion. Their jobs, then, are to provide information to donors in understandable yet compelling terms and to continue to help donors feel empowered by offering ongoing opportunities to designate their gifts. Ultimately, to maintain their credibility, the NGOs naturally need to follow through and actually achieve what they promise to do as an organization.

The study of direct giving in this case suggests that despite its high praise, direct giving has not yet revolutionized power relations between American Jewish donors and Israeli NGOs. For the most part, the NGOs hold the cards in the relationship—closer knowledge of Israel, a platform and reputation that allows them to frame issues, and a proactive desire to use their power to stay one step ahead of a donor base it does not especially respect and believes it can manipulate. Overall, in direct giving relationships, though there have been some important changes in attitudes and behavior, the essential power dynamics that underlay the Weizmann school of philanthropic power sharing have not yet disappeared.

CHAPTER 7

# Power Sharing in the Twenty-First Century in New Federated Arrangements

While observers of philanthropy have devoted considerable attention to the growth of direct giving, it is not direct giving but another new form of philanthropy that this book terms "new federated" giving, which represents the most popular way American Jews donate to Israel in the twenty-first century. In new federated giving relationships, donors still give non-earmarked contributions directly to organizations to spend at their own discretion. But unlike in the classic federation model, instead of a single common pot, each American donor chooses a smaller pot aligned with their interests—either an ideological umbrella or a "friends of" organization. The trust and abdication of choice exercised by donors are nonetheless similar to the classic federation model.

What many donors are likely not aware of, however, is that when they donate via new federated arrangements, their money is going not to the Israeli organizations they have chosen to support but rather to their affiliated American 501(c)(3) umbrella and "friends of" organizations. By IRS regulations, it is the American boards of these organizations, alone, that are free to decide what to do with contributions—which NGOs to support, how much they will give them, and the specific activities or projects at each NGO they will or will not support. The Israeli NGOs supported by "friends of" organizations and ideological umbrellas cannot tell the American organizations what to do and they must comply with American stipulations.

For example, as discussed in chapter 4, if the board of Friends of Ir David— an organization constituted for the express purpose of supporting the activities of the Israeli NGO El'ad, including its archaeological exploration in the Silwan neighborhood of East Jerusalem—decided that it no longer wanted to support El'ad's work, it would be within its legal right to do so. Friends of Ir David could allocate the donations it receives to *anything* so long as it complied with the IRS's stated list of permissible charitable activities. It could offer the money to El'ad on the condition that it do different work. It could instead give money to a different organization in Israel working on the same project or something else. Or it could support any charity doing any kind of charitable work in the United States, Israel, or anywhere else in the world. Thus, if an American board wanted to have a say in deciding allocations, its affiliated Israeli organization would have one of two choices: it would be forced to either accept the American demands for a seat—or many—at the allocations table; or, if it did not want to accept this, it would have to risk not receiving funds from the American organization.

This chapter looks at the power-sharing relationship in new federated giving relationships: between the American stewards—the boards of the organizations—and the Israeli NGOs they support. Gone are the days of the almost across-the-board automatic deference practiced by the UJA. Instead, there are now a range of relationship types, differing in levels of trust, collaboration, and participation of Americans. This study identified three main modes the Americans and Israelis in this case typically used for sharing power over use of funds and agenda setting: the "Loyalist Model," resembling traditional deferential power sharing; the "Attempted Symbiosis Model," a form that intends to build a more inclusive partnership between Americans and Israelis; and the "American Power Play Model," which largely sidelines Israelis and vests Americans with allocation decision-making powers over the money they donate.

This chapter closely explores each of the three models, detailing their characteristics and design and outlining how American umbrellas and "friends of" organizations and their counterpart Israeli NGOs negotiate over issues of money and power.

## MODEL 1: THE LOYALIST MODEL

In the loyalist model of interaction between Israeli NGOs and their affiliated American "friends of" organizations, Israelis retain control over most allocation decision-making powers. In a number of ways, it closely mirrors the dynamics from the long-standing UJA–Jewish Agency relationship. Within this case study, the loyalist model is the most common type of relationship, operative in five of the NGOs in the study.[1] In most of the cases, the leadership of the Israeli NGO orchestrated the establishment of an affiliated American "friends of" organization, usually recruiting like-minded Americans to undertake the legal process of establishing the 501(c)(3) organization with the IRS.

The boards of these American "friends of" organizations are usually populated by Americans who still hold deference as a value, believing that their Israeli partners are both much more qualified and entitled to decide how to spend donated funds. For a smaller portion of American board members at loyalist "friends of" organizations, their abdication of a role in a de facto sharing of power is less ideologically driven—perhaps more closely resembling the early situation in the Jewish Agency following the 1971 reconstitution (recounted in chapter 3), in which the Americans were often just "glad to be part of the conversation"[2] and thus remained willing to let the more qualified, knowledgeable Israelis guide the agenda. Often, American board members are hand selected by the leadership of the associated Israeli NGOs. The result is that even though the "friends of" organizations are legally "independent" bodies, they do not exactly act *independently*. Instead, they often serve mainly as conduits for raising tax-deductible donations from Americans to support the desires of the Israeli NGO—and, typically, the involved parties understand the arrangement to be such.[3]

The relationship between the Rebuilders of the Jewish Community in Hebron and its American affiliate, the Hebron Fund, is a good example of the loyalist model. Although the Hebron Fund raises most of the Rebuilders' budget, it is the Israelis who typically set the policy and make decisions over use of the funds donated by Americans. A leader from the Rebuilders explained that his NGO takes the lead in setting priorities and strategies, deciding what it wants the American donations from the Hebron Fund to support. In turn, the Hebron Fund—like most of the loyalist "friends of" organizations in this study—usually okays the Rebuilders' proposals.

A longtime board member of the Hebron Fund agreed with his Israeli counterpart's account of the power-sharing dynamics. He explained that usually the Rebuilders make a specific request for funding and the Hebron Fund sends them the money for it. Though the Hebron Fund may sometimes have its own ideas, he continued, "we check in with [the Rebuilders]" because the American board does not want to be "influencing decisions over there." He stated that the overall objective of the Americans on the Hebron Fund's board is to raise money for what the Hebron community determines its needs to be. Noting that only those living in Hebron have the full legitimacy to make decisions, he explained that since his "prerogative is to live in New York" and that his kids would not ever have to go to war to defend Israel, as kids of those living in Hebron might, he "would never tell them that they have to do A, B, C." He continued that most of his counterparts have trust in the leaders of the Rebuilders and thus share the general attitude of "[we're] fine with whatever."

However, as a fundraiser for the Hebron Fund explained, the Fund does maintain the legal right to opt out of participating in funding certain projects if it chooses to do so. And on some—albeit rare—occasions, it actually has declined to support some proposals put forward by the Rebuilders. But this should not be mistaken as a significant exercise of American power. As was discussed last chapter, NGOs' budgets are fungible.[4] The NGOs can usually adjust how they report things without changing any real expenditure decisions, so as to make it appear that Americans are not technically funding certain activities. Between these accounting acrobatics and the rarity of loyalist American organizations in this case study actually opting out of supporting something on the Israeli NGOs' agenda, this seeming "exercise of independence" by the American organization appears negligible.

The relationship between Ateret Cohanim and American Friends of Ateret Cohanim functions similarly. An executive at Ateret Cohanim explained that it is the Israeli NGO that decides the budget and direction of the organization. "We dictate projects [their funding will support]," he said. "[We tell them] this is what we need money for and this is what you should send it for." He explained that the American board typically complies. However, in an article on Ateret Cohanim published in *Haaretz* in 2009, Ateret Cohanim chairman Mati Dan spoke of the relationship in more symbiotic terms. According to the article, "Dan insisted that the Friends organization 'is an independent organization that decides for itself whom to fund.'"[5]

While this is technically true, both Americans and Israelis affiliated with the organization painted a picture of close coordination in following the agendas set forth by the Israeli-based leadership. To that end, American Friends of Ateret Cohanim, like most loyalist groups, neither operates any domestic programming in the United States nor supports any other foreign activities aside from those carried out by its Israeli partner organization. It is rather clear from its tax returns that year after year, whatever amount American Friends of Ateret Cohanim raises in the United States (beyond its operating expenses) is sent along to its Israeli counterpart. From 2007 to 2011, for example, American Friends of Ateret Cohanim sent $5.7 million, representing 78.6 percent of the total funds it raised, along to Ateret Cohanim.[6]

One of the founding and longtime members of the board of American Friends of Ateret Cohanim shed light on what it means to technically be "an independent organization" from the Israeli group but in actuality still work together in near lockstep: "While we support them, we are an independent organization. . . . We try to hear their point of view. They hear our point of view. It's very nice. We've been getting along all of these years." To the question of whether the American Friends organization desires to exercise independent decisions for how to use funds, he explained, "Unless they are doing something that can in some way affect our . . . tax-exempt status . . . we don't try to tell them what to do over there."

Though the loyalist model is more common among the prosettlement NGOs in this study, it also characterizes the relationship between one antisettlement NGO, B'Tselem, and its "friends of" organization, B'Tselem USA. B'Tselem had long gone without a "friends of" organization, instead receiving its American Jewish philanthropy via either PEF, donor-advised giving through the New Israel Fund, or the nondenominational progressive umbrella group Democracy in Action. In 2009, B'Tselem established B'Tselem USA to serve as its fundraising branch in the United States as well as to undertake some lobbying and education work.[7] To those involved, there was no ambiguity that the power center in this relationship lay with the Israeli NGO. A former development director for B'Tselem explained that the Israeli NGO intentionally established B'Tselem USA in a way so that its fundraising operation would be "completely under the control and supervision" of B'Tselem. Though it was acknowledged that B'Tselem USA's American board would hold titular governance responsibility over the organization and its allocations as legally mandated, practically speaking all decision making and money flows would be supervised and controlled by leadership in Israel. B'Tselem was therefore careful to populate the board with Americans fully supportive of this power structure. Even B'Tselem USA's executive director was, himself, appointed by B'Tselem—not hired by the American board, as would typically be done with a truly "independent" organization. He explained that even irrespective of IRS insistence that a 501(c)(3) be understood as a separate organization from the group it supports, both B'Tselem and the officials chosen to legally head B'Tselem USA, conceived of B'Tselem USA as the "American branch of B'Tselem" and not an independent organization.

Though not all of the loyalist "friends of" groups publish their list of board members, in looking at those that do, one sees extraordinary continuity in board membership.[8] For some, the same cadre of leaders sitting on the boards in the early 1990s were still the legal guardians of the groups twenty years later. The subtext is that it is plausible to believe that, barring changes in organizational leadership, the culture of governance and collaboration each organization has established over time vis-à-vis its partner Israeli NGO will continue.

### Alternative Loyalist Board Structures

One common characteristic in the cases of loyalist organizations discussed so far is that the American boards embrace a deferential relationship to their counterpart Israeli NGOs. But in other instances, groups have structured themselves in even less ambiguous ways so as to maintain a dominant Israeli influence over the governance of the American organization's board. In some cases, Israeli NGOs have made use of the IRS stipulation that only 50 percent of a 501(c)(3)'s board needs to be American citizens and have put key Israeli figures, themselves, onto the American boards.[9] In the cases of the American Friends of Ariel as well as the Gush Etzion Foundation, a similar American "friends of" organization that exists to support development of the Gush Etzion settlement community,[10] the boards are composed of five members: three Americans, the Israeli director of the corresponding Israeli NGO (the Ariel Development Fund and Keren Gush Etzion, respectively), and the mayors of the municipalities themselves—Ron Nachman in Ariel and Shaul Goldstein in Gush Etzion.[11] Incidentally, Israeli law considers it a conflict of interest for mayors to sit on the boards of Israeli NGOs supporting their communities. Yet there is no such ban on them sitting on the governing board of the American organizations *that fund* the NGOs that support their community. It is reasonable to assume that the effective presence of such towering Israeli figures has influence over how the boards make decisions. A fundraiser at the Ariel Development Fund explained that the American board members of the Friends of Ariel hold Ron Nachman in deeply high esteem and follow his lead. For example, if Nachman, a five-term mayor and community founder of Ariel,[12] explains that the organization should allocate funds for after-school education programs in Ariel, who are the American board members to insist—or perhaps even recommend—that the funds instead be used to build a playground or a synagogue? All the more so because, as a fundraiser at the Ariel Development Fund explains, the board really likes and supports Nachman. "Ron Nachman is the kind of person that what he says, goes. . . . That's how it works." He added, "Whatever he says, that's what everyone is going to work on." This attitude was shared by one of the American Friends of Ariel's longtime American board members. He explained, "When it comes to charity: at the end of the day, even though they're taking your money, it's got to be what they want to do." He added, "I don't live in Ariel and I'm not going to tell [Mayor Nachman] what he needs money for." By injecting the voice of esteemed or expert Israelis onto what is designed be a voice of *American* governance, Israeli NGOs can influence Americans to put aside whatever pangs for an independent exercise of power they might otherwise have held.

American Friends of New Communities in Israel (AFNCI), an ideological umbrella organization that supports a number of humanitarian projects in settlements, challenged the issue of what constitutes an "American" populated board even one step further. The founders of AFNCI—all Israeli—wanted to establish a loyalist American board for their organization. They were not willing to have Americans insert their own ideas into allocations and planning discussions whatsoever. According to one of the founders, though they tried several times over their first few years to set up a board composed of adequately deferential Americans, they were unsuccessful. As she explained, she and her associates concluded that Americans did not "understand the issues, and you can't move them." So they came up with a novel way to solve their problem, while still abiding by the IRS requirements.

The U.S. government ideally wants "friends of" organizations to be under the discretion of *American-oriented* trustees—that is, U.S. citizens who, as Bjorklund and Reynoso explain, "are not acting on behalf of the supported foreign charity."[13] Therefore, according to IRS regulations, in order to ensure that the board operates with some kind of "American interest" in mind, the majority of board members of an American 501(c)(3) must be American *citizens*.[14] Since the degree to which individual board members will operate with "American interest" is not something that can be assessed, much less monitored, the IRS settled for the stipulation that more than half be citizens.

AFNCI's Israeli founders ultimately decided that they would compose the organization's board *entirely* of what academic Avi Kay has termed American-born Israelis (ABIs), American expatriates who immigrated to Israel and often hold dual citizenship.[15] Though ABIs can still legally be Americans, they are not *only* American in whose national interests they support. As individuals who chose to leave the United States and become part of a different society, taking on Israeli citizenship, one can assume that the allegiance of most ABIs is at least split between the two countries, if not tilted toward Israel. Even for those who are "more American than Israeli" in their orientation—whatever that might mean—they most likely do not embody the unadulterated "American interest" that the IRS desires in the stewards of American 501(c)(3)s. Yet, by IRS standards, ABIs who retain their American citizenship are as American as any other American. Though such a move is completely legal, it is arguably not in the spirit of the IRS's vision of proper stewardship of American "friends of" organizations.[16] In this way, the AFNCI's Israeli founders managed to skirt the American-Israeli power sharing question entirely by filling the organization's board entirely with a group of ABIs, who in this specific case would, by their own admission, view their primary interest as Israel-oriented.

The most extreme form that an NGO in this case study took to guarantee that its affiliated American "friends of" organization would be adequately loyalist was to initially establish a board only "on paper." In this case, the organization submitted a list of American board members in its official articles of incorporation and subsequent treasury forms, as per usual practice. And like with any other American 501(c)(3) organizations, once active, the board members for this organization were granted the legal control and responsibility for financial oversight of donations and allocations. Yet in this case the board played no active role at all. It is unclear from accounts whether they ever met. They instead left *all* decision making up to those running the NGO in Israel. A former fundraiser for the NGO, who requested anonymity for both himself and the organization, described how the "friends of" organization linked to his NGO operated. As soon as the American "friends of" organization was officially granted its 501(c)(3) status, the Israeli fundraiser was instructed by the NGO's director in Israel to open a post office box in New York City under the name of the "friends of" organization. American donors wanting to receive a tax deduction for supporting the Israeli NGO would mail checks to that address. Each week the fundraiser, who was based in New York, would collect the mail from the box and mail it directly to the NGO's director in Israel, who would cash the checks and spend the money as he saw fit. This arrangement is not legal by IRS regulations because tax-deductible donations from Americans must actually be in the hands of an American body—even if only briefly.[17] But legality aside, it is apparent in this case that such a practice may happen, nonetheless. The organization was never sanctioned for this arrangement and was possibly never caught. Yet eventually, as it grew larger and was likely subject to greater scrutiny, it adopted a more traditional loyalist relationship with an active—albeit deferential—board.

While it cannot be known for sure, it is conceivable that, over time, this kind of set up has not been unique to this one organization. Assuming they could get away with it, an arrangement like this might be thought of as ideal by some Israelis and loyalist Americans who believe all decision making should be in the hands of Israelis.

In sum, loyalist organizations array themselves in such a way that the Israeli NGOs control the allocations of donated funds. This model is a contemporary embodiment of the Weizmann philosophy of philanthropic relations. Whether the typical American Jewish donor giving to the general campaigns of these organizations is aware of this or not is unknown. But what is clear in the case of the loyalist organizations is that by design, the legal American stewards running the "friends of" organizations maintain only minimal influence in determining how the funds given by their American donors are being used.

## MODEL 2: THE ATTEMPTED SYMBIOSIS MODEL

In the second relationship type, the attempted symbiosis model, an Israeli NGO and its partner "friends of" organization attempt to create a more reciprocal relationship in which power is shared between them to some degree. Leaders in the United States and Israel see a role in governance and decision making for both groups and attempt to overcome typical barriers to collaborative decision making to strive for an enhanced partnership. The attempted symbiosis model characterizes only one of the ten NGOs in this study with a dedicated "friends of" organization—Settlement Watch / Peace Now and its American counterpart organization, Americans for Peace Now (APN). But it also characterizes New Israel Fund (NIF). Though an ideological umbrella, not a "friends of" organization, NIF is the chief sources of American Jewish funding for two NGOs in this case study—Yesh Din and Ir Amim.

The two organizations define their symbiosis differently. Peace Now and APN operate with much more of a "divide-and-conquer" mentality, in which each has its specialty and autonomy from the other to execute it as it wishes. NIF has a similar mentality to a degree, but it simultaneously tried to bridge the divide between Israelis and diasporans by intimately involving a critical mass of Americans in the grant making process—an altogether anomalous situation in this book's case study. By design, NIF's board is split between Israelis and diaspora Jews (mostly American, but from other diaspora communities as well),[18] and, as a result, unlike with other groups in this study, NIF's negotiations over power sharing take place within its own board.

### Why Israelis and Americans See Merit in This Type of Relationship

One reason why groups might choose the attempted symbiosis model is if they see merit in having an American organization execute a unique agenda, aside from simply raising money for the Israeli NGO. APN was started like the loyal-ist "friends of" organizations in this study. Initially, the leaders of the Israeli NGO decided they would benefit from having a sister American organization that could raise money from American Jews.[19] However, in this case, the leader-ship in Israel also felt that their "friends of" organization would be most valu-able if its work also included a policy advocacy component. Thus, over time, APN built up a domestic U.S. agenda, recruiting education and lobbying staff to con-duct policy advocacy in Washington, D.C. To succeed in this realm, APN needed leadership that knew the ins and outs of the American scene. And so APN devel-oped both lay and professional leadership that acted out of the interests of a distinct organization with a distinct agenda from Peace Now. Over time this has meant that, for APN to achieve its own organizational goals, it has sometimes had to pursue agendas that, though not necessarily antithetical to Peace Now's, were not viewed as a priority by the Israeli NGO. In other words, leaders of both organizations came to see that APN could best help Peace Now if the two groups pursued sometimes independent agendas from one another. Though APN is still the crucial vehicle for Peace Now's American fundraising, the two groups have decided it best that somewhere between 24 and 34 percent of APN's annual fund-raising receipts be remitted to Peace Now. According to executives at Peace Now, as of 2013 this accounted for approximately half of Peace Now's overall budget. The funds APN remits to Peace Now are unrestricted, so Peace Now can spend them as it chooses, but the two organizations hold the idea of an ongoing collaborative dialogue in high esteem.

From its founding, NIF's reason for establishing this type of relationship had less to do with pragmatic concerns like Peace Now's, and more with the ideo-logical belief that Israelis and diaspora Jews all stood to benefit if they tried to generally forge a new kind of collaborative relationship based on regular com-munication, transparency, respect for one another, and a commitment to the vir-tue of joint governance. Through this arrangement, NIF sought to break the classic model of Rich Uncle-Poor Nephew that was so central in defining most formal Israel-diaspora philanthropic relationships up until that point.[20] As NIF cofounder and former president Jonathan Cohen explained in a 1982 letter to donors, NIF's founding vision was one of "Americans and Israelis working together in a new partnership,"[21] establishing, as he would write later that year in the organization's annual report, a new "structure for exchange of informa-tion and involvement among Israelis and Americans committed to a healthy, secure State of Israel."[22] By establishing a board equally composed of diaspora Jews and Israelis and rotating the chairmanship, NIF attempted to offer to its American board members equal say in decision making. Though a more in-depth study awaits on how power dynamics have actually played out within the decision-making process at NIF, by giving American board members something at least close to an equal seat at the table in organizational strategy and grant evaluation conversations, American NIF participants are afforded more power than in most organizations in this study.

### How the Relationships Are Executed

In each of the relationships, Israelis and Americans continually strive to find ideal models for communication. Peace Now and APN work to maintain what one of Peace Now's leaders described as "joint thinking," in which neither group makes big decisions unless the other is involved. At the center of this model is a network of regular communication channels, through which the two groups share information, interpret local nuance and context for one another, and collaborate on big-picture strategic vision. As one leader at Peace Now explained, "No one makes a political decision that has major impact without checking with the other." Yet at the same time, as a former chair of APN insisted, "We don't tell each other what to do." Another former chair explained, "We are an independent organization. We make our own policy, but consult with Peace Now. They don't always develop the same policies. We sometimes stick our necks out more first. But, we don't issue statements that deviate from main line because we don't want to seriously deviate from them."

Included in their communication is an annual visit of the APN board to meet with Peace Now's leadership in Israel, and receive tours and briefings from the research and field staff of Settlement Watch, monthly conference calls between the executive committees of the two boards, weekly conference calls between the staffs of the two organizations, and daily email summaries of the Israeli press sent to APN staff from Peace Now's perspective. In these communications, much of the information exchanged is based on what is happening in Israel, but Peace Now relies heavily on APN for reporting and interpretation on the American policy scene as well. Notably, to ensure consistency in their messaging, the two organizations share a common communications department.

By its own account, NIF has worked for over three decades in refining the concept of joint Israeli-diaspora governance over both its diaspora fundraising and Israeli grant making/grant management processes. It is unclear how large a role NIF board members' nationalities play in their decision making. An Israeli senior grants officer at NIF noted that divides on organizational priorities and agendas on the board typically do not run down national lines between Israeli and American members. But, on the other hand, old lingering patterns are hard to break, she explained. As one would expect, there is a nationality-based divide in familiarity with and arguably expertise in Israel and perhaps, as a result, also in the degree to which the opinions of individual board members are respected within the board. For one, the day-to-day management of and work with grantees is naturally conducted by Israeli staff, while American staff typically focus on raising funds in the United States. One senior NIF American professional explained that, at the actual discussion table, the credibility of Israeli board members is based on their "on-the-ground knowledge," while the credibility of the Americans stems from on their level of financial contribution—perhaps an inevitable result of the logistical realities, but ironically closely mirroring old patterns in relationships. This may be an unbridgeable reality, and, as a result, it is unclear whether Israeli board members truly equally respect the perspectives of most diaspora board members when evaluating needs in Israel. The one check on this dynamic is that by design the CEO of NIF is always an American. Unlike with some NGOs, the CEO of NIF is intimately involved in all important board work, so automatically there is consistently a voice coming from the top of the organization giving an American perspective and advocating for maintaining the organization's ideals of mutual respect in joint governance.

## Why the Attempted Symbiosis Model Appears as It Infrequently as It Does

Among the NGOs in this case study, Peace Now is in an almost unique position at this point in that it recognizes that American policy advocacy work will help its activities in Israel. As a result, it understands that it is in its organization's best interest pragmatically to allow for APN, its American affiliate, to have the autonomy necessary to pursue its own agenda. The two sister organizations have thus been in a position in which they have had to find an arrangement for power sharing and collaboration that would best help them collectively meet their common goals. The result has been their creation of their (attempted) symbiotic model.

The fact that most NGOs in this study have such specific agendas in Israel makes it so that it would be costly and possibly pointless for them to have their own American policy advocacy branches. However, if, for example, an organization like Women in Green were to shift the focus of its activities much more heavily to advocacy work (i.e., its campaign for the extension of Israeli sovereignty over Area C of the West Bank),[23] such a focus on advocacy in the United States could be conceivable. Women in Green would then be left to determine how best to array power sharing between the two wings of its organization. But there is a very low likelihood that groups like Ateret Cohanim, Mishmeret Yesha, Emek Shaveh, or Madaa, with their particularistic agendas, for example, would ever have broad enough American policy agendas to necessitate a dedicated American-based operation that did more than fundraise. Some of the NGOs have broad enough agendas that they could conceivably benefit from an American branch (i.e., Rabbis for Human Rights, Regavim, or Yesh Din), but to date they have focused their advocacy activities domestically in Israel. The one other NGO that has entered the realm of U.S.-based advocacy is B'Tselem. But, as discussed in the section on loyalist organizations, at least in its earliest years B'Tselem has preferred to keep the decision making of both the Israeli and the American organizations under the control of its leadership in Israel. Unless and until its perspective changes, B'Tselem will not be emulating the Peace Now–APN model. As a result, unless Israeli NGOs see symbiotic partnership as an ideal, in and of itself, they are unlikely to shift their relationship structures with their American support organizations away from the loyalist model that most employ.

Regarding NIF's model of joint governance, it is little surprise that this has not been a commonly pursued model. As was discussed in chapter 5, there remains in Israel a deeply held belief that non-Israelis are not capable of—and perhaps not entitled to be—having an equal voice. Among those affiliated with the organizations in this case study, this has not changed substantially over time, nor does it appear likely to change soon. Even as an organization that actively strives to overcome these old biases, NIF itself still struggles with them. A high-ranking Israeli professional at NIF indicated how to her and other Israelis at NIF "it can be annoying" that a non-Israeli, "someone who doesn't [even] really understand how I'm speaking," has an equal voice in the conversation. Still, she explained, Israelis at NIF work to get past these feelings because they continually recognize the inherent merit in a symbiotic multinational governance arrangement. "When I'm [being] rational," she added, "I know that the fact that they are foreign gives them a different way of looking at things that is extremely important and it's easier for them to see it this way than for the Israelis who live here, so I actually believe it's a good thing."

### MODEL 3: THE AMERICAN POWER PLAY MODEL

Among the NGOs in this study, there are two cases in which the designated American fundraising organization insisted on having the bulk of control over the decision-making process. In each case, this caused major tension with the Israeli organization, ultimately leading to a formal severing of ties between the two organizations and the creation of independent entities competing with one another for support among their American donor base.

### Case 1: One Israel Fund and the Yesha Council

In the early 1990s, a group of American *olim* living in settlements in the West Bank observed what they regarded as a major problem with how the Moetzet Yesha (Yesha Council), the central planning and advocacy body for Jews living in settlements, was mishandling its relationship with a potentially supportive American Jewish community. As one from the group explained in an interview, they believed the Council was missing a big opportunity to develop overseas support, because it "didn't understand the importance of media, or government, or fundraising or anything else." The group decided to put the expertise some of its members had in marketing and development, and in American sensibilities more generally, to use for the Council. So in 1991, they set up an American 501(c)(3) known as the Israel Community Development Fund (ICDF). Its purpose would be to generate greater support among American Jews for the settlement enterprise through promoting humanitarian charity efforts for Jewish residents living in settlement communities in the West Bank and Gaza Strip.[24] The ICDF would serve as the de facto "Friends of the Yesha Council." It would raise the money from American Jews and give the Yesha Council the latitude to decide how to allocate it. For its part, the Yesha Council was pleased to work with the ICDF, and once the ICDF started successfully bringing in funds from American Jews, all the more so.

But by 1994, the relationship between the two organizations had become strained. ICDF board members were concerned that the Yesha Council was not adequately adhering to IRS regulations in how it was spending the tax-exempt contributions it received from American supporters. As one former ICDF board member explained, the Yesha Council had had no experience raising money in the United States nor a good understanding of the intricacies of U.S. tax laws. It was not accustomed to the legally dictated fiscal limitations as stipulated by the IRS and U.S. treasury department. As he explained, "We had some issues with Moetzet Yesha . . . where they were not being particularly sensitive to these restrictions." Another board member recounted that due to American tax law regarding permissible uses for charitable funds: "We [at ICDF] did not want to have anything to do with . . . political money. In other words, money for campaigns. For banners. Anything outside what was strictly charitable, tax-exempt money. The Yesha Council at that time had a different point of view. . . . When '93 came, and they felt that their campaign [to oppose the newly signed Oslo Accords] was the most important thing, they didn't give a damn about the law, and they felt that [they would take] anything they could get." A third leader of the ICDF explained, "Eventually we had it out. We felt Moetzet Yesha did not have the sensitivity to divide up the money . . . [in a way] that would be considered legal." The ICDF thus severed its relationship with the Yesha Council in 1994 but continued its work on behalf of the settlement movement. The ICDF turned to other Israeli partners, specifically the leaders from a number of individual settlement communities, to help with planning and allocation decisions.

Yet prior to the split, as the gulf between the two groups was developing, the Yesha Council was also plotting to develop an alternative partnership for overseas fundraising to working with the ICDF. The Council had come to see the merit of raising funds from American Jews but had also determined that it would more fully be able to achieve its aims without the ICDF constantly nitpicking about its expenditure decisions. New Yesha Council director general Uri Ariel tasked one of his deputies, an ABI still holding American citizenship, with quietly setting up a new 501(c)(3) in the United States to be known as the One Israel Fund (OIF) and recruiting an American board that would be loyal to the Council. As one leader from the Yesha Council at the time recounted, "We decided that [our American "friends of" organization] . . . wouldn't be run by the people outside of the Council because . . . they had their own agenda. . . . [It] had to be something that we would run."

When the ICDF broke off its affiliation with the Yesha Council in 1994, the OIF quickly swept in. OIF made the case to the ICDF's donors that it, as the new partner of the Yesha Council, now represented the more "legitimate" voice for the interests of Jews living in the territories, rather than the now-independent ICDF. Its campaign proved successful, as it managed to convince the bulk of the ICDF's donors to henceforth direct their giving to OIF instead. In no small part, the OIF's success was due to the work of celebrated Israeli war hero and former defense minister Ariel Sharon, who campaigned community to community in the United States, urging donors to shift their affiliation for settlement-support fundraising to the OIF.[25] The ICDF, a mostly volunteer-run organization without a professional staff or office in the United States, was not prepared for the concerted efforts of the OIF. Stunned, it watched as its donor base was taken from under its nose. But with neither the affiliation with the Yesha Council nor the support of its American donors, the ICDF could no longer survive and, within a year, ceased to exist.[26]

In the first years of its existence, OIF, though titularly an independent organization, was the prototypical loyalist American "friends of" organization. The Yesha Council was thus mostly unchallenged in how it used the funds OIF raised from American Jews. However, by the late 1990s, the American donors who had originally been handpicked by the Yesha Council to sit on the board of OIF were becoming disgruntled with this arrangement. According to a former member of the Yesha Council familiar with the conflict, the American board was tiring of what it considered being "dictated to" by the Yesha Council. "You can't have people here [in Israel] giving orders to their supporters [abroad]," he said. "It just doesn't work, because people don't want to be [pushed around]." Thus, in a strikingly similar maneuver to the Yesha Council's sidestepping of the ICDF a few years earlier, OIF's American trustees decided to make their own bid for control of the organization and cut the Yesha Council out of the equation. From the standpoint of one of OIF's longtime trustees involved in this decision, "There came a time when we just wanted a little more control—a lot more control. . . . Our donors . . . have somewhat different priorities than people at the other end did. . . . We decided that we would make more decisions over here . . . that determined the use of the donations."

In a dramatic turn, the resultant incarnation of OIF, from that point forward, vested control over allocation decisions *exclusively* with its American trustees. It believed that its American donors should be making the decisions about what work to do in Israel. Israelis on the ground would advise, but Americans would answer to no one but themselves. To keep its power consolidated in this way, OIF decided it would not retain a formal partner body in Israel. Instead, it would take requests from and make grants directly to a variety of municipalities, small

NGOs, and charity collectives in the West Bank and Gaza Strip. It would vet funding requests and conduct necessary due diligence over already granted money, including a sometimes close line-item evaluation of the budgets of the grant recipients in Israel through the Israeli-based ABI grants officer it would employ. Though the grants officer would make allocations recommendations to the American board and professional staff, the Americans would make all decisions. This arrangement put great faith in the lone Israeli grants officer to shape the narrative of the most pressing needs as he, personally, saw fit. But by the testimonies of both the Israeli grants officer and the American decision makers, the relationship works seamlessly: the Americans see themselves as the decision makers and view their ABI grants officer as just a trusted adviser in the process. Such hands-on management from afar by an organization governed exclusively by Americans aligns closely with what Louis Brandeis had in mind and is without equal among organizations in this study.

The Yesha Council was not surprisingly furious at the new power arrangement OIF imposed. One longtime representative of the Council described the move as the treachery of a small group of American "demagogues" who co-opted the Yesha Council's legitimate place as the representative voice of the needs of settlers to the world, including the American Jewish community. But the move, nonetheless, left the Yesha Council powerless in raising money from American Jews. Unlike when it took on the ICDF a few years earlier, the Yesha Council was in a much worse position to fend off the challenge. It was not ready for the American power play and now faced off against an OIF board, who, unlike the board of the ICDF, had a genuine interest in holding the reins of allocations power themselves and was savvy enough to conduct its own proactive campaign with its donors aimed at permanently cementing its own legitimacy as the most effective American charitable body for supporting Israelis living in settlement communities.

Eventually, after several unsuccessful attempts to set up a new funding vehicle that it would again be in control of, members of the Yesha Council established the AFNCI in 2001. As discussed earlier, the leaders of the Yesha Council felt they could only maintain the type of advantageous power-sharing relationship they desired if they packed the American board completely full of ABIs who were either members or strong supporters of the Yesha Council. Since 2001, AFNCI has operated in this manner, raising funds from Americans to support charitable agendas in the West Bank commensurate with the priorities of the Yesha Council. Nonetheless, OIF remained deeply entrenched as the body of choice for American Jews supporting humanitarian work in Yesha, with AFNCI collecting only a fraction of what OIF brings in. For example, in the five-year span from 2009 to 2013, OIF raised almost five times as much as AFNCI. According to their 2013 IRS documents, OIF raised $11.3 million in the previous five-year period to AFNCI's $2.74 million.[27]

### Case 2: Rabbis for Human Rights and Rabbis
### for Human Rights–North America

In 2002, a group of American Rabbis interested in supporting human rights activism in Israel learned of the work of Rabbi Arik Ascherman and his NGO, Rabbis for Human Rights (RHR). They decided to establish Rabbis for Human Rights–North America (RHR-NA) as an American organization to support RHR's work and raise funds on its behalf.[28]

By the admission of its own leadership, RHR had never been a wealthy organization nor one with a highly developed organizational infrastructure. Compared to other NGOs in this study of similar age, RHR's fundraising activities in the United States were somewhere between ad hoc and haphazard. Though RHR leaders would visit the United States a few times each year, conduct speaking engagements, and meet with donors, the organization had never worked with its close American supporters to establish a "friends of" organization in the United States as so many others had. Instead, those interested in donating were able to do so via NIF's pass-through donor-advised giving option. Even so, at the time of RHR-NA's founding in 2002, RHR's English-language website neither included instructions for how to donate via NIF nor even mentioned solicitation.[29] As comparisons, the sites for Ateret Cohanim, Rebuilders of Hebron, Peace Now, and B'Tselem, for example, all prominently discussed how to donate. The effects of not having a better fundraising infrastructure or strategy in the United States to advocate, coordinate, and market RHR likely led to a large amount of lost potential revenue.

It made sense, therefore, why leaders at RHR jumped at the opportunity to affiliate with RHR-NA when offered. Both the potential for bringing in higher totals from the American Jewish community than it had ever done and suddenly having a "friends of" organization spring up without it having to do the legwork itself to create one were appealing.

However, the founders of RHR-NA were not like the loyalist founders of most of the "friends of" groups in this study. An RHR-NA board member explained that the founding members of the group had originally discussed the idea of creating a "friends of" organization to help RHR fundraise in the United States but ultimately decided they wanted to be active beyond just raising money. But unlike an organization like Americans for Peace Now that initiated unique American-based activities specifically geared to support Peace Now's work in Israel, RHR-NA devised an agenda focused on unrelated human rights issues in the United States in addition to supporting RHR's work in Israel.

Originally, the two groups had a good working relationship. Though RHR-NA operated as a distinct entity, RHR did have input in how the American group fundraised and branded itself, as well as how much of its budget it granted to RHR. From 2004 to 2005, RHR-NA granted 69 percent of the funds it raised to

RHR, not substantially less than the loyalist "friends of" groups in this study.[30] But as RHR-NA developed its other human rights work outside of Israel, such as lobbying the U.S. government to take a more vocal role in the international campaign against torture, the two organizations began to diverge. RHR started to discover that this meant that its agent in the United States—which was increasingly becoming the face and the mouthpiece of the Israeli organization to its current and potential U.S. donors—was operating with a different agenda and, as it would find out, also different politics. Not only was RHR-NA using the RHR brand to build support for its portfolio of human rights work outside of Israel, but, from RHR's perspective, it was not even properly representing the positions of the Israeli NGO to American Jews. RHR considered the political perspective of RHR-NA's leadership to be to the political left of its own, which, as one RHR leader indicated, "cause[d] no small amount of tension." For example, RHR had vocally staked its claim in the Israeli organizational scene as both a human rights organization and avowedly Zionist—an important mantle in a political environment that increasingly associated human rights advocacy groups as being anti-Zionist, and thus not legitimate actors in Israel. The leaders of RHR-NA nevertheless shied away from any overt affiliation to Zionism. While early promotional material from RHR-NA emphasized its affiliation to Zionism,[31] by the early 2010s statements RHR-NA put out regarding mission and values did not mention Zionism,[32] and, in the opinion of some at RHR, RHR-NA tried to stay away from using the term "Zionism" altogether.

Furthermore, RHR-NA had almost completely taken over relationships with American donors. A development professional at RHR noted how the group's American counterpart at RHR-NA shut them out of donor relationships. "She left us out completely," the professional explained. "She didn't want me to have any contact with the donors." Another executive at RHR recounted examples of RHR-NA "poaching" top American donors. The implications were that RHR's funding base from the United States, an important part of the NGO's overall financial lifeblood, was vulnerable.

RHR found itself in the peculiar situation of being an Israeli NGO that had allowed for its ability to raise funds in the United States to be solely at the discretion of an independent group of Americans. It played out like this: According to the RHR-NA executive, twice each year, when Ascherman would visit the United States to meet with donors and raise money for RHR, RHR-NA would set up the meetings and handle post-meeting contact with donors, directing those interested in supporting the work of RHR in Israel to forward their gifts to RHR-NA. She explained that though, technically, donors could designate that a larger portion of their funds be forwarded to RHR, RHR-NA would discourage this. The RHR leader believed that North American donors would have given directly to RHR, rather than to RHR-NA, if Ascherman would have asked them to—even knowing that it would have meant foregoing their tax deduction.

However, due to the nature of the agreement between the two organizations, RHR refrained from doing so. Thus, donors who may have been most interested in RHR were essentially intercepted and redirected by RHR-NA. Donors—whose giving was intended principally or exclusively to support the work of RHR in Israel—were likely unaware of the details of the arrangement yielded such a small percentage of the funds they gave actually going to the Israeli counterpart organization. "The donors had absolutely no idea about this," an RHR executive explained. "Nor did [we] really know how much was going to RHR-NA."

RHR had very little leverage in the relationship. Unlike in the cases of most American support organizations for Israeli NGOs, the problem for RHR was that it neither chose the RHR-NA board members nor had any of its own representation on the RHR-NA board and was thus forced to live with whatever RHR-NA decided. According to Cerny and McKinnon, "friends of" organizations usually include "several board members associated with the supported organization."[33] So RHR's lack of voice within the RHR-NA board's policy development process was rather exceptional. As a result, what was initially a lucrative financial arrangement for RHR became gradually less so, as RHR-NA was becoming much more focused on promoting its non-Israeli agenda. The 69 percent of total raised funds that RHR-NA had originally been granting to RHR dropped to 42 percent in 2006–2007, 36 percent in 2008–2009, and 30 percent in 2010–2011. As a point of comparison to loyalist "friends of" organizations, in 2010, when RHR-NA granted 30 percent of the funds it raised to RHR, American Friends of Ariel, Friends of Ateret Cohanim, and the Hebron Fund, for example, passed on respectively 87 percent, 76 percent, and 71 percent of the funds they raised to their counterpart Israeli NGOs.[34] Though there were tense ongoing negotiations over allocations percentages between RHR and RHR-NA, RHR ultimately had little recourse. RHR-NA controlled the money as well as the contact with donors.

It is little surprise that the relationship between the two organizations eventually collapsed. In January 2013, the groups issued a joint statement notifying that they were formally severing ties, arguing that the split was mutually beneficial for the two groups.[35] A representative at RHR explained that the split was nowhere near as amicable as the official statement suggested. "It was a real mess" she said, "and not a healthy situation before the split nor after the split."

To minimize future confusion, RHR-NA changed its name to "T'ruah: The Rabbinical Call for Human Rights." But it still claimed a desire to work on human rights issues in Israel. RHR meanwhile reverted to its pre-2002 method of trying to raise funds in the United States from afar without an American-based fundraising operation and using NIF and PEF—as well as the new online pass-through, Israelgives—as its conduits. The long-term implications of the split to RHR are not yet clear. Though RHR began the process of trying to extricate what it believed were *its* donors from T'ruah, by RHR's accounts, donors were confused. Not having the donor database and personal contacts that RHR-NA had long managed made this even more of a difficult process. In addition, RHR and RHR-NA found themselves directly competing for the same donors. In an interview regarding the first years after the split, an RHR development professional reported languishing fundraising numbers from American Jews. Though no specifics were offered, according to Israeli tax documents, as of 2018, RHR's total annual donations were still an inflation-adjusted 35 percent below what they were at the time of the split.[36] While it is not clear what percentage of this decline was from its American fundraising, based on the recent history and accounts from those involved it is safe to say that between some and much of the decline came from a loss in ability to fundraise from American Jews.

T'ruah, by contrast, found itself well placed to raise money and conduct its activities as it wished without having to affiliate and share its donations with RHR. During roughly the same few-year period after the split, T'ruah enjoyed a 54 percent inflation-adjusted increase in donations.[37]

### Factors Contributing to the "American Power Play" Model

Among the case study NGOs, this American Power Play model of relationship has not been common. In the two examples we saw in which Americans tried to take control of an organization, there were two common characteristics not seen in any of the other case study organizations. In each case, unlike in any of the other "friends of" organizations in this study, RHR-NA and ICDF were started exclusively by American initiative and therefore originally placed at the helm of their organizations Americans who had not been handpicked by Israelis—and, as it turned out, were not supporters of the classic pattern of American deference. Similar to the classic Brandeis school of philanthropic relations, the Americans believed they had a right to be involved in deciding how American funds should be allocated in Israel. And when the Israelis gave them resistance, they were willing to cut them out of the relationship entirely.

In each case, the American "friends of" organization initially used its relationship with the Israeli organization as a tool for establishing its own credibility. Once it came to be viewed by American Jews as the bearer of the legitimate brand and controlled the contacts with the donors, each organization was in a position to be able to wrest control from the Israeli partner, and the Israelis could do little to stop them. OIF took control of the whole operation; RHR-NA just extracted much of the donor base.

Perhaps RHR-NA and OIF are exactly the kinds of situations that David Ben-Gurion, Henry Montor, and Henry Morgenthau feared that Abba Hillel Silver would try to create with the UJA/UIA or that Chaim Weizmann feared that Louis Brandeis would do within the ZOA. In an era in which Israelis were considered by the masses of American Jews as the authoritative voices over what should be done in Israel, there was no popular backlash, even when the most notable American Zionist leaders of the day were excommunicated from the organizational leadership structure—and, in the case of Silver, in a humiliating fashion. But in a new environment in which most American Jews believe they have greater rights regarding Israel, groups like RHR-NA and OIF cannot be kicked aside like in former times. Still, it is unlikely that this kind of arrangement will become anything like the norm any time soon. While some American Jews feel more entitled to assert their say, it is likely that most do not feel that they should—or would even want to—subsume the Israeli voices, as was done in these two cases.

## CONCLUSION

In the decades since the 1980s, new federated relationships have become the most common form for how American Jews give to Israel. This chapter has explored the question of the degree to which a more diversified field of giving has also led to one with notably different power dynamics between Americans and Israelis. The typology introduced in this chapter is a helpful tool for parsing this question out.

Most organizations in this study adhere to the "loyalist" model, in which Israelis and Americans are in cahoots to perpetuate the kind of Israeli control of old. While top American leaders in these cases see this arrangement as a virtue, it is unclear the extent to which rank-and-file donors would as well. Though most donors to new federated arrangements do not appear to typically clamor for greater control, they may not have full awareness of just how little of an actual voice in decision making the American board members theoretically representing their interests are having.

The second relationship form, the "attempted symbiosis" model, seeks to bridge the gap between the dichotomy of the Brandeis and Weizmann schools, through the promotion of values such as transparency, communication, and mutual respect. In this case, and likely within the wider field of organizations, this enhanced partnership is a fairly uncommon model. It appears difficult to execute, even for those who want it to work. That is not to say that it could not work, but it is with its own unique set of challenges around cultural barriers, physical distance, and some lingering vestiges of prejudgments and resentments left over from nearly a century of institutionalized Checkbook Zionism.

Finally, for organizations falling into the "American power play" model, top American leadership has indeed rewritten the classic power-sharing relationship by dispensing of their Israeli partners at some point. But in protest of a domineering and opaque Israeli decision making body, have Americans replaced it with their own domineering and opaque leadership? In each of the cases presented, it was unclear whether American donors understand who really made decisions about how money was spent. Did the American donors to OIF know that the organization was run by Americans and that all Israeli decision makers have been kicked out? Did donors to RHR-NA know that the organization kept most of the money they donated to use for its domestic programs? Did they even know that after 2013, T'ruah did not pass *any* money at all on to Rabbis for Human Rights?

The characteristics of power sharing that this chapter identifies represent the first step in mapping contemporary relationship dynamics between American Jews and Israelis in new federated relationships. The insights gleaned through this case will offer a helpful theoretical frame for evaluating the larger field of relationships.

# Conclusion

The philanthropic relationship between American Jews and Israelis is dramatically different than it was during the heyday of Checkbook Zionism—from a structural perspective, at least. The common giving modes and centralized organizations that dominated the relationship for four decades gave way in the 1980s and beyond to a much more variegated system. Instead of donating to centralized federated bodies, most American Jewish donors opted to support whichever Israeli NGOs fit their particular interests and priorities. And many donors weighed in further by selecting the specific projects they wanted their donations to support. The results of these changes are striking and undeniable: American Jews now make their presence felt in every type of charitable endeavor in Israel. They give perhaps more than they ever have and spread it among hundreds of American organizations that fund thousands of Israeli NGOs.

But has the underlying nature of the partnership between American givers and Israeli recipients changed quite so dramatically? On the surface, it appears that it has. For one, American Jews no longer seem willing to give Israelis the free hand to decide how to spend their donations, as they long did. Well over 90 percent of all American Jewish donations now go to some kind of cause that allows them input into use of funds. In addition, the literature on donor-directed giving corroborates that in an era in which evaluation and reporting on NGO activity are evermore at a premium, one should assume that American Jewish donors—savvier and more attuned than they had been in the past[1]—want more information so they can direct their giving strategically.[2] The days of JNF representatives cynically toying with the Birnbaums and Sonnenscheins of the world have been replaced by an era of greater partnership, mutual respect, and close collaboration, the argument goes.

Yet, the data from this study suggest something very different: at least in this one specific case study, pronouncements of a new era of partnership appear to be overblown; and changes to the essential power relationship more cosmetic than systemic. Indeed, many of the central dynamics that characterized the classic Checkbook Zionist power-sharing arrangements appear more operative in the current environment than one might expect. As the next pages argue, despite assumptions to the contrary, some of the most important paradigms that observers of the Israel-diaspora relationship had used in the past to describe attitudes and power dynamics at the core of the Israeli-diaspora relationship were alive and well in the relationships in this study. Rather than a new *concept* of partnership having emerged, relationships were largely characterized by the old imbalanced patterns of power sharing relations—even if now shrouded in the language of partnership and mutual responsibility.

## RELATIONSHIP PARADIGMS

Some of the important characteristics at the center of the classic Checkbook Zionism relationship were the following: (1) the Israeli partner in the relationship (probably a fundraiser) portraying a version of Israel not necessarily accurate but intended to be appealing to American Jews' needs or agendas; (2) American Jewish donors being made to feel like indispensable partners in Israel's future; and (3) Israeli representatives reassuring and redirecting any American Jews looking too closely at what they were being sold. These characteristics constitute some of the main paradigms that will be explored below: Israel as *heim*, the embattled Israel, the rich American uncle, and the naïve, easily deceived donor.

### The Old Home

In his seminal work, *Pressure without Sanctions*, Charles Liebman identified two predominant motifs that explained how American Jews regarded Israel from the time of its inception through when he wrote in the 1970s: "Israel as the '*heim*'" (the Yiddish word for home) and what he called the "exodus image."

Liebman explained that American Jews saw Israel as something of a quaint "old country." Irrespective of whether American Jews ever had any intention of moving to Israel—or even visiting there, for that matter—it nonetheless held an eternally warm spot in their hearts.[3] "Because Israel is a symbol," Liebman argued, "its particular policies are not very important to American Jews." So therefore, "while American Jews do have potential influence on Israeli policy," he continued, "they will not generally exercise their power."[4] This phenomenon manifested in Americans' consistent willingness to open their wallets to support Israel, but not demanding the same kind of information or accountability that they did in their other giving.

In a series of articles written over three and a half decades, Chaim Waxman traced the development of this idea. Waxman agreed with Liebman that

American Jews did at one point definitely relate to Israel as their *heim*.[5] As he argued, however, as time passed, the level of their sentimentality eventually faded, and as it did, they came to see Israel as simply a political entity like any other, he argued.[6] Thus the partial "family rules" that American Jews once applied to Israel were replaced with more rational, interest-driven rules.[7] Their support for Israeli policy, and even Israel itself, would no longer be automatic—an allegedly more rational, discerning generation of givers picks their own giving destinations based on *their* interests and *their* considerations—not a blind love for the old home. In fact, he argued in 2010, American Jews "are pro-Israel for much the same reason that other Americans are" and that American Jews relate to Israel as a "political entity . . . subject to the same, if not more, criticism as in any other state."[8]

Recent analyses echo a similar idea of a waning of the *automatic* love affair American Jews have for Israel. For example, Dov Waxman indicates that though ideas like what he calls "familism" and a "fantasy"-driven understanding of Israel still resonate, "growing numbers of American Jews have become less willing to unquestioningly support Israel."[9] A similar point was made by Daniel Gordis. He argued that "not that long ago, if there was a single issue that could unite Jews of all stripes, it was Israel," then added, "those days are gone."[10]

However, the evidence that came to light in this case study suggests that irrespective of what Americans may actually think, to many Israelis, this idea of the mythic *heim* probably is still a resonant message they use to tug on American heart strings (and purse strings). This is largely how many of the NGOs in this case study—especially the prosettlement NGOs—brand themselves toward their American donors. One need only glance at their websites to see this message of the *heim* front and center. The Hebron Fund, the American counterpart to the Rebuilders of Hebron, proclaims, "Our founding parents lived here. . . . They are precious. Guard them."[11] El'ad's tagline on their English language website is "Ir David: Where it All Began,"[12] and Ateret Cohanim implores its donors to "be part of Jewish history as it unfolds."[13] The messages from antisettlement NGOs played to emotions in an almost inverse way, featuring words like "violence,"[14] "violations of human rights,"[15] and "apartheid"[16] meant to drum up outrage and perhaps bring the degree of support that may likely come only from people who truly cared about a problem as if it were their own—people who would be deeply saddened to see a symbol they loved marred by values they would otherwise find anathema.

Almost all interview subjects affiliated with Israeli NGOs in this study did not believe the narrative that Americans were rational consumers of Israel, as Chaim Waxman argued. To them, American Jews' disinterest in truly learning about Israel was as clear a sign as any that Israel was still principally a symbol to them. Supporting it was driven more by a reflexive commitment than any information-driven assessment.

## *The Embattled Hero*

Liebman's other motif for explaining uncritical American Jewish commitment to Israel was what he called the "exodus image." In it, the prototypical Israeli was understood as "tough, hardheaded, courageous, and shrewd . . . something of a superman, albeit in an underdog's clothing."[17] He was on the front lines of a war slanted heavily against him, but continued to fight the good fight, and due to the rightness of his cause and his strength of character and mind, he was winning; but an uphill battle, nonetheless, still remained.

The UJA used this image of exodus—or what can perhaps better be termed "embattled" Israel as the basis of its fundraising narrative for decades. Wertheimer recounts that in part to maximize overseas allocations, the UJA presented an Israel in perpetual crisis and need. Under the leadership of Herbert Friedman (UJA executive vice president from 1956 to 1969), the UJA "routinely identified a dramatic situation and raised money to cope with the 'special rescue, or survival, or special Emergency, or Emergency Rescue Fund' of the year." In so doing, he explains that the UJA developed a persuasive rationale for why it should receive so large a percentage of federated campaign funds relative to domestic Jewish communal needs. In the 1970s, Israel was largely presented as a perpetual target, subject to one international attack after another.[18] In the 1980s, as Israel was more convincingly proving its long-term ability to withstand pressure and survive, the UJA rebranded Israel as still embattled, but for a different reason. Due to the heavy burden that Israel's defense needs had put on its overall budget, the UJA argued, Israel needed the assistance of its brothers and sisters in the diaspora to help it deal with some of its consequently neglected domestic issues like urban renewal.[19]

However, as Israel emerged from its more challenging origins, the UJA (and eventually its successor organizations, the UJC and the JFNA) came to reason that it was not so easy for donors to reconcile that a country with a growing first world economy, among the world leaders in technological innovation—and for anyone visiting, replete with modern infrastructure and amenities—was the same country being sold as one in perpetual struggle. As long as there were no wars actively going on, Israel appeared to be standing strongly on its own. The idea of helping a "needy" Israel thus no longer made much sense. Of course, there were still poor neighborhoods in need with crumbling infrastructures, inadequate services, and at-risk youth, but why was this something that the diaspora should foot the bill for? Should not a wealthy country address its own social service needs? The federation system's answer to this disconnect was to rebrand how it presented Israel from "embattled" to "emergent." It would replace Project Renewal, its urban revitalization program in the 1980s and 1990s, with a program called Partnership 2000 and eventually Partnership2Gether. These programs would be based not on social services but rather on supporting the work of proactive community development and local training, civil society, and advocacy NGOs.[20]

This strategy of branding Israel as emergent has been used by other organizations as well, including some of the Israeli organizations raising the most in the diaspora—from universities to hospitals to Birthright Israel. In it, Israel is depicted no longer as a charity case but as a rising power. Nonetheless, it is still in an emerging stage. Though Israel may have achieved incredible accomplishments in recent years, the narrative goes, it was not easy for a state that was for so long living a hand-to-mouth existence to be able to fully stand on its own overnight—especially when such a high portion of taxpayers' money still goes to support the country's defense and deterrence needs in what remained a very hostile neighborhood.[21] Therefore, as strong as Israel had become, it still stood to benefit greatly from support from foreign partners in order to help it get to the next level. This support might include the advice, expertise, or coplanning from diaspora Jewish partners, but it would certainly also mean money.

Interestingly, this paradigm of Israel as emergent is almost nowhere to be found in how NGOs in this case study brand themselves. The classic image of Israel as the embattled hero, on the other hand, appears all over the place with both pro- and antisettlement NGOs. Why might that be?

One fundraiser for prosettlement NGOs that exclusively supports educational work in settlements explained how he managed to double the size of his organization's fundraising campaign in just a few years in the late 2000s, specifically because he heavily leaned on a portrayal of Israel as embattled. He explained that in his regular fundraising trips in the United States he always brings along a retired Israeli general. The presentations and meetings they have consist of 90 percent of the general sharing his impressions of Israel's overall security situation and only the last 10 percent having to do with anything directly relevant to the cause or organization for which they are fundraising. Yet he claims that his success in fundraising is due to this model. "When you have a street show [with a performer] and then he has his monkey with the hat . . . I'm the monkey. He [the general] draws all the attention, and I'm running around [collecting money]." It matters little to the donors that the problems the general is outlining are barely related to this NGO's work. They are moved in some way by what he says, and they respond by giving money.

This is similarly the case with most NGOs in this study. They are working on a deeply divisive issue within Israeli society, offering a very particular vision of how best to address it. Regardless of where they fall on the issue, each presents its work as a race against time, and, interestingly, each also bills itself as an underdog struggling against much bigger and better-funded adversaries. The work of each is presented to potential donors as the last line of defense that is upholding a certain vision of Israel otherwise on the verge of falling apart: if there is one more eviction of a Palestinian family from the Sheikh Jarrah neighborhood of Jerusalem, or one more hill falling under Palestinian control near Gush Etzion, or one more missed opportunity for Jews to buy an apartment in the Muslim quarter of the Old City of Jerusalem from an otherwise willing Palestinian seller because there is not enough Jewish interest to make the financial investment, things will go down an irreversible course, leading to the destruction of the state or at least the collapse of the most pure, noble version of the Zionist ideal, they argue. Donors are given an image of a sinking ship that desperately needs their help plugging because the majority of Israelis have been tricked into believing that the ship is not really sinking.

To donors who support these organizations, Israel is therefore not the emerging powerhouse it may be in other fields. It is truly still embattled. It is not clear whether each NGO actually *believes* that its work is really saving Israel or Israel's soul or whether it is mostly presenting itself that way because it sees that it is able to raise a lot of money by tapping into the existential concerns of supporters.

So while the motif of Israel as the emergent modern intellectual, economic, and technological powerhouse is on full display in how Israel is sold to many American Jewish donors, the embattled Israel of the exodus myth, at least within this case study's NGOs, is also alive and well—both in how the Israelis present their situation and based on how well most of the NGOs have performed in raising funds from American Jews, likely also in the eyes of those donors that support it as well. Apparently, at least with organizations in this case study, in 2013, as in 1948 or 1967, the exodus image still resonates as donors gaze starry-eyed at the general and hand their money to the proverbial monkey.

### The Rich Uncle

The "rich uncle" paradigm is constructed based on similar themes to *heim* and exodus. In it, the wealthy community of diaspora Jews is cast as the wise, generous, and loving wealthy uncle who sends funds along to help his struggling little nephew make it through hard times. This was a classically propagated frame for how the relationship between Israel and diaspora Jews should be understood: one should do anything for family members in need.[22] It famously came under criticism in the late 1990s from Israeli politician Yossi Beilin. In his book, *His Brother's Keeper: Israel and Diaspora Jewry in the Twenty-first Century*, Beilin asserted that the old paradigm for the American Jewish-Israeli philanthropic relationship was no longer appropriate. Railing against what he saw as a "facade of dependence" still existing in how Americans understood Israel perpetuated by the rich uncle image, Beilin questioned why this was a healthy or productive way for the world's two largest Jewish communities to interact when there were actually real problems facing them collectively that could best be addressed through real collaboration, rather than propagating the farcical theater play. He wondered how a real dialogue "could develop between someone rattling a cup and someone dropping coins into it."[23]

In this case study, there was a difference of opinion among interviewees on the extent to which the rich uncle frame of relating still existed. In the opinions of the limited numbers of American donors interviewed, the idea of America as the rich uncle was only a part of the past relationship—not still operative in any way. Most interviewed Israelis, however, disagreed with this assessment. While none saw themselves as *in need* of a rich uncle, per se, they (1) believed that Americans still clung to the notion that they were the rich uncle (whether or not they realized they were doing it), (2) cynically recognized how perpetuating the relationship benefited them, and, as such, (3) did not go out of their way to dispel it.

One prosettlement fundraiser who had raised money for Americans to build a Beit Midrash (Torah study hall) in the settlement she lived in explained that her community is certainly affluent enough to afford its own Beit Midrash. Yet she still chose to raise most of the funds from American Jews—which she successfully did—because she believes that Americans still see themselves as rich uncle and therefore are willing to fund something like a Beit Midrash even in an affluent community. If they were looking at the relationship more honestly, she explained, they would realize they should not be paying for it. But nevertheless, she understands that based on how American Jews think about Israel, she could easily raise the funds she needed from them with far less effort than if she had to convince the residents of her own community to reach into their pockets to pay for the Beit Midrash, themselves.

Another Israeli fundraiser made the point that Americans may not want to be viewed as rich uncle, with all of the aloof and parochial connotations that go along with it. And so language of "partnership" had become a more palatable way for them to view their role—even if on some level they still viewed themselves as the rich uncle. He explained that many "Israeli NGOs have fundraisers whose positions [are] . . . called things like 'Coordinator of Partnerships,' but that is often only a euphemism for: 'I need to raise money.'" "A real partnership," he explained, "can only exist when each side can . . . see each other as equals that they each have responsibilities to the other and each has expectations from the other that are legitimate and fair." It is not "partnership," he continued, "when either side sees it as a front for taking advantage of the other." So based on what a real partnership would actually mean, he questioned whether either side really wanted a partnership. Instead, he believed they were much more comfortable with the familiar role-play.

One grant recipient from a prosettlement organization indicated how the old relationship format really worked best for her group. Over the years, she explained, there had been efforts to expand the relationship her religious journal had with its donors from money-based alone to greater substance. "We had explored building what we were calling a 'transatlantic partnership'" with Rabbis and teachers from the diaspora contributing articles to her journal. But, she explained, "I don't need their second-rate teachers to write articles in my journal just to say 'we're connected.'" The bottom line, she admitted, is that her organization "just want[s] their money."

An expectation has taken root among several of the Israeli groups in this study that Americans who want to support Israel really *should* still be that rich uncle even if Israel has, itself, become a rich nephew. One leader at an antisettlement NGO, for example, explained that though his group's work was supported in large part by like-minded American Jews, they ought to be giving more. "We get some money for them," he explained, "[but] actually not enough money . . . I think." According to this organization's 2012 tax documents, it received over 60 percent of its revenue from donations from Americans. It is striking then that an Israeli organization that received so much of its money from Americans still believed it should receive even more.

In a more poignant articulation of the same point, one fundraiser for a pro-settlement NGO exhibited an almost entitlement to receive money from American Jews to support his group's work. But at the same time he revealed a perspective that few other Israelis discussed. He was disgusted at what he regarded as the degradation that sometimes comes along with playing the role of poor nephew. "I'm not happy to go [to the United States for fundraising]. I think it's disgusting that we have to go there at all in the first place. These people should be crawling here and begging to give us money." But, as he explained, he still has to do it because many American Jews like to be regarded in their traditional exalted role in the relationship and "get a kick out of you coming to them and begging for their money."

This kind of parochialism that he pointed to—likely inherent in an unequal power relationship like the rich uncle paradigm—was still operative in the minds of some of the American Jews interviewed, regardless of what they claimed about "partnership" replacing the rich uncle model. One example of this was conveyed by an American fundraiser for a "friends of" organization that supported a pro-settlement NGO. He explained that Israeli recipients of American donations through his organization need to show appreciation and respect for their benefactors abroad.

> There's a certain amount of training the Israelis [that we have to do]. We make it very, very clear to our donors here that when they go there [if they have sponsored a project] an $18,000 or $25,000 project . . . , I want a dedication ceremony for them when they go. Not for them—although some of them do need it. Not only for them. It's for the Israeli counterparts. They need to show their thanks and gratitude for being given this project, whatever it is. . . . It also sends a message to the kids of the community, that this is how we show respect.

We don't have anything coming to us. This is somebody's hard-earned money that they're donating to a new playground for my children. My children are going to be there at that dedication ceremony saying thank you.

While some of the ideas in his explanation—like gratitude and acknowledgment—are arguably objectively positive values to instill, there is a certain arrogant or patronizing attitude that comes through as well.

But perhaps, from another perspective, as industrialized and affluent as Israel has become as a society, there are some causes in Israel—whether due to a slowly maturing culture of philanthropy among Israelis or a lack of resonance among the Israeli donor class—that need to, or at least see themselves as needing to, raise money in the diaspora. In other words, regardless of Israel's economic strength, writ large, certain specific causes or organizations may indeed still need a rich uncle.

Overall, it was clear in this case study that contrary to Beilin's pronouncement, the uncle is not dead. Maybe he should be dead. But Israelis continue to propagate the image, and Americans, regardless of what they might say to the contrary, continue to take on—and perhaps even enjoy—the traditional role.

### *The Dog and Pony Show: The Sallah Shabati Phenomenon*

As discussed extensively in chapter 5, despite the fact that most American giving suggests that they have some interest in playing a role in allocation decisions, the NGOs in this case study invest heavily in trying to neuter whatever power American Jews believe they have. Except in the few cases of organizations attempting to create a symbiotic relationship between Israelis and American donors, most Israelis demonstrated they wanted to keep the old power-sharing dynamics as alive as possible. From their perspective, if they could offer things that sound good on the surface but do little to fundamentally change core relationship patterns—like the Jewish Agency did with its reconstitution in 1971 and Project Renewal in the 1980s—and they can get away with it, then why would they not?

But in an age in which the Americans in the relationship are asking for something more—whether that is a true voice in decision making or just the illusion of control and/or psychic gratification they get from designating gifts[24]—the old heavy-handed Israeli approach seems that it will no longer work, as more and more Americans, at least nominally, favor Louis Brandeis's perspective of donors retaining control over the use of their donations. In addition, due to advances in availability of information and frequency of travel, American Jews are, in some ways, far more sophisticated customers than the Birnbaums and the Sonnenscheins from *Sallah Shabati*. To see what an Israeli tells them is "their" forest is not enough for most donors anymore.

Yet, despite all of this, many NGOs believe they actually *can* continue to use similar smoke-and-mirror techniques like the JNF agent did in *Sallah Shabati*, so long as they do it with a more sophisticated presentation. One example of how this is being done in a way that satisfies the supposedly more discerning, demanding donor but still allows the NGO the type of latitude that the JNF officer enjoys in *Sallah Shabati* can be seen with one antisettlement NGO that was considered as a candidate but ultimately not included as part of the case study. This organization produces publications that have the appearance of being very high quality. Whether or not they are actually high-quality reports is not even relevant. The heavy stock paper, attractive full-color covers, and heavily footnoted research give them the appearance of being impressive, authoritative documents. The NGO's director of development noted that though some of her organization's big donors visit, typically the reports provides them "the only way that donors know what the organization is doing." In this example, perhaps the glossy reports can fairly be seen as a modern-day equivalent of the certificates donors to the JNF used to get certifying "their" tree. This is especially so if it is accurate that many or most donors do not even read the reports, as several interviewees contended.

These types of polished presentations—publications, guided tours, or annual fundraising dinners—are practiced by all NGOs in this study. They showcase the version of reality NGOs want their donors to believe. While it is reasonable to expect that any charity anywhere would want to do the same types of things, most interviewees noted how rare it was for their donors, as one fundraiser for an antisettlement organization put it, "to look underneath the hood."

Between positioning themselves as the new middleman and at times using slick representations (or misrepresentations if need be), most organizations in this case expressed few qualms about propagating the relationship parodied in *Sallah Shabati*. Even if everyone—Israelis and Americans—speaks in Brandeis's language of sharing decision making, the NGOs in this case study are happy to do what it takes on the surface in order to propagate the traditional power-sharing relationships advocated for by Chaim Weizmann, in which Israelis still call the shots.

## CHALLENGES TO IDEAS OF POWER SHARING GROWING AT THE MARGINS

While the proceeding pages have emphasized just how little certain aspects of power sharing have changed over time, it is important to acknowledge two developing trends that, though only marginal at this point, have the potential to substantially impact the nature of Israeli-diaspora power sharing down the road. One is related to opportunities for greater Israeli power, the other to greater diaspora power.

### Israeli Resistance to Foreign Influence?

It is a hallmark of open democratic societies that NGOs are free to operate, in much the same way as citizen activists, labor unions, or clubs. So long as they do not break the law, NGOs are supposed to have the latitude to run their organizations and conduct programming, protest, and advocacy activities as they wish.

It therefore came as a surprise to the worldwide community of democracies in the early 2010s when members of the Israeli parliament pushed for a series of bills that would curtail the freedom of some Israeli NGOs receiving funds from overseas sources. Legislation passed by the Knesset called on these NGOs to make their sources of funding public.[25] Other proposed bills looked to levy draconian tax rates on such organizations, make their registration as NGOs contingent on them passing certain ideological tests, or even force the Israelis running the organizations to wear badges labeling themselves as foreign agents when they were testifying or lobbying at the Knesset.[26]

The legislators advocating for these laws argued that by virtue of receiving large amounts of funding from foreign sources, some Israeli NGOs were operating at the behest of their non-Israeli benefactors and possibly, therefore, against the best interest of Israeli society. They argued that such regulations on NGO funding would not only promote transparency but, more importantly, protect Israel's sovereignty against undue foreign influence.[27]

Critics of the proposed laws, on the other hand, argued that they were politically motivated attacks launched by right-wing politicians and specifically targeting only certain left-wing NGOs. They pointed to how the laws were written in such a way that left-wing NGOs receiving foreign funding would be subject to the regulations, but the right-wing NGOs also receiving large portions of their budgets from, abroad—albeit from different sources—were not required to report. Being labeled as an agent of foreign interests, they claimed, would delegitimize and ultimately make less effective the work of the various propeace and human rights NGOs under scrutiny—which included some of the antisettlement NGOs in this study.[28]

While this debate centered on the issue of left versus right, it is worth considering the wave of proposed laws through a different lens. This was the first high-profile instance on record of Israeli leaders toying with using their power to officially limit the influence of foreign philanthropic voices in Israel under the claim that it violated the state's sovereignty. It is possible that the right-wing Knesset members calling for the laws—aside from aiming to defang a handful of specific NGOs critical of government policies—may have been looking to block certain types of foreign influence *on principle*. Drawing a distinction between "legitimate" and "less legitimate" (i.e., foreign) sources of funding could call the validity of agendas pushed for by non-Israelis into question. It could be a notable first step of powerful forces in Israel pushing back against non-Israeli donor influence—which in some ways would be like institutionalizing the philosophy of the Weizmann school of power sharing into public culture and law.

The fact that some Israelis were willing to raise this as an issue suggests the possibility that if American Jewish donors eventually grew too interested in using their financial might to push for certain agendas in Israel, they too may be subject to backlash from the Israeli state flexing its muscles to retain control over the use of donations from abroad.

### Greater American Control?

As referenced in chapter 4, Jewish family foundations are becoming a rising force within American Jewish philanthropy. While foundations are legally allowed to give directly to Israeli NGOs, most choose instead to do so through "friends of" organizations, pass-throughs, and umbrella groups. Those foundations that do give directly to Israeli NGOs in many ways resemble "direct giving." Both individual donors giving directly and foundations pick their own grantees, can designate their gifts, and reserve the right to pull their funding if dissatisfied. Implicit in this is that the donors in both giving modes believe they are entitled to some say in how their donations are used.

However, the two modes of giving also differ significantly—especially regarding the increasing numbers of foundations that hire professional staffs to administer their grant-making operations ("staffed foundations").[29] As was argued in chapter 6, donors giving directly are often very dependent on the progress reports and overall contextualizations of events provided by the NGOs, themselves. In this way, NGOs can position themselves as "new middlemen" and, through this role, seek to win and cement donor confidence. Staffed foundations, however, often have the resources to take on the functions of research and evaluation themselves and thus have much less need for NGOs to be a "new middleman" for them. This essentially strips Israeli NGOs of much of the power they have been able to maintain in direct giving arrangements vis-à-vis their donors. Staffed foundations have greater leverage to demand accountability than most individual donors giving directly because of their knowledge and attentiveness to what is really happening, not to mention the relatively larger size of the grants they give. NGOs thus have to work much harder to retain funding support as compared to individual donors, in which they must present actual compelling cases as to why they should continue to fund them. NGOs cannot retain foundations as supporters based largely on clever packaging, as they are able to do with many individual donors. They have to show more definitive evidence of their performance.[30]

While foundations played only a marginal role in supporting the NGOs in this specific case study, their influence was on the rise. An executive at one of the antisettlement NGOs reported that its foundation donors were "very hands-on,"

TABLE C.1

DEGREE OF DONOR CONTROL IN VARIOUS GIVING MODELS

| | Donors pick the organizations they fund | Donors pick the projects within the organizations to fund | Donors dependably receive accurate information on the organizations and status reports on their funding |
|---|---|---|---|
| Classic federated relationships | — | — | — |
| New federated relationships | Yes | — | — |
| Direct giving relationships | Yes | Yes | — |
| Staffed foundation giving | Yes | Yes | Yes |

*Note:* Shaded areas typically represent power vacuums within which NGOs can assume the role of middleman between donors and projects.

demanding an "exact accounting" of their activity, even requiring the organization "to ask permission to move money from budget line to budget line." Another explained that the foundation donors to her NGO required so much reporting that it had to maintain a full-time staff member exclusively devoted to preparing reports for them.

The issues that the growth of staffed Jewish family foundations raise to possible donor-NGO power-sharing relationships in the future are intriguing. When faced with more powerful, focused, and informed donor entities than ever before, how, if at all, will NGOs be able to retain the degree of power that—if the case study is a good indication of the larger field—they have been able to keep in many direct giving and new federated relationships? Indeed, foundation-NGO relationships might result in levels of donor power not seen since the days of Rothschild and the first *aliya*. As table C.1 shows, the decline of federation and the direct giving "revolution" have allowed donors to pick destination organizations and earmark within them. But as argued in chapter 6, the increase in power this afforded them is exaggerated—at least, in many cases. Staffed foundations, on the other hand, give donors independent evaluative eyes and ears on the ground that can provide reliably accurate information on what the NGOs are doing.

Theoretically, the relatively limited opportunities NGOs have to shape the narrative of their work to staffed foundation donors stands to level the playing field between NGOs and these donors to an unprecedented magnitude. The kind of honest relationships and real accountability it forces may have substantial ripple effects in the greater power relationship between NGOs and all of their donors.

## CONCLUSION

How likely is it that a much broader range of Israeli NGOs still employ similar tactics and attitudes vis-à-vis their donors as was true with the organizations in this case study? There are aspects of this particular case that make it unique, such as the politically and emotionally charged nature of the settlement debate. But as argued earlier, in numerous ways this case may be as good a window as any into the larger workings of the contemporary philanthropic relationship between Israeli NGOs and American Jewish donors and, from a larger perspective, homeland-diaspora relationships in general. So while it cannot be known for sure without further research, it is certainly plausible that the findings in this study apply to much of the Israeli nonprofit sector. Israeli NGOs searching for funding abroad similarly target a population of donors who presumably give to Israel in the first place out of a similar degree of emotional attachment. They have a similar focus on heavily investing their organizational resources into ways to draw in and hook donors: promotion, tours, branding, websites, English-speaking development professionals, and naming possibilities for donors. So why then would they not also use the same tried and true methods—if they could get away with them—for attracting and retaining donors and controlling use of funds straight out of the playbook of the classic Checkbook Zionist relationship?

In this study, we saw widely held opinions regarding American Jews as limited in their knowledge level and understanding of Israel. We also saw Israeli NGOs as having little confidence in American Jews' ability to share decision making and a desire on their part to cede as little real control as possible, not unlike how Israelis in the Jewish Agency had long been uncomfortable with sharing decision making with American Jews. Yet, at the same time, they also understood that they could not behave like the Jewish Agency had in the old days. The era of Israeli organizations taking their American Jewish donors for granted or strong-arming them in any noticeable way had to be over. They acknowledged they needed different ways of acting within the partnership. And they similarly understood that they had to be ready to demonstrate accountability if called on to do so by their donors.

If the arguments put forth throughout this chapter—that images of *heim* and exodus, and relationship dynamics of rich uncle and *Sallah Shabati* remain prevalent in the contemporary era—are indeed true on a broader scale beyond this one case study, it suggests an interesting idea. Perhaps Americans actually exercised *more* authority as a collective before the growth of directed forms of giving supplanted the old giving channels of Checkbook Zionism. American Jews—despite giving 90 percent to some donor-directed giving option—ironically may have considerably less control over their donations than they believe they do. While it is true that most individual donors at the peak of the UJA–Jewish Agency dominance in the sixties, seventies, and eighties were voiceless—subject to the federation/UJA leadership—they at least, collectively, had an advocate in the UJA/federations. Granted, that advocate did not exercise its voice much in its dealings with the Jewish Agency, though it increasingly did so from the 1980s on. This now-cast-aside middleman, no matter how docile or bumbling he may have been in the opinion of donors eventually fleeing the centralized system, was theoretically an advocate for them and their funds.

But in the new direct philanthropy arrangements, there are only two agents in the relationship—the individual donors and the organizations they give to that are operating thousands of miles away. The same can be said in the new federated relationships with loyalist American "friends of" organizations—in which the alleged advocates on the American board of the "friends of" group mostly defer to the NGO's leaders in Israel. This seems to create a situation in which supposedly empowered donors giving directly are perhaps just as vulnerable as the Birnbaums or the Sonnenscheins—at the mercy of the narrative and proprietary decision making of the organizations they are supporting. Multiply that disempowered donor by thousands or tens of thousands or hundreds of thousands of similar disproportionate power-sharing relationships between Israeli NGOs and individual American donors, and one is left to wonder whether the aggregate American power over the use of its funds in Israel has not increased but actually declined. It would certainly be an ironic twist in an era in which the Brandeis ideas of power sharing have finally become the norm among American Jews that Israelis can hold as much of the power in the relationship as they ever have had.

# Acknowledgments

I have been fortunate over the course of this project to receive incredible support from a number of colleagues, family, and friends.

First, thank you to my terrific mom and dad, Phyllis and Alan Fleisch, for their unending support each step of the way. I love you both and appreciate all you've done and continue to do for me.

I want to acknowledge just how blessed I was to have three of my grandparents in my life through adulthood. They provided an anchor and a model that I can only hope to do one day for my own grandchildren. Even though they all passed before I completed this project, I know they'd be *kvelling* if they were here.

Thanks also to my other wonderful and supportive family members, including my brother Dave and his family, my stepmom Judi, and the whole Hartman clan, who have always had my back. To Mindi, who helps me to remember who I am and what life can be. And finally, of course, to the other members of my own fab four: my sons, Oren, Eli, and Emmett—respectively, the John, Paul, and George to my Ringo. You keep me going and laughing, and regardless of what you think, you keep me young.

I have had the benefit of being trained in this profession by two living legends, Professors Ilan Troen and Jonathan Sarna. I am truly grateful to you both for firing my interest in Jewish history and Israel studies, for mentoring me in how to be both a scholar and a *mensch*, and for always having an open door for me.

Over the past few years while finishing this project, I have found a home at Penn State University. Thank you to Dean Clarence Lang, Jewish Studies Chair Tobias Brinkmann, and others for the opportunity to be a part of the community and interact with so many terrific students and faculty members.

Thank you to my colleagues from all over the country and world who have been supportive of my work and open to helping me over the years whenever

I've reached out, including Hannah Shaul Bar-Nissim, Rachel Fish, Benny Gidron, Motti Inbari, Sherry Israel, Kristen Johnson, Chaim Kaufmann, Hartley Lachter, Daniel Parmer, Norrin Ripsman, Aaron Rubin, Kim Rubin, Ted Sasson, Marlene Schultz, Gabi Sheffer, Susan Shevitz, Oles Smolansky, and Jack Wertheimer.

I would be remiss if I did not acknowledge a handful of late scholars whose work was of particular importance to me as I learned about diaspora philanthropy and power sharing. Thank you especially to Daniel Elazar (z"l), Charles Hoffman (z"l), and Charles Liebman (z"l) for the amazing scholarship you produced and left behind for us all to learn from. I want to especially single out Ernest Stock (z"l), whose research and commentary I leaned on heavily. I was fortunate to have had the chance to correspond with Dr. Stock a few times before his passing and discuss both his work and my own. It was such an honor and a pleasure to be in touch with him. I am sorry he was not able to see my finished product.

I truly appreciate the opportunity to have my first book published with Rutgers University Press. I have long admired the work published by RUP. Thank you to my editor Christopher Rios-Sueverkruebbe, who has been a joy to work with. Thank you also to my former editor Elisabeth Maselli as well as Marlie Wasserman and all the other members of the team, present and past, who have helped shepherd me through this process.

Finally, this project would not have been possible without the contributions of my 120-plus interview subjects—most of whom have been kept intentionally anonymous in the pages of this book. Thank you all for your time, your perspective, and your candor. Though you represent the gamut of political perspectives on Israel and the diaspora, I (as probably the only person in the world who has spoken to all of you) can attest that you all share a deep passion for making Israel the best place possible. With God's help, we can hope that one day you'll all agree on what that means!

# Notes

## INTRODUCTION

1. *Sallah Shabati*, dir. Ephraim Kishon (Sallah Company, 1964).

2. See, for example, Gabriel Sheffer, ed., *Modern Diasporas in International Politics* (St. Martin's, 1986); Stéphane Dufoix, *Diasporas* (Berkeley: University of California Press, 2008); Robin Cohen, *Global Diasporas: An Introduction* (London: Routledge, 2022); Gabriel Sheffer. *Diaspora Politics: At Home Abroad* (Cambridge: Cambridge University Press, 2003).

3. According to the Migration Policy Institute, "The number of people worldwide living outside their origin countries as of 2020 was at its historical high—almost quadruple the level in 1960 when this population stood at 77.1 million. In the last decade alone, nearly 60 million more people became international migrants" (Jeanne Batalova, "Top Statistics on Global Migration and Migrants" [Migration Policy Institute, July 21, 2022], https://migrationpolicy.org. See also, for example, Stephen Castles, Hein De Haas, and Mark J. Miller, *The Age of Migration: International Population Movements in the Modern World* (New York: Guilford, 2014); Steven Vertovec, *Transnationalism* (London: Routledge, 2009).

4. Dennis Dijkzeul and Margit Fauser, eds., *Diaspora Organizations in International Affairs* (London: Routledge, 2020).

5. Paula Doherty Johnson, *Diaspora Philanthropy: Influences, Initiatives, and Issues* (The Philanthropic Initiative (TPI) and the Global Equity Initiative of Harvard University, 2007), 4.

6. Johnson, *Diaspora Philanthropy*, 3.

7. Sonia Plaza and Dilip Ratha, eds., *Diaspora for Development in Africa* (Washington, DC: World Bank Publications, 2011).

8. Jennifer M. Brinkerhoff, "David and Goliath: Diaspora Organizations as Partners in the Development Industry," *Public Administration and Development* 31 (2011): 37–49; Brinkerhoff, "Diaspora Philanthropy in an At-Risk Society: The Case of Coptic Orphans in Egypt," *Nonprofit and Voluntary Sector Quarterly* 37, no. 3 (2008): 411–433; Shawn Teresa Flanigan, "Crowdfunding and Diaspora Philanthropy: An Integration of the Literature and Major Concepts," *Voluntas* 28, no. 2 (2017): 492–509; Kathleen

Newland, Aaron Terrazas, and Roberto Munster, *Diaspora Philanthropy: Private Giving and Public Policy* (Washington, DC: Migration Policy Institute, 2010), 25.

9. Vivien Collingwood, "Assistance with Fewer Strings Attached," *Ethics & International Affairs* 17, no. 1 (2003): 55–67; Terje Tvedt, *Angels of Mercy or Development Diplomats? NGOs and Foreign Aid* (Trenton, NJ: Africa World Press, 1998); Liesl Riddle, Jennifer M. Brinkerhoff, and Tjai M. Nielsen, "Partnering to Beckon Them Home: Public-Sector Innovation for Diaspora Foreign Investment Promotion," *Public Administration and Development* 28, no. 1 (2008): 54–66. Jennifer M. Brinkerhoff, "Creating an Enabling Environment for Diasporas' Participation in Homeland Development," *International Migration* 50, no. 1 (2012): 77.

10. Victoria Licuanan, Omar Mahmoud Toman, and Andreas Steinmayr, "The Drivers of Diaspora Donations for Development: Evidence from the Philippines," *World Development* 65 (2015): 94; Newland, Terrazas, and Munster, *Diaspora Philanthropy*; Johnson, *Diaspora Philanthropy*, 11.

11. Brinkerhoff, "David and Goliath"; Brinkerhoff, "Creating an Enabling Environment," 88–89; Terrence Lyons, Harald Svein Ege, Birhanu Teferra Aspen, and Bekele Shiferaw, "The Ethiopian Diaspora and Homeland Conflict," *Power* 44, no. 2 (2007): 215–231.

12. Brinkerhoff, "Creating an Enabling Environment," 78; Matthias Lücke, Omar Mahmoud Toman, and Peuker Christian, "Identifying the Motives of Migrant Philanthropy" (Working paper, Kiel Institute for the World Economy, 2012); Hillel Rapoport and Frédéric Docquier, "The Economics of Migrants' Remittances," *Handbook of the Economics of Giving, Altruism and Reciprocity* 2 (2006): 1135–1198; René Bekkers and Pamala Wiepking, "A Literature Review of Empirical Studies of Philanthropy: Eight Mechanisms That Drive Charitable Giving," *Nonprofit and Voluntary Sector Quarterly* 40, no. 5 (2011): 924–973; Licuanan, Mahmoud, and Steinmayr, "Drivers of Diaspora Donations," 95; Newland, Terrazas, and Munster, *Diaspora Philanthropy*, 26.

13. Lücke, Toman, and Christian, "Identifying the Motives of Migrant Philanthropy."

14. Johnson, *Diaspora Philanthropy*, 21. In their study about foundations, Anheier and Daly argue that foundations are inherently political because they represent agendas operating in public arenas outside direct majoritarian public control. A similar argument applies here with donors of every amount. Helmut K. Anheier and Siobhan Daly, eds., *The Politics of Foundations: A Comparative Analysis* (London: Routledge, 2007).

15. In her study of the Bialystok, Poland, diaspora in the period between the two world wars, Rebecca Kobrin discusses such a case. At the time, a number of newspaper editors in Bialystok were struggling to keep their publications open until they connected with American Bialystocker ex-patriots who supported their ideas and funded their papers, keeping the doors open. As a result, they were able to vocally promote certain ideas about Jewish autonomy and critique Polish rule to a broad audience—which they certainly would not have been able to do without the support of foreign donors—that did not reflect the dominant perspectives of Jews in Bialystok and arguably led to greater strife with Polish authorities than they were otherwise likely to have. Kobrin, *Jewish Bialystok and Its Diaspora* (Bloomington: Indiana University Press, 2010).

16. Paula Doherty Johnson, Stephen P. Johnson, and Andrew Kingman, *Promoting Philanthropy: Global Challenges and Approaches* (International Network for Strategic Philanthropy [INSP], 2004).

17. Helmut K. Anheier and Diana Leat, *Creative Philanthropy: Toward a New Philanthropy for the Twenty-First Century* (London: Routledge, 2006).

18. Some important perspectives on these ideas are discussed in the following sources: Johnson, *Diaspora Philanthropy*; Julie Fisher, *Nongovernments: NGOs and the Political Development of the Third World* (Kumarian Press, 1998); L. M. Salamon and Helmut K. Anheier, "Social Origins of Civil Society: Explaining the Nonprofit Sector Cross-Nationally," *Voluntas* 9, no. 3 (1998): 213–248; Judith M. Brown, *Global South Asians: Introducing the Modern Diaspora* (Cambridge: Cambridge University Press, 2006).

19. Those studies that do exist on the philanthropic relationship between donating diasporas and recipient homelands typically focus on the dynamics only within a single diaspora-homeland relationship. Jeremaiah M. Opiniano, "Filipinos Doing Diaspora Philanthropy: The Development Potential of Transnational Migration," *Asian and Pacific Migration Journal* 14, no. 1–2 (2005): 225–241; Kathleen Dunn, "Diaspora Giving and the Future of Philanthropy," *Philanthropic Initiative* (2004); Choo Chin Low, "Malaysian Diaspora Philanthropy: Transnational Activism, Mobilization and Resistance," *Diaspora Studies* 10, no. 2 (2017): 152–174; Jennifer M. Brinkerhoff, "Diaspora Philanthropy: Lessons from a Demographic Analysis of the Coptic Diaspora," *Nonprofit and Voluntary Sector Quarterly* 43, no. 6 (2014): 969–992. And even most of those focus not on power sharing dynamics but on topics such as donor motivation, organizational mechanics, or government policy to promote diaspora philanthropy (e.g., Flanigan, "Crowdfunding and Diaspora Philanthropy").

20. Kathleen Newland and Erin Patrick, "Beyond Remittances: The Role of Diaspora in Poverty Reduction in Their Countries of Origin" (Washington, DC: Migration Policy Institute, 2004); Mark Sidel, "A Decade of Research and Practice of Diaspora Philanthropy in the Asia Pacific Region: The State of the Field" (University of Iowa Legal Studies Research Paper 08–09, 2008); Brinkerhoff, "Diaspora Philanthropy"; Johnson, *Diaspora Philanthropy*.

21. Some key works include David Lewis and Nazneen Kanji, *Non-governmental Organizations and Development* (London: Routledge, 2009); Tvedt, *Angels of Mercy or Development Diplomats?*; Jean-Philippe Thérien, "Debating Foreign Aid: Right versus Left," *Third World Quarterly* 23, no. 3 (June 2002): 449–466.

22. Jennifer N. Brass, Wesley Longhofer, Rachel S. Robinson, and Allison Schnable, "NGOs and International Development: A Review of Thirty-Five Years of Scholarship," *World Development* 112 (2018): 136–149; Patrick Kilby, "Accountability for Empowerment: Dilemmas Facing Non-governmental Organizations," *World Development* 34, no. 6 (2006): 951–963.

23. Katie Willis, *Theories and Practices of Development* (London: Routledge, 2011); Kilby, "Accountability for Empowerment."

24. Willem Elbers and Lau Schulpen, "Corridors of Power: The Institutional Design of North–South NGO Partnerships," *Voluntas* 24, no. 1 (2013): 48–67.

25. Elbers and Schulpen, "Corridors of Power." See also D. W. Binkerhoff and J. M. Brinkerhoff, "Partnerships between International Donors and Nongovernmental Development Organizations: Opportunities and Constraints," *International Review of Administrative Sciences* 70, no. 2 (2004): 253–270.

26. Sally Reith, "Money, Power, and Donor–NGO Partnerships," *Development in Practice* 20, no. 3 (2010): 446–455.

27. Wilhelmus Johannes Elbers, "The Partnership Paradox: Principles and Practice in North-South NGO Relations" (PhD diss., Radbound University, 2012).

28. Yossi Shain, *Kinship and Diasporas in International Affairs* (Ann Arbor: University of Michigan Press, 2007); Cohen, *Global Diasporas*.

29. It should be noted that this study intentionally chose not to include Israel Bonds, a program that allowed individual supporters of Israel abroad to make loans directly to the Israeli government. Though Israel Bonds helped the nation-state raise billions of dollars and deepened the connection between individual diaspora Jews and Israel, the purchase of such bonds was a profit-seeking investment, not philanthropy. Eric Fleisch, "Israeli NGOs and American Jewish Donors: The Structures and Dynamics of Power Sharing in a New Philanthropic Era (PhD diss., Brandeis University, 2014), 59–60. For excellent work on the history of Israel Bonds, see Dan Lainer-Vos, *Sinews of the Nation: Constructing Irish and Zionist Bonds in the United States* (New York: John Wiley, 2013). Daniel J. Elazar, *Community and Polity: The Organizational Dynamics of American Jewry* (Philadelphia: Jewish Publications Society of America, 1976); Ernest Stock, *Partners and Pursestrings: A History of the United Israel Appeal* (Lanham, MD: University Press of America, 1987); Philip Bernstein, *To Dwell in Unity: The Jewish Federation Movement in America, since 1960* (Philadelphia: Jewish Publication Society of America, 1983); Mitchell Bard, "American Jewish Contributions to Israel" (Jewish Virtual Library, 2016), https://www.jewishvirtuallibrary.org/american-jewish-contributions-to-israel; Marc Lee Raphael, *A History of the United Jewish Appeal, 1939–1982* (Chico, CA: Scholars Press, 1982); Mark I. Rosen, *Responding to a World of Need: Fundraising at the American Jewish Joint Distribution Committee* (Bloomington, IN: iUniverse, 2009).

30. Ernest Stock, *Chosen Instrument: The Jewish Agency in the First Decade of the State of Israel* (New York: Herzl Press, 1988); Ernest Stock, *Beyond Partnership: The Jewish Agency and the Diaspora, 1959–1971* (New York: Herzl Press, 1992); Ben W. Lappin and Morton I. Teicher, *Distant Partners: Community Change through Project Renewal* (Lanham, MD: University Press of America, 1990); Raviv Schwartz, "Partnership 2000: A New Model for Diaspora-Israel Relations," *Jerusalem Letter/Viewpoints* 410 (July 15, 1999).

31. Eliezer Schweid, "The Rejection of the Diaspora in Zionist Thought: Two Approaches," *Studies in Zionism* 5, no. 1 (1984): 43–70.

32. Eliezer Don-Yehiya, *Israel and Diaspora Jewry: Ideological and Political Perspectives* (Ramat Gan: Bar-Ilan University Press, 1991); Matti Golan, *With Friends Like You: What Israelis Really Think about American Jews* (New York: Free Press, 1992); Eli Lederhendler, "The Diaspora Factor in Israeli Life," in *Israeli Identity in Transition*, ed. Anita Shapira (Westport, CT: Praeger, 2004).

33. Daniel J. Elazar and Alysa M. Dortort, eds., *Understanding the Jewish Agency: A Handbook* (Jerusalem: Jerusalem Center for Public Affairs, 1984); Daniel J. Elazar, *Reinventing World Jewry: How to Design the World Jewish Polity* (Jerusalem: Jerusalem Center for Public Affairs, 1996); Charles Hoffman, *The Smoke Screen: Israel, Philanthropy, and American Jews* (Silver Spring, MD: Eshel Books, 1989); Eliezer David Jaffe, *Giving Wisely: The Israel Guide to Nonprofit and Volunteer Organizations* (Hewlett, NY: Gefen, 2000).

34. Arye Carmon, "Roundtable on Yossi Beilin's 'The Death of the American Uncle': Toward an Inclusive Definition of Jewishness: Remarks on Beilin's 'The Death of the American Uncle'," *Israel Studies* 5, no. 1 (2000): 355–360; Gabriel Sheffer, "The Israelis and the Jewish Diaspora," in *Jews in Israel: Contemporary Social and Cultural Patterns*, ed. Uri Rebhun and Chaim Isaac Waxman (Lebanon, NH: University Press of New England, 2004); Charles S. Liebman, *Pressure without Sanctions: The Influence of World Jewry on Israeli Policy* (Rutherford, NJ: Fairleigh Dickinson University Press, 1977).

35. Elazar, *Community and Polity*; Jonathan Woocher, *Sacred Survival: The Civil Religion of American Jews* (Bloomington: Indiana University Press, 1986); Melvin I. Urofsky, *We Are One! American Jewry and Israel* (Garden City, NY: Anchor Press, 1978).

36. Jerold S. Auerbach, "Are We One? Menachem Begin and the Long Shadow of 1977," in *Envisioning Israel: The Changing Ideals and Images of North American Jews*, ed. Allon Gal (Detroit: Wayne State University Press, 1996); Melvin I. Urofsky, *American Zionism from Herzl to the Holocaust* (Garden City, NY: Anchor Press / Doubleday, 1976), 89; Jack Wertheimer, "American Jews and Israel: A 60-Year Retrospective," *American Jewish Year Book* 108 (2008): 60; Gabriel Sheffer, *Diaspora Politics: At Home Abroad* (Cambridge: Cambridge University Press, 2003).

37. Israeli Central Bureau of Statistics, "Immigrants by Period of Immigration, Country of Birth and Last Country of Residence" (2018), https://www.cbs.gov.il/he/publications /doclib/2018/4.%20shnatonimmigration/st04_04.pdf.

38. Harry L. Lurie, *A Heritage Affirmed: The Jewish Federation Movement in America* (Philadelphia: Jewish Publication Society of America, 1961); Raphael, *History of the United Jewish Appeal*; Stock, *Partners and Pursestrings*; Elazar, *Community and Polity*; Bernstein, *To Dwell in Unity*.

39. Fleisch, "Israeli NGOs and American Jewish Donors."

40. Gottlieb Hammer, *Good Faith and Credit* (New York: Cornwall Books, 1985); Charles Hoffman, *The Smoke Screen: Israel, Philanthropy, and American Jews* (Silver Spring, MD: Eshel Books, 1989).

41. Steven M. Cohen, "Relationships of American Jews with Israel: What We Know and What We Need to Know," *Contemporary Jewry* 23 (2002): 132–155; Steven T. Rosenthal, *Irreconcilable Differences? The Waning of the American Jewish Love Affair with Israel* (Hanover, NH: University Press of New England, 2001).

42. Eric Fleisch and Theodore Sasson, *The New Philanthropy: American Jewish Giving to Israeli Organizations* (Waltham, MA: Brandeis University, Maurice and Marilyn Cohen Center for Modern Jewish Studies, April 2012).

43. Fleisch and Sasson, *New Philanthropy*.

44. Eric Fleisch and Theodore Sasson, "$2.4 Billion and Counting: The Burgeoning Field of American Jewish Philanthropy for Israel in 2020 and Beyond" (forthcoming). One might wonder whether the broadened heterogeneity in available charitable destinations demonstrably improved the philanthropic support received by some of the more marginalized populations within Israel—principally Palestinian-Israeli communities. While certain organizations like the New Israel Fund began raising $10 to $20 million each year for a portfolio of progressive causes—including pro-peace organizations, dialogue groups, and community empowerment work for some Palestinian communities, among other work—and federations eventually set up projects to specifically aid more neglected communities through their sister city/regions relationships, the vast, vast majority of funding coming into Israel still went to support mostly apolitical organizations and nonmarginalized populations. See Fleisch and Sasson, *New Philanthropy*.

45. Fleisch and Sasson, *New Philanthropy*.

46. Fleisch and Sasson, "$2.4 Billion and Counting."

47. Liebman, *Pressure without Sanctions*, 197.

48. A few important works have touched on aspects of these questions, but there has yet to be a thorough update to Liebman's analysis. See, for example, Lederhendler,

"Diaspora Factor in Israeli Life"; Oded Haklai, "Helping the Enemy? Why Transnational Jewish Philanthropic Foundations Donate to Palestinian NGOs in Israel," *Nations and Nationalism* 14, no. 3 (2008): 581–599; Michael N. Barnett, *The Star and the Stripes: A History of the Foreign Policies of American Jews* (Princeton, NJ: Princeton University Press, 2016).

## CHAPTER 1 — THE MECHANICS OF CHECKBOOK ZIONISM

1. Jacob Rader Marcus, "The American Colonial Jew: A Study in Acculturation," in *The American Jewish Experience*, ed. Jonathan D. Sarna (New York: Holmes & Meier, 1997), 11.

2. Jonathan D. Sarna, *American Judaism* (New Haven, CT: Yale University Press, 2004), 60.

3. Lila Corwin Berman, *The American Jewish Philanthropic Complex: The History of a Multibillion-Dollar Institution* (Princeton, NJ: Princeton University Press, 2020), 22.

4. The three biggest exceptions would seem to be B'nai B'rith (founded in 1843) and the Board of Delegates of American Israelites (founded in 1859). While B'nai B'rith was indeed the first large-scale national Jewish organization, it was more accurately a loose confederation of local fraternal lodges with local memberships and local agendas than it was a nationally oriented organization. The Board of Delegates of American Israelites, on the other hand, did work on international issues that were of common concern to American Jews. However, it remained a relatively small organization, attracting the attention and support of only a small portion of American Jews. The one most relevant to the forthcoming discussion was the North American Relief Society, an organization that sent funds to Jews living in the Holy Land. However, most of its revenue came from interest from the original bequest left by Judah Touro. As Baron and Baron noted, "It was rare for anyone to send a contribution [to the society] on his own initiative." Salo W. Baron and Jeannette M. Baron, "Palestinian Messengers in America, 1849–79: A Record of Four Journeys" (Part 3), *Jewish Social Studies* 5, no. 2 (July 1943): 225.

5. Gerald Sorin, *A Time for Building: The Third Migration, 1880–1920* (Baltimore: Johns Hopkins University Press, 1992), 7.

6. Harry L. Lurie, *A Heritage Affirmed: The Jewish Federation Movement in America* (Philadelphia: Jewish Publication Society of America, 1961), 26.

7. Lurie, *Heritage Affirmed*.

8. Lurie, *Heritage Affirmed*, 38.

9. This idea was simultaneously becoming apparent in wider non-Jewish circles in American cities. For a good description of the broader trend, see Robert H. Bremner, *American Philanthropy* (Chicago: University of Chicago Press, 1960), 124.

10. It should be noted that though the spread of federation was fairly slow among Jewish communities in the first decades of the twentieth century, it was still a faster pace than general American communities in their adoption of the federated community chest model (Lurie, *Heritage Affirmed*, 115–121; Bremner, *American Philanthropy*, 140–141).

11. Lurie, *Heritage Affirmed*, 41.

12. Jonathan S. Woocher, "Sacred Survival: American Jewry's Civil Religion," *Judaism* 34, no. 2 (1985): 155.

13. Daniel Soyer, *Jewish Immigrant Associations and American Identity in New York, 1880–1939* (Cambridge, MA: Harvard University Press, 1997).

14. In contemporary philanthropic parlance they would be known as HTOs (hometown organizations) and are a prevalent form of early diaspora philanthropy among immigrant communities worldwide. See Paula Doherty Johnson, *Diaspora Philanthropy: Influences, Initiatives, and Issues* (Cambridge, MA: The Philanthropic Initiative (TPI) and Global Equity Initiative of Harvard University, 2007).

15. Though from time to time there was interest among some diaspora community leaders in arranging a more regular and orderly system of *halukkah* collection, by and large giving was done in a haphazard fashion. Salo W. Baron and Jeannette M. Baron, "Palestinian Messengers in America, 1849–79: A Record of Four Journeys" (Part 1), *Jewish Social Studies* 5, no. 2 (April 1943): 115.

16. Walter Lehn and Uri Davis, *The Jewish National Fund* (London: Kegan Paul, 1988).

17. Urofsky notes the weaknesses of the FAZ: "[The FAZ had] dependent relations with affiliated societies. Individual Zionists belonged to different lodges, benevolent associations, and clubs rather than to the FAZ. Moreover, since the . . . [FAZ] had no real coercive power over the societies, it could only act through moral suasion." Melvin I. Urofsky, *American Zionism from Herzl to the Holocaust* (Garden City, NY: Anchor Press / Doubleday, 1976), 147.

18. More than in other diaspora Jewish communities the JNF was central in how American Jews supported Zionist efforts, as American Jewry had a far less developed Zionist movement than did the Jewish communities in Europe and Russia.

19. Urofsky, *American Zionism*, 99–100.

20. Mark I. Rosen, *Mission, Meaning, and Money: How the Joint Distribution Committee Became a Fundraising Innovator* (Bloomington, IN: iUniverse, 2010), 18.

21. Sarna, *American Judaism*, 208.

22. Bremner, *American Philanthropy*, 140–141.

23. Bremner, *American Philanthropy*, 140–141.

24. Rosen, *Mission, Meaning, and Money*, 5.

25. Federation was clearly an important trend in American philanthropy. Jewish communities seized upon it as the best model at a rate that surpassed the general trend line. Federated fundraising had grown from 14 Jewish communities in 1914 to 260 cities by 1941 (Lurie, *Heritage Affirmed*, 115–121). In a similar time frame, general, nonsectarian community chests were operating in 40 cities in 1919 and in 350 a decade later (Bremner, *American Philanthropy*, 140–141).

26. Derek Penslar, "Solidarity as an Emotion: American Jews and Israel in 1948," *Modern American History* 5 (2022): 27–51.

27. Urofsky, *American Zionism From Herzl to the Holocaust*, 142

28. Morton Mayer Berman, *The Bridge to Life: The Saga of Keren Hayesod, 1920–1970* (Tel Aviv: Shifrin and Na'aman, 1970), 12.

29. Ernest Stock, *Partners and Pursestrings: A History of the United Israel Appeal* (Lanham, MD: University Press of America, 1987), 11.

30. Stock, *Partners and Pursestrings*, 45, 53, 87.

31. Stock, *Partners and Pursestrings*, 45, 53, 87–88; "Joint Conference Agrees on Details of Combined $6,000,000 Campaign; $3,500,000 to J. D. C., $2,500,000," *Jewish Telegraphic Agency*, January 19, 1930.

32. For example, the UPA's proceeds plummeted from $2.2 million in the 1928 campaign to less than $600,000 in the 1929 campaign (Stock, *Partners and Pursestrings*, 53, 88). The JDC experienced a similar cascade.

33. Stock, *Partners and Pursestrings*, 83.

34. Marc Lee Raphael, *A History of the United Jewish Appeal, 1939–1982* (Chico, CA: Scholars Press, 1982), 5–10.

35. One additional organization, known as the National Refugee Service (NRS), was also a partner in the agreement. The NRS helped settle German Jewish refugees in the United States. Though it received a relatively small portion of the UJA budget (usually between $1 and $3 million per year), its draw on the scarce UJA resources intensified the already strained allocation conversations held between the JDC and UPA.

36. Data for these figures were gathered from various sources: Raphael, *History of the United Jewish Appeal*, 7–10; Stock, *Partners and Pursestrings*, 100–109; Samuel Halperin, "Ideology or Philanthropy? The Politics of Zionist Fund-Raising," *Western Political Quarterly* 13, no. 4 (December 1960): 962; "Committee Distributes $2,800,000 among JDC, UPA and NRS," *Jewish Telegraphic Agency*, October 26, 1941; "United Jewish Appeal Renewed for 1942 by JDC, UPA and NRS to Meet Wartime Needs," *Jewish Telegraphic Agency*, January 11, 1942; "J.D.C. Annual Report Published; Shows $7,257,000 Spent in 1942," *Jewish Telegraphic Agency*, February 23, 1943. Whereas JDC allocations roughly doubled UPA allocations in 1940 ($6.9 million to $3.5 million), by 1944 the UPA received only slightly less ($13.5 million to the JDC's $17.5 million), and by 1948 the UPA had overtaken the JDC in allocations ($85.3 million to $68.4 million). As we will see, this was to change even more dramatically in the years after.

37. Daniel J. Elazar, *Community and Polity: The Organizational Dynamics of American Jewry* (Philadelphia: Jewish Publications Society of America, 1976), 297.

38. Carmel Ullman Chiswick, "The Economics of American Judaism," *Shofar: An Interdisciplinary Journal of Jewish Studies* 13, no. 4 (1995): 1–19.

39. Raphael, *History of the United Jewish Appeal*, 136; Elazar, *Community and Polity*, 297.

40. Monty Noam Penkower, "American Jewry and the Holocaust: From Biltmore to the American Jewish Conference," *Jewish Social Studies* 47, no. 2 (Spring 1985).

41. This approximate division would remain for the next fifty years. Stock, *Partners and Pursestrings*, 152; Raphael, *History of the United Jewish Appeal*, 155; Rosen, *Mission, Meaning, and Money*, 120; Mitchell Bard, "American Jewish Contributions to Israel" (Jewish Virtual Library, 2016), https://www.jewishvirtuallibrary.org/american-jewish -contributions-to-israel.

42. Irving Bernstein, *Living UJA History: Irving Bernstein: An Oral History Anthology* (Jerusalem: Avraham Harman Institute of Contemporary Jewry, Hebrew University of Jerusalem, 1994–1995), 5.

43. Raphael, *History of the United Jewish Appeal*, 136. Elazar, *Community and Polity*, 297.

44. Philip Bernstein, *To Dwell in Unity: The Jewish Federation Movement in America, since 1960* (Philadelphia: Jewish Publication Society of America, 1983), 338; Bard, "American Jewish Contributions"; Raphael, *History of the United Jewish Appeal*, 136; Rosen, *Mission, Meaning, and Money*, 120.

45. Stock, *Partners and Pursestrings*, 123.

46. Stock, *Partners and Pursestrings*, 125.

47. Stock, *Partners and Pursestrings*, 125–126.

48. Raphael, *History of the United Jewish Appeal*, 23.

49. Jack Wertheimer, "Current Trends in American Jewish Philanthropy," *American Jewish Year Book* 97 (1997): 11–12.

50. Dan Lainer-Vos, "Masculinities in Interaction: The Coproduction of Israeli and American Jewish Men in Philanthropic Fund-Raising Events," *Men and Masculinities* 17, no. 1 (2014): 43–66.

51. Elazar, *Community and Polity*, 297.

52. Avraham Doron and Ralph M. Kramer, *The Welfare State in Israel: The Evolution of Social Security Policy and Practice* (Boulder, CO: Westview, 1991), 13.

53. Jewish Agency–American Section, *The Story of the Jewish Agency for Israel* (New York, 1964), 27.

54. The British Mandate administration proved uninterested in providing these services. The only social legislation the Mandate government provided was limited worker's compensation for those suffering from certain types of industrial injuries. Dan Horowitz and Moshe Lissak, *Origins of the Israeli Polity: Palestine under the Mandate* (Chicago: University of Chicago Press, 1978), 13.

55. Doron and Kramer, *Welfare State in Israel*, 13.

56. The JDC's principal social work in the Yishuv had been its hunger relief during World War I and orphan services in the war's immediate aftermath. Together, its support for these programs totaled roughly $4.1 million and much more worth of in-kind donations of food and supplies, given to Palestinian Jewry between 1914 and 1920. In the 1920s, the JDC continued to invest in work in Palestine, including some public health programs, but most of its work was instead dedicated to financing various economic development projects. American Jewish Joint Distribution Committee, "Our Story" (n.d.), http://www.archives.jdc.org. Erica Simmons, *Hadassah and the Zionist Project* (Lanham, MD: Rowman & Littlefield, 2006), 29–49.

57. Ilana Silber and Zeev Rosenhek, *The Historical Development of the Israeli Third Sector* (Beer Sheva: Ben-Gurion University of the Negev Press, 1999), 12.

58. *Reports of the Executive of the Jewish Agency for Palestine*, no. 10 (March 10, 1935), 22, Goldfarb Library, Brandeis University.

59. Berman, *Bridge to Life*, 111.

60. Eric Fleisch, "Israeli NGOs and American Jewish Donors: The Structures and Dynamics of Power Sharing in a New Philanthropic Era" (PhD diss., Brandeis University, 2014), 47.

61. Boris Bittker and George K. Rahdert, "The Exemption of Nonprofit Organizations from Federal Income Taxation," *Yale Law Journal* 85, no. 3 (January 1976); Harvey Dale, "Foreign Charities," *Tax Law Review* 48, no. 3 (1995): 655–704.

62. For a discussion on the connection between philanthropic giving and tax deductibility, see Charles T. Clotfelter, "The Economics of Giving," in *Giving Better, Giving Smarter: Working Papers of the National Commission on Philanthropy and Civic Renewal*, ed. John W. Barry and Bruno V. Manno (Washington, DC: National Commission on Philanthropy and Civic Renewal, 1997).

63. Ernest Stock, *Chosen Instrument: The Jewish Agency in the First Decade of the State of Israel* (New York: Herzl Press, 1988), 29.

64. Mike Lowy, *Thirty Years of Global Jewish Action: Resolutions of the Jewish Agency Assembly 1971–2001* (Jerusalem: Jewish Agency for Israel, 2002).

65. There were an astounding 445 nonprofit organizations operating in the Yishuv in 1933 (Simmons, *Hadassah and the Zionist Project*, 35–36).

66. Tamar Hermann, "New Challenges to New Authority: Israeli Grassroots Activism in the 1950s," in *Israel: The First Decade of Independence*, ed. S. Ilan Troen and Noah Lucas (Albany: State University Press of New York, 1995), 118.

67. Benjamin Gidron, Michal Bar, and Hagai Katz, *The Israeli Third Sector: Between Welfare State and Civil Society* (New York: Kluwer/Plenum, 2004), 6.

68. Hermann, "New Challenges to New Authority," 118.

69. Tamar Hermann, "The Sour Taste of Success: The Israeli Peace Movement, 1967–1998," in *Mobilizing for Peace: Conflict Resolution in Northern Ireland, Israel/Palestine, and South Africa*, ed. Benjamin Gidron, Stanley Nider Katz, and Yeheskel Hasenfeld (Oxford: Oxford University Press, 2002), 110.

70. Raphael, *History of the United Jewish Appeal*, 155; Rosen, *Mission, Meaning, and Money*, 120; Bard, "American Jewish Contributions".

71. Woocher, "Sacred Survival," 155–158; Francie Ostrower, *Why the Wealthy Give: The Culture of Elite Philanthropy* (Princeton, NJ: Princeton University Press, 1995), 45–59.

### CHAPTER 2 — THE CULTURE OF CHECKBOOK ZIONISM

1. Thank you to Brill Publishers and *Diaspora Studies* for allowing material in this chapter to be republished (Eric Fleisch, "Building a Culture of Deference: American Jewish Givers, Israelis, and Control over Donations to Israel, 1920–1989," *Diaspora Studies* 14, no. 2 (2021): 121–142).

2. Eliezer Schweid, "The Rejection of the Diaspora in Zionist Thought: Two Approaches," *Studies in Zionism* 5, no. 1 (1984): 43–70.

3. Melvin I. Urofsky, *We Are One! American Jewry and Israel* (Garden City, NY: Anchor, 1978), 255–277.

4. Eliezer Don-Yehiya, *Israel and Diaspora Jewry: Ideological and Political Perspectives* (Ramat Gan: Bar-Ilan University Press, 1991); Gabriel Sheffer, "The Israelis and the Jewish Diaspora," in *Jews in Israel: Contemporary Social and Cultural Patterns*, ed. Uri Rebhun and Chaim Isaac Waxman (Lebanon, NH: University Press of New England, 2004).

5. Simon Schama, *Two Rothschilds and the Land of Israel* (New York: Knopf, 1978), 67.

6. Schama, *Two Rothschilds*, 69–70.

7. Chaim Waxman, "American Jewish Identity and New Patterns of Philanthropy," in *The Call of the Homeland: Diaspora Nationalisms, Past and Present*, ed. Allon Gal, Athena S. Leoussi, and Anthony D. Smith (Leiden: Brill, 2010), 85.

8. Schama, *Two Rothschilds*, 22–23.

9. Walter Lehn and Uri Davis, *The Jewish National Fund* (London: Kegan Paul, 1988).

10. Charles Hoffman, *The Smoke Screen: Israel, Philanthropy, and American Jews* (Silver Spring, MD: Eshel Books, 1989), 124.

11. Ben Halpern, *A Clash of Heroes—Brandeis, Weizmann, and American Zionism* (New York: Oxford University Press, 1987).

12. Naomi W. Cohen, *American Jews and the Zionist Idea* (New York: Ktav, 1975); Mark A. Raider, *The Emergence of American Zionism* (New York: New York University Press, 1998).

13. Melvin I. Urofsky, *American Zionism from Herzl to the Holocaust* (Garden City, NY: Anchor/Doubleday, 1976).

14. Halpern, *Clash of Heroes*, 237.

15. Halpern, *Clash of Heroes*, 222.

16. Halpern, *Clash of Heroes*, 228.

17. Halpern, *Clash of Heroes*, 232.

18. Ernest Stock, *Partners and Pursestrings: A History of the United Israel Appeal* (Lanham, MD: University Press of America, 1987), 16.

19. Stock, *Partners and Pursestrings*.

20. Philip Goodman, *66 Years of Benevolence: The Story of PEF Israel Endowment Funds* (New York: PEF Israel Endowment Funds, 1989); Philip Bernstein, *To Dwell in Unity: The Jewish Federation Movement in America, since 1960* (Philadelphia: Jewish Publication Society of America, 1983); "American Jewish Contributions to Israel"; Marc Lee Raphael, *A History of the United Jewish Appeal, 1939–1982* (Chico, CA: Scholars Press, 1982), 136; Mark I. Rosen, *Responding to a World of Need: Fundraising at the American Jewish Joint Distribution Committee* (Bloomington, IN: iUniverse, 2009), 120.

21. Ofer Shiff, "Abba Hillel Silver and David Ben-Gurion: A Diaspora Leader Challenges the Revered Status of the 'Founding Father,'" *Studies in Ethnicity and Nationalism* 10, no. 3 (2010): 391–412.

22. Marc Lee Raphael, *Abba Hillel Silver: A Profile in American Judaism* (New York: Holmes & Meier, 1989), 173–174.

23. Stock, *Partners and Pursestrings*, 134.

24. Ernest Stock, *Chosen Instrument: The Jewish Agency in the First Decade of the State of Israel* (New York: Herzl Press, 1988), 40.

25. Stock, *Partners and Pursestrings*, 135–136.

26. Gottlieb Hammer, *Good Faith and Credit* (New York: Cornwall Books, 1985), 131–132; Emanuel Neumann, *In the Arena: An Autobiographical Memoir* (New York: Herzl Press, 1976), 270–287.

27. See chapter 1. This is evidenced by how the JDC dwarfed the performance of the UPA for so many years.

28. Hoffman, *Smoke Screen*, 154.

29. Future Israeli finance minister Eliezer Kaplan estimated, for example, that Morgenthau's participation in UJA fundraising, alone, would single-handedly boost campaign receipts by $20 million per year. Stock, *Partners and Pursestrings*, 138.

30. Stock, *Partners and Pursestrings*, 125.

31. Stock, *Chosen Instrument*, 42–44; Neumann, *In the Arena*, 277–289.

32. Arnold Gurin, "Impact of Israel on American Jewish Community Organization and Fund Raising," *Jewish Social Studies* 21 (1959): 46–59.

33. Zohar Segev, "American Zionists' Place in Israel after Statehood: From Involved Partners to Outside Supporters," *American Jewish History* 93 (September 2007): 277–302.

34. "Full Transcript of Proceedings for First Day of 'Conference on Multiple Campaigns' in Tel Aviv Israel," July 27, 1949, Isadore Hamlin Files, Z6-159, doc. no. 92, p. 4, Central Zionist Archives, Jerusalem, 10.

35. "Full Transcript of Proceedings."

36. "Full Transcript of Proceedings."

37. Committee on Control and Authorization of Campaigns, "Copy of Full-Page Ad Printed in the New York Times, Entitled 'For Contributors to Israel Philanthropy,'" November 17, 1949, Isadore Hamlin Files, Z6-159, doc. no. 38, Central Zionist Archives.

38. This refrain appeared in the text of the CCA's "Information Bulletin," published annually since 1966. Isadore Hamlin Files, Z6-159, doc. no. 127, Central Zionist Archives).

39. Dr. Nachum Goldman, "Letter to Rabbi Herbert S. Goldstein," March 15, 1950, Isa-dore Hamlin Files, Z6-413, doc. no. 37, Central Zionist Archives.

40. More broadly, there are examples of the CCA coordinating with the Israeli government and the Jewish Agency to actually have the Israeli bodies reduce their own allocations to organizations engaged in any "unauthorized" fundraising. In one instance, such a "corrective action" was taken when the American Friends of Hebrew University—an authorized campaign—overstepped the parameters of its CCA-permitted fundraising activities in the United States, and the Israeli Finance Ministry actually withheld funds allocated in its budget to Hebrew University. Herman L. Sainer, "Memo to Members of the National Committee on Control," August 24, 1977, Isadore Hamlin Files, Z6-241, doc. no. 11, Central Zionist Archives.

41. Isadore Hamlin, "Letter to Mordecai Danzis, President of Achdut Israel," June 20, 1949, Isadore Hamlin Files, Z6-158, doc. no. 8, Central Zionist Archives.

42. Isadore Hamlin, "Letter to Maximilian Moss, President of the Brooklyn Jewish Community Council and Dr. Arthur J.S. Rosenbaum, Executive Director of the Brook-lyn Jewish Community Council," June 27, 1949, Isadore Hamlin Files, Z6-158, doc. no. 19, Central Zionist Archives.

43. Isadore Hamlin, "Memorandum—Some Developments on Multiple Campaign Matters," July 1, 1949, sent to D. Nahum Goldman, Isadore Hamlin Files, Z6-158, doc. no. 14, Central Zionist Archives.

44. "Summary of Meeting—Committee on Control and Authorization of Campaigns," November 7, 1951, Isadore Hamlin Files, Z6-159, doc. no. 33, Central Zionist Archives.

45. Committee on Control and Authorization of Campaigns, "Minutes of Meeting The Committee on Control and Authorization of Campaigns," December 16, 1949, Isa-dore Hamlin Files, Z6-159, doc. no. 6, Central Zionist Archives.

46. Untitled and undated internal document, reviewing the work of the Committee on Control and Authorization of Campaigns, likely produced in late 1949, Isadore Hamlin Files, Z6-159, doc. no. 16, pp. 4–5, Central Zionist Archives.

47. United Jewish Appeal, "Minutes of Meeting with Representatives of Agudath Israel and Members of the UJA," November 2, 1949, Isadore Hamlin Files, Z6-180, doc. no. 27, Central Zionist Archives.

48. United Jewish Appeal, "Minutes of Meeting."

49. Stock, *Partners and Pursestrings*, 39.

50. Raphael, *History of the United Jewish Appeal*, 71.

51. Stock, *Chosen Instrument*, 237.

52. "First Israel Education Fund-UJA High School Is Dedicated in Israel," *JTA*, Sep-tember 15, 1965; "Racoosin High School to Be Established in Israel; Philanthropist Hon-ored," *JTA*, December 13, 1965; Stock, *Partners and Pursestrings*, 167–168.

53. Ilana Silber and Zeev Rosenhek, *The Historical Development of the Israeli Third Sector* (Beer Sheva: Ben-Gurion University of the Negev Press, 1999).

54. Jonathan Woocher, *Sacred Survival: The Civil Religion of American Jews* (Bloom-ington: Indiana University Press, 1986), 164; Raphael, *History of the United Jewish Appeal*, 69–70.

55. Stock, *Partners and Pursestrings*, 139.

56. Stanley Stone (Executive Vice President, Jewish Federation of Central New Jersey), interview, Scotch Plains, NJ, December 8, 2010.

57. Stock, *Partners and Pursestrings*, 167.

58. Irving Bernstein, *Living UJA History: Irving Bernstein: An Oral History Anthology* (Jerusalem: Avraham Harman Institute of Contemporary Jewry, Hebrew University of Jerusalem, 1994–1995), 36–48.

59. Stock, *Chosen Instrument*, chaps. 3–7.

60. Raphael, *History of the United Jewish Appeal*, 136, 141, 155; Rosen, *Responding to a World of Need*, 120; Bernstein, *To Dwell in Unity*, 338; "American Jewish Contributions to Israel."

61. Calculations based on U.S. Bureau of Labor Statistics' "CPI [Consumer Price Index] Calculator," https://www.bls.gov/data/inflation_calculator.htm.

62. S. P. Goldberg, "Jewish Communal Services: Programs and Finances," *American Jewish Year Book* (1978).

63. Goodman, *66 Years of Benevolence*; "American Jewish Contributions to Israel."

64. Raphael, *History of the United Jewish Appeal*, 73.

65. Menahem Kaufman, "The Case of the United Jewish Appeal," in *Envisioning Israel: The Changing Ideals and Images of North American Jews*, ed. Allon Gal (Detroit: Wayne State University Press, 1996), 224.

66. Raphael, *History of the United Jewish Appeal*, 136, 141, 155; Rosen, *Responding to a World of Need*, 120; Bernstein, *To Dwell in Unity*, 338; "American Jewish Contributions to Israel."

67. Hammer, *Good Faith and Credit*, 140.

68. The CJF was technically called the CJFWF at that time.

69. Hammer, *Good Faith and Credit*, 136.

70. Stock, *Partners and Pursestrings*, 167–182.

71. Charles S. Liebman, *Pressure without Sanctions: The Influence of World Jewry on Israeli Policy* (Rutherford, NJ: Fairleigh Dickinson University Press, 1977), 180.

### CHAPTER 3 — THE DECLINE OF CHECKBOOK ZIONISM

1. Mitchell Bard, "Total Immigration to Israel by Select Country by Year (1948–Present)" (Jewish Virtual Library, 2016), https://www.jewishvirtuallibrary.org /total-immigration-to-israel-by-country-per-year.

2. Melvin I. Urofsky, *We Are One!: American Jewry and Israel* (Garden City, NY: Anchor, 1978), 353–357.

3. Menaham Kaufman, "The Case of the United Jewish Appeal," in *Envisioning Israel: The Changing Ideals and Images of North American Jews*, ed. Allon Gal (Detroit: Wayne State University Press, 1996), 232.

4. Daniel J. Elazar, *Community and Polity: The Organizational Dynamics of American Jewry* (Philadelphia: Jewish Publications Society of America, 1976), 83.

5. Philip Bernstein, *To Dwell in Unity: The Jewish Federation Movement in America, since 1960* (Philadelphia: Jewish Publication Society of America, 1983); Ernest Stock, *Partners and Pursestrings: A History of the United Israel Appeal* (Lanham, MD: University Press of America, 1987); Marc Lee Raphael, *A History of the United Jewish Appeal, 1939–1982* (Chico, CA: Scholars Press, 1982); Morton Mayer Berman, *The Bridge to Life: The Saga of Keren Hayesod, 1920–1970* (Tel Aviv: Shifrin and Na'aman, 1970); Elazar, *Community and Polity*; Urofsky, *We Are One!*

6. See chapter 1.

7. Eric Fleisch and Theodore Sasson, *The New Philanthropy: American Jewish Giving to Israeli Organizations* (Waltham, MA: Brandeis University, Maurice and Marilyn Cohen Center for Modern Jewish Studies, April 2012).

8. Eric Fleisch and Theodore Sasson, "$2.4 Billion and Counting: The Burgeoning Field of American Jewish Philanthropy for Israel in 2020 and Beyond" (forthcoming).

9. Ernest Stock, *Beyond Partnership: The Jewish Agency and the Diaspora, 1959–1971* (New York: Herzl Press, 1992), 153–155.

10. Stock, *Beyond Partnership*, 152.

11. Ernest Stock, *Partners and Pursestrings*, 191. It should also be noted that the reconstitution of the Jewish Agency was also motivated by the Agency's desire to buttress its independence and strength against an Israeli state that had been increasingly marginalizing its role over the previous years.

12. The reconstitution agreement was similar to the Pact of Glory, the defunct power-sharing agreement reached in 1929 between the WZO and non-Zionist American Jewish Committee but never really enacted. Stock, *Partners and Pursestrings*, 32.

13. "Proposal Made to Change the Functions and Structure of the Jewish Agency Board and Executive," *Jewish Telegraphic Agency*, February 24, 1981.

14. "Proposal Made to Change the Functions."

15. Charles Hoffman, *The Smoke Screen: Israel, Philanthropy, and American Jews* (Silver Spring, MD: Eshel Books, 1989), 130.

16. Daniel J. Elazar and Alysa M. Dortort, eds., *Understanding the Jewish Agency: A Handbook* (Jerusalem: Jerusalem Center for Public Affairs, 1984), 2.

17. Daniel J. Elazar, *Reinventing World Jewry: How to Design the World Jewish Polity* (Jerusalem: Jerusalem Center for Public Affairs, 1996), 38.

18. Elazar and Dortort, *Understanding the Jewish Agency*, 74.

19. Hoffman, *Smoke Screen*, 140.

20. Elazar and Dortort, *Understanding the Jewish Agency*, 2.

21. Hoffman, *Smoke Screen*, 172.

22. "Diaspora Leaders Back Simcha Dinitz to Head WZO-Jewish Agency Executive," *Jewish Telegraphic Agency*, December 3, 1987.

23. Hoffman, *Smoke Screen*, 172.

24. "Jewish Agency Assembly Ends with Delegates Disappointed at Begin's Failure to Appear," *Jewish Telegraphic Agency*, June 27, 1983.

25. "Behind the Headlines: Is Fund-Raisers' Move Against Lewinsky Constructive or Anti-Democratic?," *Jewish Telegraphic Agency*, November 5, 1987.

26. "Diaspora Leaders Tap Meir Shitrit for WZO-Jewish Agency Treasurer," *Jewish Telegraphic Agency*, March 24, 1988.

27. "Diaspora Committee Endorses Burg as Jewish Agency Chairman," *Jewish Telegraphic Agency*, February 15, 1995.

28. Rabbi Daniel Allen (former Executive Vice Chairman and Assistant Executive Vice Chairman of the United Israel Appeal, 1988–2000), interview by phone, April 5, 2012.

29. "Diaspora Leaders Back Simcha Dinitz."

30. "Behind the Headlines"; "Diaspora Committee Endorses Burg."

31. "Jewish Agency, UJA Accord Renewed," *Jewish Telegraphic Agency*, November 13, 1985; "Jewish Agency Assembly Concludes with Strained Partnership Intact," *Jewish Telegraphic Agency*, July 12, 1994; Paul King, Orli Hacohen, Hillel Frisch, and Daniel J.

Elazar, *Project Renewal in Israel: Urban Revitalization through Partnership* (Jerusalem: Center for Public Affairs / Center for Jewish Community Studies Series, 1987).

32. Eliezer David Jaffe, "The Crisis in Jewish Philanthropy," *Tikkun* 2, no. 4 (September 1987).

33. Hoffman, *Smoke Screen*, 32.

34. Jaffe, "Crisis in Jewish Philanthropy."

35. "Behind the Headlines"; "Zionists, Fund-Raisers Agree on Reforming the Jewish Agency," *Jewish Telegraphic Agency*, November 8, 1993; "Jewish Agency Assembly Concludes"; "News Analysis: Move to Review Path of Funds to Israel Reflects New Thinking," *Jewish Telegraphic Agency*, October 1, 1997.

36. "Jewish Agency Assembly Concludes."

37. David Polish, "A Memoir," *American Jewish History* 78, no. 4 (June 1989): 463.

38. "Behind the Headlines."

39. Charles Hoffman, *Project Renewal: Community and Change in Israel* (Jerusalem: Halberstadt Communications, 1986); Paul King et al., *Project Renewal in Israel: Urban Revitalization through Partnership* (Lanham, MD: University Press of America, 1987); Frederick A. Lazin, *Politics and Policy Implementation: Project Renewal in Israel* (Albany: State University of New York Press, 1994); Raviv Schwartz, "Partnership 2000: A New Model for Diaspora-Israel Relations," *Jerusalem Letter/Viewpoints* 410 (July 15, 1999).

40. Eliezer Jaffe, "Ad Hoc Repairs on a Sleeping Giant," *Jerusalem Post*, June 21, 1989.

41. Polish, "Memoir," 471.

42. Fleisch and Sasson, *New Philanthropy*.

43. Uriel Heilman, "JFNA Flexing Muscles on Allocations; At GA, New Federation Plan for Overseas Seen as Blow to Jewish Agency," *Jewish Telegraphic Agency*, November 8, 2011.

44. Gila Noam (Director-Israel and Overseas, Jewish Community Federation of San Francisco), interview in Jerusalem, June 13, 2010.

45. It is worth noting that this also speaks to the concomitant maturation of the NGO sector in Israel—even if such a restive federation had existed a decade or two earlier, it would have found few viable giving alternatives to the Jewish Agency. By 1985, there were other choices. These developments will be explored in chapter 4.

46. Martin Karp (Senior Vice President and head of Israel office, Jewish Federation of Greater Los Angeles), interviews in Jerusalem, May 9 and July 27, 2010.

47. Yael Shapira (Federation Representative, Jewish Federation of Greater Atlanta and Jewish Federation of St. Louis), interview in Rosh Ha'ayin, June 24, 2010.

48. List obtained from Israel office, Jewish Federation of Greater Los Angeles.

49. Amir Shacham (Director, Israel Operations, United Jewish Communities of Metrowest New Jersey), interview in Jerusalem, June 29, 2010.

50. "Funding Israel Outside Established Channels Attacked by Zionist Assembly," *Jewish Telegraphic Agency*, January 13, 1987.

51. Mark I. Rosen, *Responding to a World of Need: Fundraising at the American Jewish Joint Distribution Committee* (Bloomington, IN: iUniverse, 2009), 60.

52. Anonymous (Executive, Jewish Federation of Greater Philadelphia), interview in Jerusalem, July 4, 2010.

53. Gila Noam (Director-Israel and Overseas, Jewish Community Federation of San Francisco), interview in Jerusalem, June 13, 2010.

54. Linda Epstein (Associate Vice President, Jewish United Fund / Jewish Federation of Metropolitan Chicago), interview in Jerusalem, May 30, 2010.

55. See Steven F. Windmueller and Gerald B. Bubis, *Predictability to Chaos? How Jewish Leaders Re-invented Their National Communal System* (Baltimore: Center for Jewish Communal Studies, 2005).

56. MeLena Hessel, "The Life of ONAD: Its Origins, Operation, and Demise" (Waltham, MA: Brandeis University, Cohen Center for Modern Jewish Studies, 2007).

57. Rebecca Caspi (JFNA Senior Vice President for Israel and Overseas), interview in Jerusalem, July 27, 2010.

58. Hessel, "Life of ONAD," 2.

59. Hessel, "Life of ONAD."

60. Rachel Pomerance, "Few Cry over Federation System's Funding Change," *Jewish Telegraphic Agency*, March 21, 2006.

61. Heilman, "JFNA Flexing Muscles."

62. Caspi interview.

63. Shacham interview.

64. Rosen, in *Responding to a World of Need*, chronicles how the JDC identified this as a problem issue for its organizational health and has spent the better part of the last fifteen years revamping its fundraising operation to reduce its dependence on core funding from the JFNA.

65. Caspi interview.

66. Jewish Federations of North America—Israel Office, "Fact Sheet: Israel Emergency Campaign II: Enduring Impact Three Years Later" (January 4, 2010).

67. Elazar, *Community and Polity*, 341–377.

68. Offer Isseroff (Director of the Division of Priority Regions, Jewish Agency), interview in Jerusalem, July 11, 2010.

69. Roger Colinvaux, "Donor Advised Funds: Charitable Spending Vehicles for 21st Century Philanthropy," *Washington Law Review* 92 (2017): 39.

70. Eliezer Jaffe, "The 30th Zionist Circus," *Jerusalem Post*, December 20, 1982.

71. Francie Ostrower, *Why the Wealthy Give: The Culture of Elite Philanthropy* (Princeton, NJ: Princeton University Press, 1995), 8–10, 53–63; Eliezer David Jaffe, *Giving Wisely: The Israel Guide to Nonprofit and Volunteer Organizations* (Jerusalem: Gefen, 2000), 22.

72. To be discussed in chapter 4.

73. See, for example, Susan A. Ostrander, "The Growth of Donor Control: Revisiting the Social Relations of Philanthropy," *Nonprofit and Voluntary Sector Quarterly* 36, no. 2 (June 2007): 357–372; Beth Breeze, "How Donors Choose Charities: The Role of Personal Taste and Experiences in Giving Decisions," *Voluntary Sector Review* 4, no. 2 (2013): 165–183; Elizabeth T. Boris and Teresa Jean Odendahl, *America's Wealthy and the Future of Foundations* (New York: Yale University Institution for Social and Policy Studies Program for Non-Profit Organizations Foundation Center, 1987). Boris and Odendahl noted that more than half of the interview subjects in their study on giving behavior indicated "control" as their chief motive for how they chose their charitable destinations (258).

74. Helmut K. Anheier and Diana Leat, *Creative Philanthropy: Toward a New Philanthropy for the Twenty-First Century* (London: Routledge, 2006).

75. Paula Doherty Johnson, Stephen P. Johnson, and Andrew Kingman, *Promoting Philanthropy: Global Challenges and Approaches* (Gutersloh, Germany: International Network for Strategic Philanthropy (INSP), 2004).

76. Peter Frumkin, "Inside Venture Philanthropy," *Society* 40, no. 4 (2003): 7–15; Felicia Herman, "Funding Innovation," *Journal of Jewish Communal Service* 84, no. 1/2 (2009).

77. Dvora Blum, "The Ambivalent Emergence of Philanthropy in Israel," *Journal of Jewish Communal Service* 84, no. 1/2 (2009).

78. Brian Duncan, "A Theory of Impact Philanthropy," *Journal of Public Economics* 88, no. 9–10 (2004): 2159–2180.

79. Emily Barman, "With Strings Attached: Nonprofits and the Adoption of Donor Choice," *Nonprofit and Voluntary Sector Quarterly* 37, no. 1 (2008): 39–56.

80. Ostrower, *Why the Wealthy Give.*

81. See, for example, Matthew Berkman, "Coercive Consensus: Jewish Federations, Ethnic Representation, and the Roots of American Pro-Israel Politics" (PhD diss., University of Pennsylvania, 2018), 335–345.

82. Abby Santicola, "All for One," *NonProfit PRO*, October 1, 2009.

83. Fleisch and Sasson, *New Philanthropy.*

84. Veteran Israeli-based American fundraiser requesting anonymity, interview in Jerusalem, July 12, 2010.

85. "Jewish Agency Assembly Concludes."

86. Mitchell Bard, "American Jewish Contributions to Israel" (Jewish Virtual Library, 2016), https://www.jewishvirtuallibrary.org/american-jewish-contributions -to-israel. Though raw numbers indicate tiny increases, relative to inflation, donations to Israel via the federation system have decreased significantly over time.

87. Fleisch and Sasson, "$2.4 Billion and Counting."

88. Jack Wertheimer, *Giving Jewish: How Big Funders Have Transformed American Jewish Philanthropy* (New York: AVI CHAI Foundation, March 2018).

CHAPTER 4 — AN INTRODUCTION TO THE STUDY OF CONTEMPORARY
RELATIONSHIP DYNAMICS

1. Eric Fleisch and Theodore Sasson, "$2.4 Billion and Counting: The Burgeoning Field of American Jewish Philanthropy for Israel in 2020 and Beyond" (forthcoming).

2. Tamar Hermann, "New Challenges to New Authority: Israeli Grassroots Activism in the 1950s," in *Israel: The First Decade of Independence*, ed. S. Ilan Troen and Noah Lucas (Albany: State University Press of New York, 1995), 118.

3. Avraham Doron and Ralph M. Kramer, *The Welfare State in Israel: The Evolution of Social Security Policy and Practice* (Boulder, CO: Westview, 1991), 23.

4. Hermann, "New Challenges to New Authority."

5. Benjamin Gidron, Michal Bar, and Hagai Katz, *The Israeli Third Sector: Between Welfare State and Civil Society* (New York: Kluwer /Plenum, 2004), 102.

6. Sam N. Lehman-Wilzig, *Stiff-Necked People, Bottle-Necked System: The Evolution and Roots of Israeli Public Protest, 1949–1986* (Bloomington: Indiana University Press, 1990), 27–40.

7. Sam N. Lehman-Wilzig, *Wildfire: Grassroots Revolts in Israel in the Post-Socialist Era* (Albany: State University of New York Press, 1992), 174; Benjamin Gidron, Hagai

Katz, and Michal Bar, *The Israeli Third Sector 2000: Roles of the Sector* (Beersheba: Israeli Center for Third sector Research, Ben-Gurion University, 2000), 56.

8. Jennifer Oser, "Between Atomistic and Participatory Democracy," *Nonprofit and Voluntary Sector Quarterly* 39, no. 3 (2010): 431; Ilana Silber and Zeev Rosenhek, *The Historical Development of the Israeli Third Sector* (Beer Sheva: Ben-Gurion University of the Negev Press, 1999), 39-40.

9. Ḥagai Katz, Benjamin Gidron, and Esther Levinson, *Philanthropy in Israel, 2006: Patterns of Giving and Volunteering of the Israeli Pubic* (Beersheba: Israeli Center for Third Sector Research, Ben-Gurion University, 2007).

10. Gidron, Bar, and Katz, *Israeli Third Sector*, 103.

11. Gidron, Katz, and Bar, *Israeli Third Sector 2000*, 48-49.

12. Samuel Shye, Alon Lazar, Rivka Duchin, and Benjamin Gidron, *Philanthropy in Israel: Patterns of Giving and Volunteering of the Israeli Public* (Beersheba: Israel Center for Third Sector Research, 2000), 6; Trading Economics, "Israeli Shekel," http://www.tradingeconomics.com/israel/currency; Israeli Central Bureau of Statistics, "The Israeli Population" (1997), http://www.cbs.gov.il/statistical/populationeng.htm.

13. Ann E. Kaplan, ed., *Giving USA 1998: The Annual Report on Philanthropy for the Year 1997*, 43rd Annual Issue (New York: American Association of Fund-Raising Counsel (AAFRC) Trust for Philanthropy, 1998), 22; U.S. Census Bureau, Population Division, Population Estimates Program, "Historical National Population Estimates: July 1, 1900, to July 1, 1999" (June 2000), http://www.census.gov/population/estimates/nation/popclockest.txt.

14. Index Mundi, "United States—GDP per Capita," http://www.indexmundi.com/facts/united-states/gdp-per-capita.

15. Index Mundi, "Israel—GDP per Capita," http://www.indexmundi.com/israel/gdp_per_capita.

16. Fleisch and Sasson, "$2.4 Billion and Counting."

17. Fleisch and Sasson, "$2.4 Billion and Counting."

18. Nina J. Crimm, "High Alert: The Government's War on the Financing of Terrorism and Its Implications for Donors, Domestic Charities, and Global Philanthropy," *William & Mary Law Review* 45, no. 3/4 (2004).

19. Though the literature on this issue admits that there is uncertainty about the exact degree to which tax deductibility affects giving, Clotfelter notes that there is "near universal consensus" in the scholarly community that tax deductibility "has a significant effect" on individuals' giving choices. Charles T. Clotfelter, "The Economics of Giving," in *Giving Better, Giving Smarter: Working Papers of the National Commission on Philanthropy and Civic Renewal*, ed. John W. Barry and Bruno V. Manno (Washington, DC: National Commission on Philanthropy and Civic Renewal, 1997). In Boris and Odendahl's study of wealthy donors, the authors interviewed 135 donors. Of them, they noted that "fewer than ten people told us that tax considerations were not important to them, and perhaps another ten said they only have moderate influence." Elizabeth T. Boris and Teresa Jean Odendahl, *America's Wealthy and the Future of Foundations* (New York: Yale University Institution for Social and Policy Studies Program for Non-Profit Organizations Foundation Center, 1987), 231.

20. Ernest Stock, *Partners and Pursestrings: A History of the United Israel Appeal* (Lanham, MD: University Press of America, 1987), 128.

21. Paul Arnsberger, Melissa Ludlum, Margaret Riley, and Mark Stanton, "A History of the Tax-Exempt Sector: An SOI Perspective," *Statistics of Income Bulletin*, Winter 2008, 105–135.

22. Harvey Dale, "Foreign Charities," *Tax Law Review* 48, no. 3 (1995): 655–704.

23. Dale, "Foreign Charities."

24. Internal Revenue Service, Revenue Ruling 73–440, 1973.

25. Boris Bittker and George K. Rahdert, "The Exemption of Nonprofit Organizations from Federal Income Taxation," *Yale Law Journal* 85, no. 3 (January 1976).

26. See Supreme Court of the United States, Certiorari to the United States Court of Appeals for the Fourth Circuit, 461 U.S. 574, *Bob Jones University v. United States*, no. 81–3 Argued: October 12, 1982, Decided: May 24, 1983. For a good discussion of the case, see Harvey J. Dale, "Public Policy Limits on Tax Benefits: 'Bob Jones' Revisited," *Tax Forum* 459 (1990).

27. Fritz F. Heimann, ed., *The Future of Foundations* (Englewood Cliffs, NJ: Prentice Hall, 1973), 82.

28. Two instances in which this issue was raised in the context of American support for Israeli NGOs doing work in West Bank settlements are as follows: Israeli peace group Gush Shalom taking legal steps in 2009 to challenge the legitimacy the tax-exempt status of NGOs supporting work in settlements (E. B. Solomont, "Gush Shalom Seeks to Hinder Settlers' U.S. Fundraising," *Jerusalem Post*, October 21, 2009). And in 2010 the *New York Times* ran a front-page lead story criticizing settlement support organizations, also implying that their legality should be examined (Jim Rutenberg, Mike McIntire, and Ethan Bronner, "Tax-Exempt Funds Aid Settlements in West Bank," *New York Times*, July 5, 2010, sec. 1, A1).

29. Roy G. Blakey and Gladys C. Blakey, "The Revenue Act of 1938," *American Economic Review* 28, no. 3 (1938): 447–458.

30. Dale, "Foreign Charities," 6–10.

31. Internal Revenue Service, Revenue Ruling 63–252, 1963.

32. Internal Revenue Service, Revenue Ruling 63–252.

33. U.S. Treasury Department Regulation 53.4942–3(a)(6)(i), 53.4945–5(a)(5).

34. Dale, "Foreign Charities"; Nina J. Crimm, "Through a Post–September 11 Looking Glass: Assessing the Roles of Federal Tax Laws and Tax Policies Applicable to Global Philanthropy by Private Foundations and Their Donors," *Virginia Tax Review* 23, no. 1 (2003): 55–67.

35. Bittker and Rahdert.

36. Foreign equivalency is defined in Internal Revenue Code sec. 4945 (pt. d4). See Dale, "Foreign Charities" and Crimm, "Through a Post–September 11 Looking Glass."

37. Fleisch and Sasson, "$2.4 Billion and Counting."

38. Eric Fleisch and Theodore Sasson, *The New Philanthropy: American Jewish Giving to Israeli Organizations* (Waltham, MA: Brandeis University, Maurice and Marilyn Cohen Center for Modern Jewish Studies, April 2012).

39. Stephen G. Greene, "Making Friends in America," *Chronicle of Philanthropy*, June 13, 1996, 1, 29–31; David M. Roth, "American Friends" Organizations of Israeli Nonprofits: An Exploration of Challenges and Opportunities (master's thesis, Regis University, 2005).

40. Eric Fleisch and Theodore Sasson, "$2.4 Billion and Counting."

41. Greene, "Making Friends in America"; Rutenberg, McIntire, and Bronner, "Tax-Exempt Funds."

42. Internal Revenue Service 1983 EO CPE (Exempt Organizations Continuing Professional Education), "Text O," 6.

43. Samuel B. Finkel, "American Jews and the Hebrew University," *American Jewish Year Book* 39 (1937–1938): 193–201.

44. Philip Goodman, *66 Years of Benevolence: The Story of PEF Israel Endowment Funds* (New York: PEF Israel Endowment Funds, 1989).

45. Mitchell Bard, "American Jewish Contributions to Israel" (Jewish Virtual Library, 2016), https://www.jewishvirtuallibrary.org/american-jewish-contributions-to-israel; Goodman, *66 Years of Benevolence*.

46. Information obtained from IRS form 990 documents PEF—Israel Endowment Funds Inc., (tax years 2010–2017); 990 forms were available via Economic Research Institute (https://www.erieri.com). PEF—Israel Endowment Funds Inc., 2017 Annual Report.

47. Information obtained from IRS form 990 documents Central Fund of Israel (tax years 1991–2017); 990 forms were available via Economic Research Institute (https://www.erieri.com).

48. Eric Fleisch, "Israeli NGOs and American Jewish Donors: The Structures and Dynamics of Power Sharing in a New Philanthropic Era" (PhD diss., Brandeis University, 2014), 125.

49. New Israel Fund, 1982 Annual Report.

50. Information obtained from IRS form 990 documents New Israel Fund (tax years 2010–2017); 990 forms were available via Economic Research Institute (https://www.erieri.com).

51. Fritz F. Heimann, ed., *The Future of Foundations* (Englewood Cliffs, NJ: Prentice Hall, 1973).

52. Jack Wertheimer, "Giving Jewish: How Big Funders Have Transformed American Jewish Philanthropy" (New York: AVI CHAI Foundation, 2018).

53. Stefan Toepler, "Foundation Roles and Visions in the U.S.," in *The Politics of Foundations: A Comparative Analysis*, ed. Helmut K. Anheier and Siobhan Daly (London: Routledge, 2007).

54. Gary A. Tobin, *Mega-Gifts in American Philanthropy: General & Jewish Giving Patterns between 1995–2000* (San Francisco: Institute for Jewish & Community Research, 2003).

55. Fleisch and Sasson, *New Philanthropy*.

56. Hanna Shaul Bar Nissim and Matthew A. Brookner, "Ethno-Religious Philanthropy: Lessons from a Study of United States Jewish Philanthropy," *Contemporary Jewry* 39, no. 1 (2019): 31–51.

57. "Yesha" is a Hebrew acronym for Judea, Samaria, and Gaza. Even though Israel removed its settlements from Gaza in 2005, the "Yesha" acronym is still used.

58. Israel annexed East Jerusalem officially in 1980 but de facto in 1967–1968, while it never annexed the West Bank.

59. Shlomo Gazit, "Yes Mr. Lieberman, I'm a Proud Jewish Terrorist," *Haaretz*, July 19, 2011.

60. Ezra HaLevi and Josh Shamsi, "Heroism and Miracles in Gush Etzion," *Arutz Sheva*, February 6, 2008.

61. Magnus Norell, *A Dissenting Democracy: The Israeli Movement "Peace Now"* (London: Frank Cass, 2002).

62. Eyal Hareuveni, Yael Stern, and Zvi Shulman (B'Tselem), *By Hook and by Crook: Israeli Settlement Policy in the West Bank* (Jerusalem: B'Tselem, July 2010).

63. Nadia Matar (Co-Founder and Co-Chair, Women in Green), interview in Alon Shvut, West Bank, August 11, 2011.

64. Ezra HaLevi, "Protests Pay Off, East Gush Etzion-Jerusalem Road to Open Friday," *Arutz Sheva*, August 30, 2007; Hillel Fendel, "Keeping a Former IDF Base Jewish," *Arutz Sheva*, December 2, 2010.

65. Nathan Jeffay, "Rabbi David Forman, 65, Leading Human Rights Activist in Israel," *Jewish Daily Forward*, May 21, 2010.

66. Yehiel Grenniman (Rabbis for Human Rights), "9 October 2009 Entry," *Harvest Journal Blog*, www.rhr.org.il/page.php?name=human_rights_in_the_occupied_territories&id=15&language=en.

67. HCJ 9593/04 Morar v. IDF Commander in Judaea and Samaria 87—Rashed Morar, Head of Yanun Village Council and Others v. 1. IDF Commander in Judaea and Samaria 2. Samaria and Judaea District Commander, Israel Police.

68. *Israel Law Reports* (Jerusalem: Nevo Press, 2006), 77–83.

69. Grenniman, "9 October 2009 Entry."

70. Ari Briggs, "Illegal Arab Building Defies Supreme Court Ruling," *Jerusalem Post*, August 27, 2014.

71. Yonah Jeremy Bob, "Settlers Put the Heat on Palestinian Charcoal Makers," *Jerusalem Post*, November 6, 2012.

72. See, for example, Eldad Beck, "France Honors Anti-Israel Watchdog Groups, Sparks Backlash," *Cleveland Jewish News*, December 6, 2018.

73. See, for example, B'Tselem, "A Regime of Jewish Supremacy from the Jordan River to the Mediterranean Sea: This Is Apartheid" (January 12, 2021), www.btselem.org/publications/fulltext/202101_this_is_apartheid.

74. Jerold S. Auerbach, *Hebron Jews: Memory and Conflict in the Land of Israel* (Lanham, MD: Rowman & Littlefield, 2009), 65–79.

75. See, for example, "Husbands Join Wives in Hebron," *Jewish Telegraphic Agency*, July 2, 1979.

76. Elad Benari, "Beit Hamachpela to Be Evicted by April 26," *Arutz Sheva*, April 4, 2012; Tovah Lazaroff, Herb Keinon, and Joanna Paraszcz, "Border Police Evacuate Settlers from Hebron Home," *Jerusalem Post*, April 4, 2012.

77. David Wilder, "Rooting for a Roof," *Hebron Now & Forever*, Spring 2011, 5.

78. Fleisch, "Israeli NGOs and American Jewish Donors," 170–171.

79. See, for example, "Ben Eliezer: Ariel, Gush Etzion, and Alfe Menashe Not on the Agenda in Talks," *Jerusalem Post*, February 19, 2008.

80. Ir Amim, "Evictions and Settlement Plans in Sheikh Jarrah: The Case of Shimon Ha-Tazadik" (Fact sheet, May 19, 2009).

81. Nir Hasson and Gili Cohen, "Arab Families in Sheikh Jarrah Won't Be Evicted by Settlers, Israeli Court Rules," *Ha'aretz*, July 28, 2011.

82. Melanie Lidman, "East Jerusalem Activist Organization to Arrange Weekly Protests," *Jerusalem Post*, February 24, 2011.

83. Meron Rapoport, *Shady Dealings in Silwan* (Jerusalem: Ir Amim, 2009), 9.

84. El'ad's own website includes the following description: "The city was in such a state of disrepair and neglect that the former excavations that had been conducted in the area were once again concealed beneath garbage and waste" ("Ir David Foundation," http://www.cityofdavid.org.il/en/The-Ir-David-Foundation).

85. Khaled Abu Toameh, "PA: Death Penalty for Those Who Sell Land to Jews," *Jerusalem Post*, April 1, 2009.

86. The Ir David Foundation, "Discovering the City of David" (presentation, St. John's Wood Synagogue, London, November 18, 2009).

87. Katharina Galor, *Finding Jerusalem: Archaeology between Science and Ideology* (Berkeley: University of California Press, 2017), 119–131.

88. Chris Mitchell, "Scripture Comes Alive in the City of David," *CBN News*, May 22, 2008.

89. Nir Hasson, "Israel Approves New East Jerusalem Visitors' Compound, Razes Palestinian Community Center," *Haaretz*, February 13, 2012.

90. This phenomenon is widely documented by an Israeli NGO called NGO Monitor (http://www.ngo-monitor.org).

91. The most known example of this among the organizations in this case study is the Ariel Development Fund, which has intentionally cultivated support from Evangelical Christians for decades. See Göran Gunner and Robert O. Smith, eds., *Comprehending Christian Zionism: Perspectives in Comparison* (Minneapolis: Augsburg Fortress, 2014), 27; "Evangelist Hagee Pledges $6 Million to Israel," Associated Press, April 6, 2008; "Israeli Youth Center Combines Faith, Fun," *Christian Broadcasting Network*, July 16, 2010; Major Avner Mutsafy, Samaria Regional Commander, Firefighting Services of Judea, Samaria and the Jordan Valley, to Faith Bible Chapel, Arvada, Colorado, December 19, 2010, letter available at http://www.friendsofariel.org/articlenav.php?id=164.

92. See, for example, Rutenberg, McIntire, and Bronner, "Tax-Exempt Funds"; Meron Rapoport, *Shady Dealings in Silwan* (Jerusalem: Ir Amim. 2009); Edwin Black, "Funding Hate [Part 3] Transparency a Concern as Millions Go to Mideast," *Jewish Telegraphic Agency*, October 16, 2003; David Ignatius, "How a U.S. Tax Deduction Aids Israeli Settlements," *Washington Post*, March 26, 2009; Ronen Shoval, "Strategic Investment in Israel's New War," *Jewish Ideas Daily*, October 10, 2012.

93. Uri Blau, "U.S. Group Invests Tax-Free Millions in East Jerusalem Land," *Haaretz*, August 17, 2009.

94. Janet Aviad (Co-Founder and longtime leader, Peace Now), interview in her office in Jerusalem, June 1, 2010.

95. www.guidestar.org.il (מחדשי הישוב היהודי בחברון) (*M'hadashei Ha-Yishuv Ha-Yehudi B'Hevron*) ["The Rebuilders of the Jewish Community in Hebron"]).

96. www .guidestar .org .il (מ"בע הדמוקרטיה להגנת הקרן ["Sheikh Jarrah Solidarity"]); (האדסרב זכויות למען נים משפט שומרי ["Rabbis for Human Rights"]).

97. Risa Zoll (International Relations Director, B'Tselem), interview in her office in Jerusalem, May 27, 2010.

98. www.guidestar.org.il (עיר עמים) ["Ir Amim"].

99. Information obtained from IRS form 990 documents for Friends of Ir David (tax years 2002–2011); 990 forms were available via guidestar.org.

CHAPTER 5 — PROSPECTS FOR A NEW ERA OF PARTNERSHIP?

1. Charles S. Liebman, *Pressure without Sanctions: The Influence of World Jewry on Israeli Policy* (Rutherford, NJ: Fairleigh Dickinson University Press, 1977); Arye Carmon, "Toward an Inclusive Definition of Jewishness: Remarks on Beilin's 'The Death of the American Uncle,'" *Israel Studies* 5, no. 1 (2000): 355–360; Eliezer Don-Yehiya, *Israel and Diaspora Jewry: Ideological and Political Perspectives* (Ramat Gan: Bar-Ilan University Press, 1991); Gabriel Sheffer, "The Israelis and the Jewish Diaspora," in *Jews in Israel: Contemporary Social and Cultural Patterns*, ed. Uri Rebhun and Chaim Isaac Waxman (Lebanon, NH: University Press of New England, 2004).

2. Eric Fleisch and Theodore Sasson, *The New Philanthropy: American Jewish Giving to Israeli Organizations* (Waltham, MA: Brandeis University, Maurice and Marilyn Cohen Center for Modern Jewish Studies, April 2012).

3. See, for example, Lehn M. Benjamin, "Funders as Principals: Performance Measurement in Philanthropic Relationships" *Nonprofit Management and Leadership* 20, no. 4 (Summer 2010); Susan A. Ostrander, "The Growth of Donor Control: Revisiting the Social Relations of Philanthropy," *Nonprofit and Voluntary Sector Quarterly* 36, no. 2 (June 2007): 357–372; Eliezer David Jaffe, *Giving Wisely: The Israel Guide to Nonprofit and Volunteer Organizations* (Jerusalem: Gefen, 2000), 22.

4. Eric Fleisch, "Israeli NGOs and American Jewish Donors: The Structures and Dynamics of Power Sharing in a New Philanthropic Era" (PhD diss., Brandeis University, 2014), 290–294.

5. Anonymous (Executive, Midot), interview in Tel Aviv, July 27, 2010.

6. Gerald Steinberg (President and Founder, NGO Monitor), interview in Jerusalem, July 19, 2010.

7. "The State of Israel as a Jewish State," https://knesset.gov.il/constitution /ConstMJewishState.htm.

CHAPTER 6 — POWER SHARING IN THE TWENTY-FIRST CENTURY
IN DIRECT GIVING ARRANGEMENTS

1. See, for example, Sally Reith, "Money, Power, and Donor–NGO Partnerships," *Development in Practice* 20, no. 3 (2007): 446–455; Catherine Agg, "Winners or Losers? NGOs in the Current Aid Paradigm," *Development* 49, no. 2 (2006): 15–21; Joseph J. Cordes, Jeffrey R. Henig, Eric C. Twombly, and Jennifer L. Saunders, "The Effects of Expanded Donor Choice in United Way Campaigns on Nonprofit Human Service Providers in the Washington, DC, Metropolitan Area," *Nonprofit and Voluntary Sector Quarterly* 28, no. 2 (1999): 127–151.

2. Susan A. Ostrander, "The Growth of Donor Control: Revisiting the Social Relations of Philanthropy," *Nonprofit and Voluntary Sector Quarterly* 36, no. 2 (June 2007): 358.

3. Eric Fleisch and Theodore Sasson, "$2.4 Billion and Counting: The Burgeoning Field of American Jewish Philanthropy for Israel in 2020 and Beyond" (forthcoming).

4. Boris Bittker and George K. Rahdert, "The Exemption of Nonprofit Organizations from Federal Income Taxation," *Yale Law Journal* 85, no. 3 (January 1976).

5. Charles S. Liebman, *Pressure without Sanctions: The Influence of World Jewry on Israeli Policy* (Rutherford, NJ: Fairleigh Dickinson University Press, 1977), 197.

6. The analysis of the power-sharing relationships in this chapter and the next is based on the sixteen Israeli case study NGOs introduced in chapter 4. All sixteen make use of some form of direct giving. Roughly ten participate in both direct giving and new federated giving. The information discussed is based on a variety of sources but prominently through interviews with stakeholders involved in each of the organizations. For each, that includes Israelis, Americans, donors, professionals, and advocates, past and present. All perspectives presented were corroborated by multiple parties. The individuals participating in the study are not identified by name, but the organizations they are associated with are. All interviews were conducted from 2010 to 2013.

7. Fleisch and Sasson, "$2.4 Billion and Counting."

8. Fleisch and Sasson, "$2.4 Billion and Counting."

9. Gary A. Tobin, Jeffrey R. Solomon, and Alexander C. Karp, *Mega-Gifts in American Philanthropy: General and Jewish Giving Patterns between 1995–2000* (San Francisco: Institute for Jewish & Community Research, 2003); Jack Wertheimer, "Giving Jewish: How Big Funders Have Transformed American Jewish Philanthropy" (New York: AVI CHAI Foundation, 2018).

10. Eric Fleisch, "Green Lines, Red Lines, and Company Lines: The United Israel Appeal and the Complex History of American Jewish Giving over the Green Line," *Israel Studies* 25, no. 1 (2020): 198–221.

11. Ron Nachman (Mayor of Ariel / Board Member of American Friends of Ariel), interview in his office in Ariel, Israel, August 7, 2011.

12. Nachman interview.

13. "Rabbi Arik Ascherman, President of Rabbis for Human Rights, Will Speak in Bedford," *Bedford [MA] Citizen*, March 24, 2014. https://thebedfordcitizen.org/2014 /03/rabbi-arik-ascherman-president-of-rabbis-for-human-rights-will-speak-in -bedford.

14. "Lecture Tour," *Women in Green*, February 25, 2009, http://blog.womeningreen.org /?p=225.

15. Americans for Peace Now, "APN's 2nd Annual 'Professor Gerald B. Bubis Lecture' Event" (n.d.), http://peacenow.org/bubis-lecture-event-featuring-hagit-ofran.html.

16. Elaine Durbach, "A Settlers' 'Guardian' Seeks Support in America," *New Jersey Jewish News*, April 15, 2010.

17. Peter Shaw-Smith, "The Israeli Settler Movement Post-Oslo," *Journal of Palestine Studies* 23, no. 3 (1994): 105–106.

18. Adrian Sargeant, John B. Ford, and Jane Hudson. "Charity Brand Personality: The Relationship with Giving Behavior," *Nonprofit and Voluntary Sector Quarterly* 37, no. 3 (2008): 468–491.

19. Yoram Bar-Gal, *Propaganda and Zionist Education: The Jewish National Fund, 1924–1947* (Rochester, NY: University Rochester Press, 2003).

20. Friends of Ariel, "Our Stories," https://www.friendsofariel.org.

21. Mitchell Bard, "Population of Jewish Settlements in the West Bank by Community" (*Jewish Virtual Library*, 2016), https://www.jewishvirtuallibrary.org/israeli -settlements-population-in-the-west-bank.

22. Nachman interview.

23. In 2010 the longtime marketing campaign reached its pinnacle when the sitting prime minister of Israel declared publicly that Ariel was "the capital of Samaria." Tovah Lazaroff, "PM: Ariel Is the 'Capital of Samaria,'" *Jerusalem Post*, January 29, 2010.

24. The Hebron Fund, "Hebron Tours—Isn't It Time," https://web.archive.org/web/20130915005012/http://hebronfund.org/multimedia/articles/events/37-hebron-tours-isn-t-it-time.

25. Emek Shaveh, "Archaeology in the Shadow of the Conflict," https://web.archive.org/web/20130703011911/alt-arch.org/.

26. Carolyn J. Cordery and Rachel F. Baskerville, "Charity Transgressions, Trust and Accountability," *Voluntas: International Journal of Voluntary and Nonprofit Organizations* 22, no. 2 (2011): 197–213.

27. Sarah Becklake, "NGOs and the Making of 'Development Tourism Destinations,'" *Zeitschrift Für Tourismuswissenschaft* 6, no. 2 (2014): 223–242.

28. Shaul Kelner, *Tours That Bind: Diaspora, Pilgrimage, and Israeli Birthright Tourism* (New York: New York University Press, 2012).

29. See Emily Barman, "With Strings Attached: Nonprofits and the Adoption of Donor Choice," *Nonprofit and Voluntary Sector Quarterly* 37, no. 1 (2008): 39–56.

30. The seven NGOs included Ariel Development Fund, Ateret Cohanim, The Rebuilders of the Jewish Community in Hebron, Women in Green, Mishmeret Yesha, Madaa, and One Israel Fund.

31. One Israel Fund, "Feature Project: Operation: No More Jewish Victims," https://web.archive.org/web/20131027102744/http://www.oneisraelfund.org/projectsnew/.

32. Shantayanan Devarajan and Vinaya Swaroop, *The Implications of Foreign Aid Fungibility for Development Assistance* (Washington, DC: World Bank, Development Research Group, and Poverty Reduction and Economic Management Network, 1998).

33. Fleisch and Sasson, "$2.4 Billion and Counting."

34. Research note: NGOs do not publish their donor lists and rarely even report how many donors they have. The one set of data that is available is the aggregate fundraising numbers. While it is impossible to parse out the extent to which changes in the amount an organization raised from one year to another are a reflection of the number of donors or the average amount of contributions, it may not matter in considering this issue. A positive trend line suggests that an organization is doing a good job in either attracting new donors, retaining existing donors, driving up average contributions, or all of the above. Regardless of which it is, growth is an indication of effective fundraising.

35. Fleisch and Sasson, "$2.4 Billion and Counting."

36. Fleisch and Sasson, "$2.4 Billion and Counting."

37. Jonathan S. Woocher, "Sacred Survival: American Jewry's Civil Religion," *Judaism* 34, no. 2 (1985): 151–162; Francie Ostrower, *Why the Wealthy Give: The Culture of Elite Philanthropy* (Princeton, NJ: Princeton University Press, 1997).

38. Lise Vesterlund, "Why Do People Give?," in *The Nonprofit Sector: A Research Handbook*, 2nd ed., ed. Walter W. Powell and Richard S. Steinberg (New Haven, CT: Yale University Press, 2006), 577.

39. Eliezer David Jaffe, *Givers and Spenders: The Politics of Charity in Israel* (Jerusalem: E.D. Jaffe, 1985); Charles Hoffman, *The Smoke Screen: Israel, Philanthropy, and American Jews* (Silver Spring, MD: Eshel Books, 1989).

40. Gerald Steinberg (President and Founder, NGO Monitor), interview in Jerusalem, July 19, 2010.

41. Eliezer David Jaffe, *Giving Wisely: The Israel Guide to Nonprofit and Volunteer Organizations* (Jerusalem: Gefen, 2000), 22.

CHAPTER 7 — POWER SHARING IN THE TWENTY-FIRST CENTURY
IN NEW FEDERATED ARRANGEMENTS

1. The organizations that follow the Loyalist model include Ariel Development Fund / American Friends of Ariel; B'Tselem / B'Tselem—USA; El'ad / Friends of Ir David; The Rebuilders of the Jewish Community of Hebron / The Hebron Fund; Ateret Cohanim / American Friends of Ateret Cohanim.

2. Daniel J. Elazar and Alysa M. Dortort, eds., *Understanding the Jewish Agency: A Handbook* (Jerusalem: Jerusalem Center for Public Affairs, 1984), 74; Charles Hoffman, *The Smoke Screen: Israel, Philanthropy, and American Jews* (Silver Spring, MD: Eshel Books, 1989), 140.

3. David M. Roth, "American Friends" Organizations of Israeli Nonprofits: An Exploration of Challenges and Opportunities" (Master's thesis, Regis University, 2005); Stephen G. Greene, "Making Friends in America," *Chronicle of Philanthropy*, June 13, 1996, 1, 29–31.

4. For a good explanation of the concept of "fungibility," see Shantayanan Devarajan and Vinaya Swaroop, *The Implications of Foreign Aid Fungibility for Development Assistance* (Washington, DC: World Bank, Development Research Group and Poverty Reduction and Economic Management Network, 1998).

5. Uri Blau, "U.S. Group Invests Tax-Free Millions in East Jerusalem Land," *Haaretz*, August 17, 2009.

6. Information obtained from American Friends of Ateret Cohanim's IRS form 990 documents from 2007, 2008, 2009, 2010, and 2011.

7. B'Tselem Director of Outreach, Mitchell Plitnick, "Press Release Announcing Opening of U.S. Office for B'Tselem," December 19, 2008, https://web.archive.org/web/20100220065804/http://org2.democracyinaction.org/o/5664/blastContent.jsp?email_blast_KEY=1083263&t=.

8. Information obtained from IRS form 990 documents from American Friends of Ateret Cohanim, American Friends of Ariel, The Hebron Fund, Friends of Ir David, and B'Tselem USA from 1990s, 2000s, and 2010s.

9. Harvey Dale, "Foreign Charities," *Tax Law Review* 48, no. 3 (1995): 655–704.

10. Information obtained from IRS form 990 document from Gush Etzion Foundation, 2013.

11. This was the case for American Friends of Ariel until Ron Nachman passed away in 2013. Information obtained from IRS form 990 document from American Friends of Ariel, 2010. Information obtained from IRS form 990 document from Gush Etzion Foundation, 2010.

12. Yifat Madmon, *Ariel, Sipura shel Ir* [Ariel, story of a city] (Ariel, 2008).

13. Victoria B. Bjorklund and Jennifer I. Reynoso, "How a Private Foundation Can Use 'Friends of' Organizations" (Council on Foundations, 2005).

14. Dale, "Foreign Charities."

15. Avi Kay, "Citizen Rights in Flux: The Influence of American Immigrants to Israel on Modes of Political Activism," *Jewish Political Studies Review* 13, no. 3–4 (Fall 2001).

16. Internal Revenue Code, Rev. Rul. 63–252, 1963–2 CB 101 (January 1, 1963).

17. Nina J. Crimm, "Through a Post–September 11 Looking Glass: Assessing the Roles of Federal Tax Laws and Tax Policies Applicable to Global Philanthropy by Private Foundations and Their Donors," *Virginia Tax Review* 23, no. 1 (2003).

18. Jonathan Jacoby, "Report to Donors, September 1983" (New Israel Fund), Widener Library, Harvard University.

19. Frank Fisher (Founding Board Member, Americans for Peace Now), interview in Cambridge, MA, March 22, 2010.

20. Yossi Beilin, *His Brother's Keeper: Israel and Diaspora Jewry in the Twenty-first Century* (New York: Schocken Books, 2000).

21. Letter from Jonathan Cohen, President of New Israel Fund to organizational supporters, November 1982, Widener Library, Harvard University.

22. New Israel Fund, 1982 Annual Report, 2, Widener Library, Harvard University.

23. Women in Green, "Sovereignty Research Center" (January 8, 2014), http://womeningreen.org/sovereignty-research-center/.

24. Yechiel M. Leiter, *Crisis In: Israel—A Peace Plan to Resist* (New York: S.P.L. Books, 1994).

25. Peter Shaw-Smith, "The Israeli Settler Movement Post-Oslo," *Journal of Palestine Studies* 23, no. 3 (1994): 105–106.

26. Information obtained from Israel Community Development Funds' IRS form 990 documents from 1995, 1996, and 1997.

27. American Friends of New Communities in Israel, IRS form 990, 2013, schedule A, page 3, One Israel Fund, IRS form 990, 2013.

28. "Rabbis for Human Rights–North America Mission Statement," September 29, 2002, https://web.archive.org/web/20020929020001/http://www.rhr-na.org.

29. Shomrey Mishpat, "Rabbis for Human Rights—North America," https://web.archive.org/web/20021004032514/http://www.rhr-na.org/.

30. Information obtained from Rabbis for Human Rights–North America's IRS form 990 documents from 2004 to 2013.

31. See, for example, open letter from RHR-NA, "Dear Prime Minister Sharon," *The Forward*, March 29, 2004, which begins, "We Rabbis, leaders of our communities, longtime Zionists and supporters of Israel. . . ."

32. For example, "Rabbis for Human Rights–North America Mission Statement," July 18, 2011, https://web.archive.org/web/20110718033616/http://www.rhr-na.org/who-we-are/mission-statement.html.

33. Milton Cerny and Michele A. W. McKinnon, "The Globalization of Philanthropy: International Charitable Giving in the Twenty-First Century," *International Charitable Giving*, Fall 2010, 18.

34. Information obtained from Rabbis for Human Rights–North America's IRS form 990 documents from 2004 to 2013.

35. Rabbis for Human Rights and Rabbis for Human Rights, Joint Press Release, "Important News about the Future of Rabbis for Human Rights–North America and Rabbis for Human Rights (Israel)," January 15, 2013.

36. www.guidestar.org.il (שומר׳ משפט רבנים למעוזזכויות האדם) (*Shomrei Mishpat*) ["Rabbis for Human Rights"], 2018 and 2018 documents.

37. Information obtained from RHR-NA/T'ruah IRS form 990 documents from 2012 and 2016.

## CONCLUSION

1. Eliezer David Jaffe, *Giving Wisely: The Israel Guide to Nonprofit and Volunteer Organizations* (Jerusalem: Gefen, 2000), 22.

2. See, for example, Lehn M. Benjamin, "Funders as Principals: Performance Measurement in Philanthropic Relationships," *Nonprofit Management and Leadership* 20, no. 4 (Summer 2010); Alnoor Ebrahim, "Accountability in Practice: Mechanisms for NGOs," *World Development* 31, no. 5 (May 2003): 813–829; Joanne G. Carman, "Nonprofits, Funders, and Evaluation: Accountability in Action," *American Review of Public Administration* 39, no. 4 (2009): 374–390; Alexandra Kate Williamson and Kylie L. Kingston, "Performance Measurement, Evaluation and Accountability in Public Philanthropic Foundations," *Evaluation Journal of Australasia* 21, no. 2 (March 2021): 101–119.

3. Charles S. Liebman, *Pressure without Sanctions: The Influence of World Jewry on Israeli Policy* (Rutherford, NJ: Fairleigh Dickinson University Press, 1977), 200.

4. Liebman, *Pressure without Sanctions*, 202.

5. Chaim I. Waxman, "The Centrality of Israel in American Jewish Life: A Sociological Analysis," *Judaism* 25, no. 2 (Spring 1976).

6. Chaim I. Waxman, "All in the Family: American Jewish Attachments to Israel," in *A New Jewry? America since the Second World War*, ed. Peter Y. Medding (Jerusalem: Hebrew University of Jerusalem, Institute of Contemporary Jewry, 1992).

7. Chaim I. Waxman, "American Jewish Identity and New Patterns of Philanthropy," in *The Call of the Homeland: Diaspora Nationalisms, Past and Present*, ed. Allon Gal, Athena S. Leoussi, and Anthony D. Smith (Leiden: Brill, 2010).

8. Waxman, "American Jewish Identity," 97.

9. Dov Waxman, *Trouble in the Tribe: The American Jewish Conflict Over Israel* (Princeton, NJ: Princeton University Press, 2016), 4.

10. Daniel Gordis, *We Stand Divided: The Rift between American Jews and Israel* (New York: HarperCollins, 2019), 8–9.

11. The Hebron Hund, https://hebronfund.org/.

12. City of David: Ancient Jerusalem, http://www.cityofdavid.org.il/en.

13. Jerusalem Chai, https://www.ateretcohanim.org/.

14. "Settlement Watch," Peace Now, https://peacenow.org.il/en/category/settlement-watch.

15. "Who Are We?," Rabbis for Human Rights, https://www.rhr.org.il/eng.

16. B'Tselem, https://www.btselem.org/.

17. Liebman, *Pressure without Sanctions*, 200.

18. Jack Wertheimer, "Jewish Organizational Life in the United States since 1945," *American Jewish Year Book* 95 (1995): 16–17.

19. See Charles Hoffman, *Project Renewal: Community and Change in Israel* (Jerusalem: Halberstadt Communications, 1986); Paul King et al., *Project Renewal in Israel: Urban Revitalization through Partnership* (Lanham, MD: University Press of America, 1987); Frederick A. Lazin, *Politics and Policy Implementation: Project Renewal in Israel* (Albany: State University of New York Press, 1994).

20. Raviv Schwartz, "Partnership 2000: A New Model for Diaspora-Israel Relations," *Jerusalem Letter/Viewpoints* 410 (July 15, 1999).

21. In the year 1997, for example, Israel ranked fourth in the world in military expenditures as a percentage of GDP. Its rate of 9.1 percent was more than four times the international median rate of 1.9 percent—and this in the midst of arguably Israel's most peaceful time in its history to that point. World Bank Group, "Military Expenditure (% of GDP)," http://data.worldbank.org/indicator/MS.MIL.XPND.GD.ZS.

22. Harold Robert Isaacs, *American Jews in Israel* (New York: John Day Company, 1967).

23. Yossi Beilin, *His Brother's Keeper: Israel and Diaspora Jewry in the Twenty-First Century* (New York: Schocken Books, 2000), 106.

24. Eric Fleisch, "Israeli NGOs and American Jewish Donors: The Structures and Dynamics of Power Sharing in a New Philanthropic Era" (PhD diss., Brandeis University, 2014), 290–294.

25. Peter Beaumont, "Israel Passes Law to Force NGOs to Reveal Foreign Funding," *Guardian*, July 12, 2016, https://www.theguardian.com/world/2016/jul/12/israel-passes-law-to-force-ngos-to-reveal-foreign-funding.

26. Ben Sales, "NGO Bill Is Latest Shot in Israeli Government Volley Against Critics," *Times of Israel*, December 30, 2015, https://www.timesofisrael.com/ngo-bill-latest-shot-in-government-volley-against-critics/.

27. William Booth and Ruth Eglash, "Israel Doesn't Trust NGOs That Get Money from U.S. and Europe. Here's Why," *Washington Post*, January 31, 2016, https://www.washingtonpost.com/news/worldviews/wp/2016/01/31/israel-doesnt-trust-ngos-that-get-money-from-u-s-and-europe-heres-why/.

28. Association of Civil Rights in Israel, "Anti-NGO Legislation in the Israeli Knesset," updated June 2016, https://law.acri.org.il/en/wp-content/uploads/2016/06/Anti-NGO-Bills-Overview-Updated-June-2016-1.pdf.

29. Jack Wertheimer, *Giving Jewish: How Big Funders Have Transformed American Jewish Philanthropy* (New York: AVI CHAI Foundation, 2018), 26–30. On page 4, Wertheimer recounts that close to a hundred staffed foundations have been established in recent decades, "with more than a passing interest in Jewish life in the U.S. and Israel."

30. Wertheimer, *Giving Jewish*, 30–32.

# Selected Bibliography

Anheier, Helmut K. *Nonprofit Organizations: Theory, Management, Policy*. Routledge, 2005.

Anheier, Helmut K., and Siobhan Daly, eds. *The Politics of Foundations: A Comparative Analysis*. Routledge, 2007.

Anheier, Helmut K., and Diana Leat. *Creative Philanthropy: Toward a New Philanthropy for the Twenty-First Century*. Routledge, 2006.

Bard, Mitchell. "American Jewish Contributions to Israel." *Jewish Virtual Library* (2016). https://www.jewishvirtuallibrary.org/american-jewish-contributions-to-israel.

———. "Population of Jewish Settlements in the West Bank by Community." *Jewish Virtual Library*, 2016. https://www.jewishvirtuallibrary.org/israeli-settlements-population -in-the-west-bank.

———. "Total Immigration to Israel by Select Country by Year(1948–Present)." *Jewish Virtual Library*, 2016. https://www.jewishvirtuallibrary.org/total-immigration-to -israel-by-country-per-year

Barman, Emily. "With Strings Attached: Nonprofits and the Adoption of Donor Choice." *Nonprofit and Voluntary Sector Quarterly* 37, no. 1 (2008): 39–56.

Baron, Salo W., and Jeannette M. Baron. "Palestinian Messengers in America, 1849–79: A Record of Four Journeys" (Part 1). *Jewish Social Studies* 5, no. 2 (April 1943): 225–292.

———. "Palestinian Messengers in America, 1849–79: A Record of Four Journeys" (Part 3). *Jewish Social Studies* 5, no. 3 (July 1943): 225–292.

Beilin, Yossi. *His Brother's Keeper: Israel and Diaspora Jewry in the Twenty-First Century*. Schocken Books, 2000.

Bekkers, René, and Pamala Wiepking. "A Literature Review of Empirical Studies of Philanthropy: Eight Mechanisms That Drive Charitable Giving." *Nonprofit and Voluntary Sector Quarterly* 40, no. 5 (2011): 924–973.

Bensimhon-Peleg, Sarit. *Jewish Philanthropy and the Israeli Third Sector: The Case of Israeli Think Tanks*. Harold Hartog School of Government and Policy, 2008.

Berkman, Matthew. "Coercive Consensus: Jewish Federations, Ethnic Representation, and the Roots of American Pro-Israel Politics." PhD dissertation, University of Pennsylvania, 2018.

Berkowitz, Michael. *Western Jewry and the Zionist Project, 1914–1933*. Cambridge University Press, 1997.

Berman, Lila Corwin. *The American Jewish Philanthropic Complex: The History of a Multibillion-Dollar Institution*. Princeton University Press, 2020.

Berman, Morton Mayer. *The Bridge to Life: The Saga of Keren Hayesod, 1920–1970*. Shifrin and Na'aman, 1970.

Bernstein, Irving. *Living UJA History: Irving Bernstein: An Oral History Anthology*. Avraham Harman Institute of Contemporary Jewry, Hebrew University of Jerusalem, 1994–1995.

Bernstein, Philip. *To Dwell in Unity: The Jewish Federation Movement in America, since 1960*. Jewish Publication Society of America, 1983.

Bittker, Boris, and George K. Rahdert. "The Exemption of Nonprofit Organizations from Federal Income Taxation." *Yale Law Journal* 85, no. 3 (January 1976): 299–358.

Bjorklund, Victoria B., and Jennifer I. Reynoso. *How a Private Foundation Can Use "Friends of" Organizations*. Council on Foundations, 2005.

Blum, Debra E. "Ties That Bind: More Donors Specify Terms for Their Gifts to Charity." *Chronicle of Philanthropy* 14, no. 11 (March 21, 2002): 7–10.

Blum, Dvora. "The Ambivalent Emergence of Philanthropy in Israel." *Journal of Jewish Communal Service* 84, no. 1/2 (2009): 96–105.

Bremner, Robert H. *American Philanthropy*. University of Chicago Press, 1960.

———. *Giving: Charity and Philanthropy in History*. Transaction, 1996.

Brinkerhoff, Jennifer M. "Creating an Enabling Environment for Diasporas' Participation in Homeland Development." *International Migration* 50, no. 1 (2012): 75–95.

———. "David and Goliath: Diaspora Organizations as Partners in the Development Industry." *Public Administration and Development* 31 (2011): 37–49.

———. "Diaspora Philanthropy in an At-Risk Society: The Case of Coptic Orphans in Egypt." *Nonprofit and Voluntary Sector Quarterly* 37, no. 3 (2008): 411–433.

———. "Diaspora Philanthropy: Lessons from a Demographic Analysis of the Coptic Diaspora." *Nonprofit and Voluntary Sector Quarterly* 43, no. 6 (2014): 969–992.

Brown, Judith M. *Global South Asians: Introducing the Modern Diaspora*. Cambridge University Press, 2006.

Browne, Stephen. *Aid and Influence: Do Donors Help or Hinder?* Earthscan, 2006.

Castles, Stephen, Hein De Haas, and Mark J. Miller. *The Age of Migration: International Population Movements in the Modern World*. Guilford, 2014.

Cerny, Milton, and Michele A. W. McKinnon. "The Globalization of Philanthropy: International Charitable Giving in the Twenty-First Century." *International Charitable Giving* 45 (Fall 2010): 529–558.

Chinitz, Zelig. *A Common Agenda: The Reconstitution of the Jewish Agency for Israel*. Jerusalem Center for Public Affairs, 1985.

Clotfelter, Charles T. "The Economics of Giving." In *Giving Better, Giving Smarter: Working Papers of the National Commission on Philanthropy and Civic Renewal*, edited by John W. Barry and Bruno V. Manno, 31–55. National Commission on Philanthropy and Civic Renewal, 1997.

Clotfelter, Charles T., and Thomas Ehrlich. *Philanthropy and the Nonprofit Sector in a Changing America*. Indiana University Press, 1999.

Cohen, Robin. *Global Diasporas: An Introduction*. Routledge, 2022.

Cohen, Steven M. "Trends in American Jewish Philanthropy." *American Jewish Year Book* (1980): 29–51.

Cohen, Steven M., and Ari Y. Kelman. *Beyond Distancing: Young Adult American Jews and Their Alienation from Israel.* Andrea and Charles Bronfman Philanthropies, 2007.

Colinvaux, Roger. "Donor Advised Funds: Charitable Spending Vehicles for 21st Century Philanthropy." *Washington Law Review* 92 (2017): 39.

Collingwood, Vivien. "Assistance with Fewer Strings Attached." *Ethics & International Affairs* 17, no. 1 (2003): 55–67.

Corbett, E. D. "History Lessons in the City of Dawud: Jordan's Past and Complexities of Identity beyond Silwan." *Middle Eastern Studies* 47, no. 4 (2011): 587–603.

Crimm, Nina J. "High Alert: The Government's War on the Financing of Terrorism and Its Implications for Donors, Domestic Charities, and Global Philanthropy." *William & Mary Law Review* 45, no. 3/4 (2004): 1341.

———. "Through a Post-September 11 Looking Glass: Assessing the Roles of Federal Tax Laws and Tax Policies Applicable to Global Philanthropy by Private Foundations and Their Donors." *Virginia Tax Review* 23, no. 1 (2003): 1.

Dale, Harvey. "Foreign Charities." *Tax Law Review* 48, no. 3 (1995): 655–704.

———. "Public Policy Limits on Tax Benefits: 'Bob Jones' Revisited." *Tax Forum* 459 (1990).

Devarajan, Shantayanan, and Vinaya Swaroop. *The Implications of Foreign Aid Fungibility for Development Assistance.* World Bank, Development Research Group and Poverty Reduction and Economic Management Network, 1998.

Dijkzeul, Dennis, and Margit Fauser, eds. *Diaspora Organizations in International Affairs.* Routledge, 2020.

Diner, Hasia. *A Time for Gathering: The Second Migration, 1820–1880.* Johns Hopkins University Press, 1992.

Don-Yehiya, Eliezer. *Israel and Diaspora Jewry: Ideological and Political Perspectives.* Bar-Ilan University Press, 1991.

———. "Political Religion in a New State: Ben-Gurion's *Mamlachtiyut*." In *Israel: The First Decade of Independence*, edited by S. Ilan Troen and Noah Lucas, 171–194. State University Press of New York, 1995.

Doron, Avraham, and Ralph M. Kramer. *The Welfare State in Israel: The Evolution of Social Security Policy and Practice.* Westview, 1991.

Dufoix, Stéphane. *Diasporas.* University of California Press, 2008.

Duncan, Brian. "A Theory of Impact Philanthropy." *Journal of Public Economics* 88, no. 9–10 (2004): 2159–2180.

Dunn, Kathleen. "Diaspora Giving and the Future of Philanthropy." *Philanthropic Initiative* (2004).

Efrat, Elisha. *The West Bank and Gaza Strip: A Geography of Occupation and Disengagement.* Routledge, 2006.

Eisenstadt, S. N., and Ora Ahimeir, eds. *The Welfare State and Its Aftermath.* Barnes & Noble Books, 1985.

Elazar, Daniel J. *Community and Polity: The Organizational Dynamics of American Jewry.* Jewish Publications Society of America, 1976.

———. *The Federation Movement at 100.* Jerusalem Center for Public Affairs, 1995.

———. *People and Polity: The Organizational Dynamics of World Jewry.* Wayne State University Press, 1989.

Elazar, Daniel J., and Alysa M. Dortort, eds. *Understanding the Jewish Agency: A Handbook.* Jerusalem Center for Public Affairs, 1984.

England, Zahava. *Settling for More: From Jersey to Judea.* Devora, 2010.

Feige, Michael. *Settling in the Hearts: Jewish Fundamentalism in the Occupied Territories.* Wayne State University Press, 2009.

Finkel, Samuel B. "American Jews and the Hebrew University." *American Jewish Year Book* 39 (1937–1938): 193–201.

Fisher, Julie. *Nongovernments: NGOs and the Political Development of the Third World.* Kumarian Press, 1998.

Fleisch, Eric. "Building a Culture of Deference: American Jewish Givers, Israelis, and Control over Donations to Israel, 1920–1989." *Diaspora Studies* 14, no. 2 (2021): 121–142.

———. "Green Lines, Red Lines, and Company Lines: The United Israel Appeal and the Question of Permissible American Jewish Giving over the Green Line." *Israel Studies* 25, no. 1 (2020): 198–221.

———. "Israeli NGOs and American Jewish Donors: The Structures and Dynamics of Power Sharing in a New Philanthropic Era." PhD dissertation, Brandeis University, 2014.

Fleisch, Eric, and Theodore Sasson. *The New Philanthropy: American Jewish Giving to Israeli Organizations.* Maurice and Marilyn Cohen Center for Modern Jewish Studies, 2012.

Fleishman, Joel. *The Foundation: A Great American Secret; How Private Wealth Is Changing the World.* PublicAffairs, 2007.

Frumkin, Peter. "Inside Venture Philanthropy." *Society* 40, no. 4 (2003): 7–15.

Gal, Allon, ed. *Envisioning Israel: The Changing Ideals and Images of North American Jews.* Wayne State University Press, 1996.

Ganin, Zvi. *An Uneasy Relationship: American Jewish Leadership and Israel, 1948–1957.* Syracuse University Press, 2005.

Gidron, Benjamin. "The Evolution of Israel's Third Sector: The Role of Predominant Ideology." *Voluntas* 8, no. 1 (1997): 11–38.

Gidron, Benjamin, Michal Bar, and Hagai Katz. *The Israeli Third Sector: Between Welfare State and Civil Society.* Kluwer/Plenum, 2004.

Gidron, Benjamin, and Hagai Katz. "Patterns of Government Funding to Third Sector Organizations as Reflecting a *De Facto* Policy and Their Implications on the Structure of the Sector in Israel." *International Journal of Public Administration* 24, no. 11 (2004): 1133–1159.

Gidron, Benjamin, Hagai Katz, and Michal Bar. *The Israeli Third Sector 2000: Roles of the Sector.* Israeli Center for Third Sector Research, 2000.

Golan, Matti. *With Friends Like You: What Israelis Really Think about American Jews.* Free Press, 1992.

Goldberg, S. P. "Jewish Communal Services: Programs and Finances." *American Jewish Year Book* (1978): 172–221.

Golden, Peter. *Quiet Diplomat: A Biography of Max M. Fisher.* Cornwall Books, 1992.

Goodman, Philip. *66 Years of Benevolence: The Story of PEF Israel Endowment Funds.* PEF Israel Endowment Funds, 1989.

Gordis, Daniel. *We Stand Divided: The Rift between American Jews and Israel.* Harper-Collins, 2019.

Gordis, Yonatan. "On the Value and Values of Social Entrepreneurship." *Journal of Jewish Communal Service* 84, no. 1/2 (2009): 37–44.

Gorenberg, Gershom. *The Accidental Empire: Israel and the Birth of the Settlements, 1967–1977.* Times Books, 2006.

Gunner, Göran, and Robert O. Smith, eds. *Comprehending Christian Zionism: Perspectives in Comparison.* Augsburg Fortress, 2014.

Hall, Peter Dobkin. "A Historical Overview of Philanthropy, Voluntary Associations, and Nonprofit Organizations in the United States, 1600–2000." In *The Nonprofit Sector: A Research Handbook,* 2nd ed., edited by Walter W. Powell and Richard S. Steinberg, 32–65. Yale University Press, 2006.

Halperin, Samuel. "Ideology or Philanthropy? The Politics of Zionist Fund-Raising." *Western Political Quarterly* 13, no. 4 (December 1960): 950–973.

Halpern, Ben. *The American Jew: A Zionist Analysis.* Schocken Books, 1983.

———. *A Clash of Heroes—Brandeis, Weizmann, and American Zionism.* Oxford University Press, 1987.

Hammer, Gottlieb. *Good Faith and Credit.* Cornwall Books, 1985.

Handlin, Oscar. *A Continuing Task: The American Jewish Joint Distribution Committee, 1914–1964.* Random House, 1965.

Heimann, Fritz F., ed. *The Future of Foundations.* Prentice Hall, 1973.

Herman, Felicia. "Funding Innovation." *Journal of Jewish Communal Service* 84, no. 1/2 (2009): 2.

Hermann, Tamar. "Do They Have a Chance? Protest and Political Structure of Opportunities in Israel." *Israel Studies* 1, no. 1 (1996): 144–170.

———. "New Challenges to New Authority: Israeli Grassroots Activism in the 1950s." In *Israel: The First Decade of Independence,* edited by S. Ilan Troen and Noah Lucas, 105–122. State University of New York Press, 1995.

———. "The Sour Taste of Success: The Israeli Peace Movement, 1967–1998." In *Mobilizing for Peace: Conflict Resolution in Northern Ireland, Israel/Palestine, and South Africa,* edited by Benjamin Gidron, Stanley Nider Katz, and Yeheskel Hasenfeld, 94–129. Oxford University Press, 2002.

Hessel, MeLena. *The Life of ONAD: Its Origins, Operation, and Demise.* Center for Modern Jewish Studies, Brandeis University, 2007.

Hoffman, Charles. *Project Renewal: Community and Change in Israel.* Halberstadt Communications, 1986.

———. *The Smoke Screen: Israel, Philanthropy, and American Jews.* Eshel Books, 1989.

Horowitz, Dan, and Moshe Lissak. *Origins of the Israeli Polity: Palestine under the Mandate.* University of Chicago Press, 1978.

———. *Trouble in Utopia: The Overburdened Polity of Israel.* State University of New York Press, 1989.

Jaffe, Eliezer David. *Givers and Spenders: The Politics of Charity in Israel.* E.D. Jaffe, 1985.

———. *Giving Wisely: The Israel Guide to Nonprofit and Volunteer Organizations.* Gefen, 2000.

———. *Giving Wisely: The Israeli Guide to Nonprofit and Volunteer Social Services.* Koren, 1982.

———. *Pleaders and Protesters: The Future of Citizens' Organizations in Israel.* American Jewish Committee, Institute of Human Relations, 1980.

Johnson, Ann. *A United Jerusalem: The Story of Ateret Cohanim.* Ktav, 1992.

Johnson, Paula Doherty. *Diaspora Philanthropy: Influences, Initiatives, and Issues.* The Philanthropic Initiative (TPI) and Global Equity Initiative of Harvard University, 2007.

———. *Global Giving: Making a World of Difference.* The Philanthropic Initiative (TPI), 2003.

———. *Global Social Investing: A Preliminary Overview.* The Philanthropic Initiative (TPI), 2000.

Johnson, Paula Doherty, Stephen P. Johnson, and Andrew Kingman. *Promoting Philanthropy: Global Challenges and Approaches.* International Network for Strategic Philanthropy (INSP), 2004.

Kabalo, Paula. "Mediating between Citizens and a New State: The History of Shurat Hamitnadvim." *Israel Studies* 13, no. 2 (2008): 97–121.

Karp, Abraham J. *To Give Life: The UJA in the Shaping of the American Jewish Community.* Schocken Books, 1981.

Kaufman, Menahem. *An Ambiguous Partnership: Non-Zionists and Zionists in America, 1939–1948.* Magnes Press, 1991.

———. "The Case of the United Jewish Appeal." In *Envisioning Israel: The Changing Ideals and Images of North American Jews,* edited by Allon Gal, 219–253. Wayne State University Press, 1996.

Kay, Avi. "Citizen Rights in Flux: The Influence of American Immigrants to Israel on Modes of Political Activism." *Jewish Political Studies Review* 13, no. 3–4 (Fall 2001): 143–158.

Kelner, Shaul. *Tours That Bind: Diaspora, Pilgrimage, and Israeli Birthright Tourism.* New York University Press, 2012.

Knee, Stuart E. *The Concept of Zionist Dissent in the American Mind, 1917–1941.* R. Speller, 1979.

Kobrin, Rebecca. *Jewish Bialystok and Its Diaspora.* Indiana University Press, 2010.

Kobrin, Rebecca, and Adam Teller, eds. *Purchasing Power: The Economics of Modern Jewish History.* University of Pennsylvania Press, 2015.

Kolsky, Thomas A. *Jews Against Zionism: The American Council for Judaism, 1942–1948.* Temple University Press, 1990.

Korten, David C. *Getting to the 21st Century: Voluntary Action and the Global Agenda.* Kumarian Press, 1990.

Kramer, Ralph M. *The Voluntary Service Agency in Israel.* Institute of International Studies, University of California, 1976.

Lainer-Vos, Dan. "Masculinities in Interaction: The Coproduction of Israeli and American Jewish Men in Philanthropic Fund-Raising Events." *Men and Masculinities* 17, no. 1 (2014): 43–66.

———. *Sinews of the Nation: Constructing Irish and Zionist Bonds in the United States.* John Wiley, 2013.

Lazin, Frederick A. *Politics and Policy Implementation: Project Renewal in Israel.* State University of New York Press, 1994.

Lederhendler, Eli. "The Diaspora Factor in Israeli Life." In *Israeli Identity in Transition,* edited by Anita Shapira, 109–136. Praeger, 2004.

Lehman-Wilzig, Sam N. *Stiff-Necked People, Bottle-Necked System: The Evolution and Roots of Israeli Public Protest, 1949–1986.* Indiana University Press, 1990.

——. *Wildfire: Grassroots Revolts in Israel in the Post-Socialist Era.* State University of New York Press, 1992.

Lewis, David, and Nazneen Kanji. *Non-governmental Organizations and Development* Routledge, 2009.

Liebman, Charles S. *Pressure without Sanctions: The Influence of World Jewry on Israeli Policy.* Fairleigh Dickinson University Press, 1977.

Lipstadt, Deborah. "The History of American Zionist Organizations: An Ideological and Functional Analysis." In *Jewish American Voluntary Organizations,* edited by Michael N. Dobkowski., 531–544. Greenwood, 1986.

Lowy, Mike. *Thirty Years of Global Jewish Action: Resolutions of the Jewish Agency Assembly, 1971–2001.* Jewish Agency for Israel, 2002.

Lurie, Harry L. *A Heritage Affirmed: The Jewish Federation Movement in America.* Jewish Publication Society of America, 1961.

Lustick, Ian. *For the Land and the Lord: Jewish Fundamentalism in Israel.* Council on Foreign Relations, 1988.

Medding, Peter. *The Founding of Israeli Democracy, 1948–1967.* Oxford University Press, 1990.

Mittleman, Alan, Jonathan D. Sarna, and Robert A. Licht. *Jewish Polity and American Civil Society.* Rowman & Littlefield, 2002.

Moore, Deborah Dash. *At Home in America: Second Generation New York Jews.* Columbia University Press, 1981.

Norell, Magnus. *A Dissenting Democracy: The Israeli Movement "Peace Now."* Frank Cass, 2002.

Oser, Jennifer. "Between Atomistic and Participatory Democracy." *Nonprofit and Voluntary Sector Quarterly* 39, no. 3 (2010): 429–459.

Ostrander, Susan A. "The Growth of Donor Control: Revisiting the Social Relations of Philanthropy." *Nonprofit and Voluntary Sector Quarterly* 36, no. 2 (June 2007): 357–372.

Ostrower, Francie. *Why the Wealthy Give: The Culture of Elite Philanthropy.* Princeton University Press, 1995.

Penkower, Monty Noam. "American Jewry and the Holocaust: From Biltmore to the American Jewish Conference." *Jewish Social Studies* 47, no. 2 (Spring 1985): 95–114.

Penslar, Derek. "Solidarity as an Emotion: American Jews and Israel in 1948." *Modern American History* 5 (2022): 27–51.

Polish, David. "A Memoir." *American Jewish History* 78, no. 4 (June 1989): 463.

Powell, Walter W., and Richard S. Steinberg. *The Nonprofit Sector: A Research Handbook.* 2nd ed. Yale University Press, 2006.

Putnam, Robert D. *Bowling Alone: The Collapse and Revival of American Community.* Simon & Schuster, 2000.

Raphael, Marc Lee. *Abba Hillel Silver: A Profile in American Judaism.* Holmes & Meier, 1989.

——. *A History of the United Jewish Appeal, 1939–1982.* Scholars Press, 1982.

——. "The Origins of Organized National Jewish Philanthropy in the United States, 1914–1939." In *The Jews of North America,* edited by Moses Rischin, 213–223. Wayne State University Press, 1987.

————, ed. *Understanding American Jewish Philanthropy*. Ktav, 1979.

Rapoport, Meron. *Shady Dealings in Silwan*. Ir Amim, 2009.

Rehavi, Yehiel, and Asher Weingarten. *Fifty Years of External Finance via State of Israel Non-negotiable Bonds*. Bank of Israel, 2004.

Reith, Sally. "Money, Power, and Donor–NGO Partnerships." *Development in Practice* 20, no. 3 (2007): 446–455.

Ribar, David C., and Mark O. Wilhelm. "Charitable Contributions to International Relief and Development." *National Tax Journal* 48, no. 2 (1995): 229–244.

Rosen, Mark I. *Responding to a World of Need: Fundraising at the American Jewish Joint Distribution Committee*. iUniverse, 2009.

Roth, David M. "American Friends' Organizations of Israeli Nonprofits: An Exploration of Challenges and Opportunities." Master's thesis, Regis University, 2005.

Safran, William. "The Jewish Diaspora in a Comparative and Theoretical Perspective." *Israel Studies* 10, no. 1 (2005): 36–60.

Salamon, L. M., and H. K. Anheier. *Defining the Nonprofit Sector: A Cross-National Analysis*. Manchester University Press, 1997.

————. *The Emerging Non-profit Sector: An Overview*. Johns Hopkins University, Institute for Policy Studies, 1994.

Sarna, Jonathan D. *American Judaism*. Yale University Press, 2004.

Sasson, Theodore. *The New American Zionism*. New York University Press, 2014.

Sasson, Theodore, Charles Kadushin, and Leonard Saxe. *American Jewish Attachment to Israel: An Assessment of the Distancing Hypothesis*. Cohen Center for Modern Jewish Studies, 2008.

Schwartz, Raviv. "Partnership 2000: A New Model for Diaspora-Israel Relations." *Jerusalem Letter/Viewpoints* 410 (July 15, 1999).

Schweid, Eliezer. "The Rejection of the Diaspora in Zionist Thought: Two Approaches." *Studies in Zionism* 5, no. 1 (1984): 43–70.

Shain, Yossi. *Kinship and Diasporas in International Affairs*. University of Michigan Press, 2007.

————. *Marketing the American Creed Abroad: Diasporas in the U.S. and Their Homelands*. Cambridge University Press, 1999.

Shapira, Anita, ed. *Israeli Identity in Transition*. Praeger, 2004.

Shaul Bar Nissim, Hanna, and Matthew A. Brookner. "Ethno-religious Philanthropy: Lessons from a Study of United States Jewish Philanthropy." *Contemporary Jewry* 39, no. 1 (2019): 31–51.

Shaw-Smith, Peter. "The Israeli Settler Movement Post-Oslo." *Journal of Palestine Studies* 23, no. 3 (1994): 105–106.

Sheffer, Gabriel. *Diaspora Politics: At Home Abroad*. Cambridge University Press, 2003.

————. "The Israelis and the Jewish Diaspora." In *Jews in Israel: Contemporary Social and Cultural Patterns*, edited by Uri Rebhun and Chaim Isaac Waxman, 421–444. University Press of New England, 2004.

————, ed. *Modern Diasporas in International Politics*. St. Martin's Press, 1986.

————. "Transnationalism and Ethnonational Diasporism." *Diaspora: A Journal of Transnational Studies* 15, no. 1 (2006): 121–145.

Shiff, Ofer. "Abba Hillel Silver and David Ben-Gurion: A Diaspora Leader Challenges the Revered Status of the 'Founding Father.'" *Studies in Ethnicity and Nationalism* 10, no. 3 (2010): 391–412.

Shye, Samuel, Alon Lazar, Rivka Duchin, and Benjamin Gidron. *Philanthropy in Israel: Patterns of Giving and Volunteering of the Israeli Public.* Israel Center for Third Sector Research, 2000.

Silber, Ilana, and Zeev Rosenhek. *The Historical Development of the Israeli Third Sector.* Ben-Gurion University of the Negev Press, 1999.

Simmons, Erica. *Hadassah and the Zionist Project.* Rowman & Littlefield, 2006.

Sklare, Marshall. "The Future of Giving." *Commentary*, November 1962.

Smith, Hanoch. *Attitudes of Israelis towards America and American Jews.* Institute on American Jewish-Israeli Relations, American Jewish Committee, 1983.

Sorin, Gerald. *A Time for Building: The Third Migration, 1880–1920.* Johns Hopkins University Press, 1992.

Soyer, Daniel, *Jewish Immigrant Associations and American Identity in New York, 1880–1939.* Harvard University Press, 1997.

Steinberg, Kerri P. "Contesting Identities in Jewish Philanthropy." In *Diasporas and Exiles: Varieties of Jewish Identity*, edited by Howard Wettstein, 253–278. University of California Press, 2002.

Stock, Ernest. *Beyond Partnership: The Jewish Agency and the Diaspora, 1959–1971.* Herzl Press, 1992.

———. *Chosen Instrument: The Jewish Agency in the First Decade of the State of Israel.* Herzl Press, 1988.

———. *Partners and Pursestrings: A History of the United Israel Appeal.* University Press of America, 1987.

Tobin, Gary A. *Israel and the Changing Character of Fundraising.* Cohen Center for Modern Jewish Studies, Brandeis University, 1994.

Tobin, Gary A., Adam Z. Tobin, and Lorin Troderman. *American Jewish Philanthropy in the 1990s.* Cohen Center for Modern Jewish Studies, Brandeis University, 1995.

Toepler, Stefan. "Foundation Roles and Visions in the U.S." In *The Politics of Foundations: A Comparative Analysis*, edited by Helmut Anheier and Siobhan Daly, 340–355. Routledge, 2007.

Troen, S. Ilan. "Establishing a Zionist Metropolis: Alternative Approaches to Building Tel Aviv." *Journal of Urban History* 18, no. 1 (November 1991): 10–36.

———. *Imagining Zion: Dreams, Designs, and Realities in a Century of Jewish Settlement.* Yale University Press, 2003.

Tvedt, Terje. *Angels of Mercy or Development Diplomats? NGOs and Foreign Aid.* Africa World Press, 1998.

Urofsky, Melvin I. *American Zionism from Herzl to the Holocaust.* Anchor Press / Doubleday, 1976.

———. *We Are One! American Jewry and Israel.* Anchor Press, 1978.

Vesterlund, Lise. "Why Do People Give?" In *The Nonprofit Sector: A Research Handbook*, 2nd ed., edited by Walter W. Powell and Richard S. Steinberg, 168–190. Yale University Press, 2006.

Waxman, Chaim I. "All in the Family: American Jewish Attachments to Israel." In *A New Jewry? America since the Second World War*, edited by Peter Y. Medding, 134–152. Oxford University Press, 1992.

———. "American Jewish Identity and New Patterns of Philanthropy." In *The Call of the Homeland: Diaspora Nationalisms, Past and Present*, edited by Allon Gal, Athena S. Leoussi, and Anthony D. Smith, 81–104. Brill, 2010.

———. "The Centrality of Israel in American Jewish Life: A Sociological Analysis." *Judaism* 25, no. 2 (Spring 1976): 175.

———. "Roundtable on Yossi Beilin's 'The Death of the American Uncle': 'The Questions Are Much Better Than the Answers.'" *Israel Studies* 5, no. 1 (2000): 361–364.

Waxman, Dov. *Trouble in the Tribe: The American Jewish Conflict over Israel.* Princeton University Press, 2016.

Wertheimer, Jack. "American Jews and Israel: A 60-Year Retrospective." *American Jewish Year Book* 108 (2008): 3–79.

———. "Breaking the Taboo: Critics of Israel and the American Jewish Establishment." In *Envisioning Israel: The Changing Ideals and Images of North American Jews*, edited by Allon Gal, 397–419. Wayne State University Press, 1996.

———. "Current Trends in American Jewish Philanthropy." *American Jewish Year Book* 97 (1997): 3–92.

———. *Giving Jewish: How Big Funders Have Transformed American Jewish Philanthropy.* Avi Chai Foundation, 2018.

———. "Jewish Organizational Life in the United States since 1945." *American Jewish Year Book* 95 (1995): 3–98.

Windmueller, Steven F., and Gerald B. Bubis. *Predictability to Chaos? How Jewish Leaders Re-invented Their National Communal System.* Center for Jewish Community Studies, 2005.

Woocher, Jonathan. *Sacred Survival: The Civil Religion of American Jews.* Indiana University Press, 1986.

Yishai, Yael. "Civil Society in Transition: Interest Politics in Israel." *Annals of the American Academy of Political and Social Science* 555, no. 1 (January 1998): 147–162.

Zertal, Idith, Akiva Eldar, and Vivian Sohn Eden. *Lords of the Land: The War over Israel's Settlements in the Occupied Territories, 1967–2007.* Nation Books, 2007.

# Index

References to figures appear in *italics*.

ABIs. *See* American-born Israelis (ABIs)
Achdut Israel, 50–51
"advise and consent" powers, 65–66, 67
AFNCI. *See* American Friends of New
  Communities in Israel (AFNCI)
AFPI. *See* American Fund for Palestine
  Institutions (AFPI)
Agency. *See* Jewish Agency
Agudat Israel, 50, 53
Agudat Yisrael, 52
*aliya* (making), 36, 113, 121, 122, 123–124,
  127, 184
Allen, Daniel (Rabbi), 66–67
Allied Jewish Campaign, 25. *See also*
  United Jewish Appeal (UJA)
American-born Israelis (ABIs), 156–157,
  163, 165
American Friends of Ariel. *See* Friends
  of Ariel
American Friends of Ateret Cohanim.
  *See* Friends of Ateret Cohanim
American Friends of New Communities
  in Israel (AFNCI), 156–157, 165
American Fund for Palestine Institutions
  (AFPI), 51–52
American Jewish funding organizations.
  *See* foundations; "friends of"
  organizations; ideological umbrella
  organizations; pass-through
  organizations
American Jewish Joint Distribution
  Committee (JDC). *See* Joint Distribu-
  tion Committee (JDC)

American Jews: "advise and consent"
  powers, 65–66, 67; allocation of
  donations, 9, 10–11, 12–13, 39, 40–41, 61,
  124–125; battles over donations from,
  41–43, *42*, 44–46, *45*; direct giving, shift
  to, 76–78, 79–80, 88–89; donation
  amounts ($), 6, 17, 20, 23, 26, 28, 31, 34,
  55, 60, 85; Eretz Yisrael, role in, 125–128,
  148; *heim*, Israel as, 173–174, 177, 185;
  Israeli leadership's views on, 36–37;
  knowledge of Israel, 117–118, 119–121,
  122–124, 145–148, 173, 174; NGO budgets
  dependent on, 112–114; as rich uncle,
  177–180, 185; settlement history, 17–18;
  *shlilat-ha-galut* (negation of exile), 36,
  37, 41, 115, 117; Six-Day War (1967)
  donation surge, 59–60, 61; World War I
  donation efforts, 20–22, *21*, 22. *See also*
  deference; diaspora Jews; power-sharing
  relationships
American power play model, 152, 162–165,
  166–169, 170–171
Americans for Peace Now (APN), 158–159,
  160, 161, 166
APN. *See* Americans for Peace Now
  (APN)
Arabs, 27, 96, 106, 107–108, 109–110, 127
archaeology, 109, 110–111, 139, 151
Ariel, 106–107, 113, 136–137, 138, 156, 212n23
Ariel, Uri, 163
Ariel Development Fund, 106–107, 113, 136,
  138, 155–156, 210n91, 214n1. *See also*
  NGOs

# About the Author

ERIC FLEISCH holds a PhD in Near Eastern and Judaic studies from Brandeis University. He also holds an MA in Jewish communal studies from Brandeis and a BA in history from Tufts University. He has published articles on Israeli history, the American Jewish community, and diaspora philanthropy. His current project is a study of philanthropy and political activism within the Palestinian American community. He teaches courses on Israel/Palestine, Jewish history, Zionism, and Middle East studies at Pennsylvania State University. He also previously taught at Lehigh University and Brandeis University. He lives in Allentown, Pennsylvania, with his three children.